THE WANDERING PILGRIM

VOLUME II

Tasmanian Bushwalk Diaries

John S.F. Dunlop

An independent publication

This edition published in 2025 by John S Dunlop & Associates,

PO Box 443, El Arish, Queensland, Australia, 4855

First published in Australia 2025

This edition published 2025

Copyright © John Dunlop 2025

Cover design, typesetting: WorkingType (www.workingtype.com.au)

The right of John Dunlop to be identified as the Author of the Work has been asserted in accordance with the Copyright, Designs and Patents Act 1988.

All rights reserved. No part of this publication may be reproduced, stored in a retrieval system, or transmitted, in any form or by any means without the prior written permission of the publisher, nor be otherwise circulated in any form of binding or cover other than that in which it is published and without a similar condition being imposed on the subsequent purchaser.

ISBN: 978-1-7641905-6-5

Also by John S Dunlop

The Wandering Pilgrim, Vol. 1 (2024)

978-1764082815 (ebook)

978-1922958969 (print)

"He who goes to the Hills goes to his mother…"
R Kipling

Dedicated to all those who ventured into the hills with me.
For the good times and hard, the miserably cold bivouacs,
The shared elation of the summits,
And especially to those who did not return.

About the Author

John Dunlop was born in Melbourne Australia in 1950, the Chinese year of the metal tiger. Educated at Scotch College, he matriculated with honours in mathematics, chemistry and Russian language. Before leaving school he twice hitchhiked around Australia and worked underground as a miner, and on offshore oil rigs. He had also accompanied his father, "Weary" Dunlop, to war-  torn Vietnam in 1965. By the time he left school he had already seen much of the world and become an accomplished outdoorsman.

After graduating from Melbourne University in mining engineering, he spent much of the next twenty years involved in mine operations, which led to roles in senior management and as a director. Then followed thirty years as a roving minerals consultant with travel to many countries and often very remote locations.

Always he made sure he took time out to "feed the rat" – to escape to remote outdoor places and keep a written record of his travels which has grown into a unique collection spanning more than sixty years.

These records, when grouped together, fall into the categories of boyhood travels, mountain travels (his first book), Tasmanian walks (this book), polar travel and work-related trips to unique places.

When eventually published in their entirety, they will become an autobiography written progressively over a very broad timespan. The photographic images captured on most of his journeys provide a historic and rare chronological record.

John is now in his seventies and has three adult children – John, a customs officer in Melbourne; Andrew, a former Victorian policeman now living in Sweden; and Isabelle, who teaches and plays violin, based in Brussels. His only sibling, brother Alexander, qualified as a doctor and passed away in his late sixties.

Prologue

The first volume in this series was devoted to my alpine climbing career, which began in the 1970s with climbs in New Zealand's southern alps, followed by Himalayan style climbs of Changabang (India, 1980), Khan Tengri (Kyrgyzstan, 1999), Everest (China, 2001) and Broad Peak (Pakistan, 2004).

This was the start of a much larger and longer project to assemble more than sixty of my travel diaries dating back to my boyhood days and present them, as written at the time. When brought together they would become an autobiography written as my life was actually being lived rather than something written (or dictated) from an armchair in increasingly decrepit old age. After all, the memory fades with time and we tend to remember only, and then embellishing, those snatches in time that come back into the mind of the now ageing writer. To me, that would lack authenticity.

As a mining engineer, I was able to work in many countries from about 1975[1] up to the present. Some were civilised, some arid, some frozen, some tropical, some even at war. Whatever the assignment, I always kept a generally light hearted account of the trip, together with whatever images I could take and preserve[2].

So, why this volume? Why Tasmanian walks? When I left school in Melbourne in 1967, I was a seasoned bushwalker[3] and was asked to lead a school walking group through the Cradle Mountain Lake St Clair National Park. Going from north to south, the walk followed the now perhaps over popular route and made such an impression on me that I vowed then and

---

1 Beginning in PNG at the time of that country's independence.
2 In the pre-digital area, many of my slides and negatives deteriorated – some I have saved.
3 I had by then received my Queen's Scout badge from the Victorian Governor.

there to return. And return I certainly did, as set out chronologically in these pages.

After graduating from Melbourne University in 1971, I went to work at the Rosebery copper, lead and zinc underground mine on Tasmania's West Coast. The job provided the time and opportunity to extend my Tasmanian wilderness experiences. If I was working underground[4] I finished day shift on a Friday and not rostered back on afternoon shift on the following Monday, giving me almost four days to hit the trails. The Frenchman's Cap trip, described here as Trip 3a, was a case in point. I became accustomed to the dodgy weather around Rosebery and gave my equipment regular road tests, always improving it as new gadgets appeared and helped to optimise the kit. In addition, there were others working at the mine keen to tag along.

In the early days, there were very few tracks with boggy areas which more recently have required park staff to install boardwalks as more and more walkers arrived. Most of the trip notes for the traverse of the East and West Arthur ranges in 1970 refer (with relief and appreciation) to boardwalks. River crossings were another issue which have since been largely replaced by swing bridges.

Back then campfires were normal but were banned[5] by the time of the new millennium and possibly before that. In the 70s and 80s I used an Optimus 00 kerosene stove. This was later replaced by the French Camping Gaz, until the MSR spirit stoves came in and were replaced by the now familiar gas canister models. As for self-standing tents, fleece clothing and Gore-Tex, yes, they made a big difference.

I have divided the trips chronologically into three groups: early (1960s and 1970s), later (1980s to early 2000s) and recent (after 2010). Most were done in spring, summer or early autumn, though I also did some winter trips, one to Mount Anne and others to Pine Valley with my late father and my late brother.

As far as possible, the notes were compiled as the trip unfolded. For

---

4   In those days, young mining engineers were required to 'do their time' as miners.

5   https://parks.tas.gov.au/explore-our-parks/know-before-you-go/campfires-and-fire-bans/fuel-stove-only-areas

possible historical interest, I have included lists of the food, equipment and first aid for some of the trips. The quotations were noted at the time (and filled out more correctly on return), the same being the case with the music I enjoyed along the way – especially when going alone. I hope these notes are interesting and entertaining. They are at least a record of how things were at the time.

I have not included maps showing the routes taken as there are now comprehensive, dedicated National Park and 1:100,000 topographic maps for all of Tasmania, published by the Lands Department[6], Hobart.

I began in my teens and was in my seventies for the last of the walks recorded here. The accounts cover a spread of almost seventy years. I hope you enjoy reading about those journeys here. I enjoyed them all and have more trips planned.

John Dunlop,
Rum Jungle Tropical Camp,
Far North Queensland, May 2025

---

[6] https://www.tasmap.tas.gov.au

Acknowledgements

My acknowledgements for *The Wandering Pilgrim Volume 1* began as follows: 'I am not an author, neither widely recognised nor admired like historian Geoffrey Blainey who was kind enough to show an interest in my work and encourage me to publish it. And, as Bob Dylan said, "'I'm a poet, I know it, hope I don't blow it'." And look what happened—he eventually was awarded a Nobel Prize for literature. Perhaps both should continue to be blamed for what appears in the following pages.'

Nonetheless, it is still appropriate that I make significant acknowledgement of those who have helped me through this second publishing journey. There are many to name and many I will have inadvertently overlooked. All of you, however, know who you are and have my gratitude. For this book, it was more or less a three-person effort made up of myself as author, Tony Berry, who edited the text, and Luke Harris, who did the design, typesetting and on-line publishing. I am indebted to Tony and Luke.

Three other groups come to mind. First, there are family members who never stopped me from 'feeding the rat[7]' and often came with me: my father, wives Heather and Chantal, sons John and Andy, daughter Isabelle, and also Susie, who came with me to the Three Capes in 2022-23. Next are my workplace superiors over many years who allowed me time off, especially during the period of my Himalayan climbing. I'm not sure it helped my professional career but it did add a work-life balance that I always felt I needed.

Additionally there are all those who accompanied me on the journeys

---

[7] An expression coined by British climber Mo Antoine to explain the need to get back to the hills to refresh. It's all in Feeding the Rat by A. Alvarez, Bloomsbury Publishing UK, May 1989

revisited in these pages. Some are no longer with us, but those who I've been able to contact are especially acknowledged here for their pluckiness, fearless courage and determined endurance when the times were hard and the way forward seemed unsurmountable. There were times when we pushed ourselves beyond normal limits in order to pave the way for the opening of hard routes, like the Franklands traverse and the linking of the Eastern and Western Arthur Ranges in one continuous undertaking.

Finally, while the days of aerial food drops are long gone, I should mention pilot Jim England[8,] who pioneered this activity and took part in many search and rescue missions in the parks. Without accurately placed drops, our extended walks would not have been possible, or certainly less practicable and more risky. As we go to press, I am yet to track him down.

Wherever possible, where I have used quotations, I have endeavoured to provide acknowledgement and attribution in whatever detail I was able to find. The same goes for photographic images. While most of them are my own, I have used some taken by members of the teams I was with or images available on the internet that show some of the places being described at a time before or after I was actually there. This was done purely to provide a historical context to the location mentioned. Every effort has been made to acknowledge the photographer concerned.

Where I have referred to song lyrics, I have endeavoured to acknowledge the originator of the work, or at least its performer.

In some cases, I have included images of documentation that related to the trip. Again, I have done this to provide historical interest on the understanding that there are no associated copyright issues that might stem from so doing.

---

8   https://www.hobartmodelaeroclub.org.au

Contents

Early Tasmanian Walks

Walk 1, Cradle Mountain Walk, 1968
    A Christmas holiday school hike in Tasmania – The Overland Track: Cradle Mountain and Lake St Clair National Park   1

Walk 2, Lake Pedder 1970
    Southwest Tasmania: Lake Pedder and the Frankland Range   7

Walk 3, Southwest coast
    The southwest coast to the eastern and western Arthur Ranges, 1970   29

Walk 3a, Frenchman's Cap 1971
    Franklin Gordon Wild Rivers National Park – Frenchman's Cap   83

Walk 3b, Mount Anne
    Mount Anne and the Mount Anne circuit 1972   90

Walk 3c, Precipitous Bluff, 1974   92
    An aborted trip and a cold walk in the snow

Walk 4, Cradle Mountain Lake St Clair, 1983
    The Overland Track Revisited 1983-4   103

Later Tasmanian Walks

Walk 5, Overland Track
    Cradle Mountain Lake St Clair National Park and the Overland Track revisited 1987   127

Walk 6, Cradle Mountain
    The Walls of Jerusalem and Cradle Mountain, 1991   153

Walk 7, Walls of Jerusalem
    Return to the Walls of Jerusalem, December 1995   179

Walk 8, Walls of Jerusalem solo
    Solo trip back to the Walls of Jerusalem, 2003   194

Walk 9, Walls of Jerusalem *en famille*
    The Walls of Jerusalem with Chantal and Isabelle, December 2004   211

Walk 10, Walls of Jerusalem
    A short fishing trip to the Walls of Jerusalem National Park, January 2016   214

Recent Tasmanian Trips and Walks

Trip 10a, Three Capes by Kayak, 2018
    Kayaking trip to the Three Capes, Tasman Peninsula, 2018   220

Trip 11, Franklin River
    Rafting down the Franklin River in Southwest Tasmania in December 2022   226

Walk 12, Pine Valley
    Back To Pine Valley, 2022   248

Walk 13, Three Capes
    Three Capes Walk, 2022-23   260

Epilogue   **279**

Early Tasmania:
Walk 1 Cradle Mountain, 1968

A Christmas holiday school hike in Tasmania – The Overland Track: Cradle Mountain and Lake St Clair National Park

SCOTCH IN THE ALPS

This hike was organised by the staff at Scotch College, Melbourne, to provide a summer adventure for some of the boys at the school. It was about the time I was leaving the school for university and, I think, my first major Tasmanian walk. I can't recall many of the details but have set out the diary notes pretty much as I recorded them at the time, What follows is therefore the scholarship of an eighteen-year-old school leaver. I have retained much of the boyish expressions, reflecting the language we used at the time.

Opening up this diary after so many years, this is what I found written on the first page more than fifty years ago, probably written at Waldheim at the northern gateway to the Overland Track.

This chapter of my Tassie wanderings records in a rather inadequate and humble way one of the most cherished memories of my hiking days. I have no doubt when I look back that Tasmania is the key to the hiker's dreams. Central western Tassie is the place: a land of incomparable alpine scenic beauty, a land of glacial lakes and dolerite screes, wild southern blizzards and snow, precipitous peaks and historical significance. Anyway, flip through these pages, follow my travels and see for yourself.

Anyone who does a fair bit of walking around the country is sooner or later classed as an old hand or even an expert. So it happens that I find myself down here in central Tasmania leading eleven able fellows south to Cynthia Bay at Lake St Clair, about sixty miles away. The weather is fine but cold and the glacial alpine country unbelievably beautiful.

I am alone in the 'boss's tent' writing casually in the warm gaslight of my lantern. It is nightfall and we are camped on the shores of Crater Lake under the shadow of Cradle Mountain. Although I have passed my year 12 English exam, I have absolutely no words which could adequately describe the beauty of this place save to say that it is surely one of the most beautiful I have ever been to. Look around at some of the pictures of this place and then turn to a snippet of the wisdom of Kipling who said when referring to the Hill men[9]:

> Hast thou desired the sea, The site of salt water unbounded,
> The heave and the comb and the crash and the curl of the breakers wind hounded?
> So, even so do the Hill men desire their Hills.

While these words of Kipling are surely more eloquent than mine, the sentiment rings true. I am sleepy and anxious for tomorrow even though it is Friday the thirteenth of December. I think I will roll myself a black-and-white and go to sleep...

Day 1: Friday 13 December 1968, Cradle Mountain and Barn Bluff

In retrospect, the 13th was anything but unlucky. We were blessed with perfect weather, high spirits and absolutely superb country all day. But to me this meant little. I rather think of today as I am sure I always will, as the day we climbed Cradle Mountain and Barn Bluff.

These peaks must surely be two of the most strikingly rugged and

---

9   From Rudyard Kipling's Kim – the poem The Sea and the Hills

beautiful in Australia. For miles around they loom over you solemnly. They are in cahoots with the weather and with no mercy call the tune as to whether the aspiring climber will negotiate them. Pity the hiker who gets himself stranded up there during a blow, for the vertical, perilous drops are shrouded in mist and the icy southern wind calves his body to bare his very bones. We were lucky, and I have never been so grateful for fair weather since the days in the Snowy Mountains in NSW two years ago where, as Banjo Paterson wrote. 'any slip was death[10]'.

Barn Bluff's beauty is quite unsurpassed. Here we are on this stable, quiet evening camped under its eastern portal. We have conquered it and yet still it looms over our heads mysteriously in the fading shadows of sunset. The very character of the Bluff: its faces rising like palisades towards the sky, its dolerite screes defying the hiker's progress, its perilous drifts of snow hiding crevices and awesome pitfalls, its majestic cornices, it is overall majesty…these are the realm of the day that will remain in my memory for ages. I lie alone in my tent, lantern hissing, the soft alpine grass cushioning my tired limbs. My legs are red raw and throbbing from the rip and tear of the crags and vegetation, and the sunburn from the snow; my hair is knotted and stringy from the sweat and the dirt, my face is haggard and hairy; my feet are tender and I am tired still. Yet I am filled with awe and admiration for the country. Here there is untold beauty for those who love the bush. It is a splendid realm.

But enough of this. It's just another evening in a hiking camp. Tents dotted over a flat glacial plain, spongy and damp, the camp fire where wood is scarce[11], the surrounding gruesome peaks – some climbed some not, the clouds slowly rolling in to shroud us with nightfall, the gentle breeze, the distant murmur of your mates, a good hot tea steaming and burning, a cigarette, the smoke curling around your fingers and away forever.

These are the idle thoughts of a drifter. The life is here whether you are able to find it or not. And I wonder: are these things all too soon doomed to disappear like the camp fire smoke? I fear lest my dreams fall asunder

---

10   A well-known line from Paterson's The Man from Snowy River.

11   Camp fires were prohibited some years later.

before I am ready for them to do so, for I earnestly love this life. I think I'll crawl out of the tent, stoke the fire and brew myself a cuppa.

DAY 2: SATURDAY 14 DECEMBER 1968, BARN BLUFF CAMP

Sit back, draw yourself up a fag and let me tell you how we spent a beautiful sunny day here at Windermere.

At 3200 feet there is peace and beauty all around us. A pleasant swim, meal and doze with the sun warm against my back. Still, the snowy crags of Barn Bluff overshadow us, now eight miles distant. Today I truly unwound and came to grips with this place; a wild beautiful realm of snowy crags, coarse savanna, glacial lakes and the other rudiments that only nature herself can provide.

This evening the sky seemed a little less inclined to favour us tomorrow, though I detected patches of pink glazing on parts of the horizon. This worries me for the park boasts of receiving 150 inches of rain a year and what they call rain means pitiful conditions on the peaks. One wonders whether we will be veritably pissed upon up on the cornices, hey but! All is well at Windermere.

DAY 3: SUNDAY 15 DECEMBER 1968, THE PELION PLAINS

As luck would have it, it rained today just enough to make the boggy tracks and spongy growth underfoot a real test of one's tolerance. The one thing I'd really like to grumble about is the blasted mud. The mud! That's an understatement if ever I heard of one for although the peaks may be beautiful, the plains and gullies all unanimously come under the classification of one great, greasy, using lick hole[12]. No matter how superhuman your temperament is, you will certainly end up greased off literally and psychologically. So mud, you're a bastard.

Tomorrow should herald greater things as we are to climb Mount Ossa. Rising to 5304 feet, it is Tasmania's highest peak, which is why I have preferred to leave my writing for today with a note of suspense.

---

12   This was well before the gradual installation of boardwalks to protect the vegetation.

DAY 4: MONDAY 16 DECEMBER 1968, PELION GAP AND KIA ORA HUT

The morning dawned with mist and fog and visibility of almost half a mile. Leaving late we made an arduous march up through the mud and swamps to Pelion Gap where, to my extreme annoyance and despair, Mount Ossa and Pelion West were swathed in swirling dangerous mist. Even the lower slopes were deep in heavy dangerous snowdrifts and rock falls which made the proposed climbs more impossible than inadvisable. So here we are at Kia Ora hut within hearing of the local waterfall. Our morale is good but we are nonetheless crapped off over not getting up Mount Ossa. After all it is Tasmania's highest peak.

DAY 5: TUESDAY 17 DECEMBER 1968, PINE VALLEY

Today the weather began to clear and here we are at Pine Valley hut[13]. It is 6:15 pm and I am quietly reposing outside the hut in a truly beautiful setting, smoking one of my last Camels. Looming above me to my right is Mount Gould with the Guardians sloping away to the Acropolis behind me. There are some beautiful bird calls in the cool evening air. The setting of eucalypts and alpine 'bastard bush'[14] around the shingle hut, which is smoking lazily from a rusty corrugated tin chimney, gives me a wonderful feeling of tranquility and a sense of being at one with outdoor life. Inside, the chaps are happily churning out hot pancakes with chocolate and sultanas, hot tea and coffee, while some are playing 500 at cards.

The light is slowly fading and high above me the lighter lower clouds are intermittent, mist swirling past the peaks, while high saddles are treeless and deep in summer snow drift. My cigarette butt is slowly suffering a smouldering death and an old one is lying near the edge of the brown leafy clearing. Some strange form of small biting insects flitter round my head. I wonder why they are not interested in my rather gnarled and dirty suntanned hands. The day is dying as I sit here on an old discarded kitchen safe. Since I started to write it has become a rather chilly unpleasant dusk. I will stop here before I lose interest in this beautiful spot.

---

13   This hut, which I returned to many times in later years, has now been rebuilt and has a separate out house toilet, pot belly stove and coal supply. No fires!

14   Richea scoparia, very prickly, sometimes called kerosene bush as drier parts burn well.

Day 6: Wednesday 18 December 1968, Acropolis and Geryon

No entry. Too buggered to write!

Day 7: Thursday 19 December 1968, Narcissus and Echo Point huts, Cynthia Bay

Yesterday's entry needs some explanation. The day was a very hard one. First, we scaled the Acropolis. Second, we walked with packs from Pine Valley hut to Narcissus hut without a stop taking two hours and, third, we walked from Narcissus to Echo Point without a stop – a further one and a half hours. We trudged so long and so far that day that I was half asleep before we even reached Echo Point at 8.30 in the evening.

A fifteen-mile hike not counting the scaling of Acropolis. It was a long day.

Not much can be said about the Acropolis save that it was as impressive and as beautiful as are all the peaks in the area. The view of the notorious sheer faced Mount Geryon was awesome to say the least. It is without a doubt the most precipitous peak I have seen. Perhaps it is no wonder I was so tired yesterday as twice I nearly lost my life down the icy blue, terrifying, mini crevasses in the snow.

Looking back, however, I must remark on the beauty of the Lake St Clair last night in spite of my exhaustion at the time. The golden sun was setting in all its splendour all across the high ridge bordering the lake, its water was glassy smooth and tranquil. The trout were rising and the idyllic setting of the hut rounded off the scene. Wednesday was beauty and exhaustion.

Thursday rolled around and with it, arrival at Cynthia Bay and our journey's end. Park bungalows, tourists, dirt and civilisation! An end to our completion of a traverse of the overland track from north to south and eight days of beauty.

My current amusements are first the Derwent Bridge pub[15] and second the ranger down here who seems determined to run his kiosk[16] at a loss.

---

15   The Derwent Bridge hotel is about 6 km from Cynthia Bay and park headquarters.
16   Years later this became an elaborate park HQ and visitor centre with more rangers and a restaurant.

Early Tasmania: Walk 1 Cradle Mountain, 1968

Fishing licence, Tassie 1968

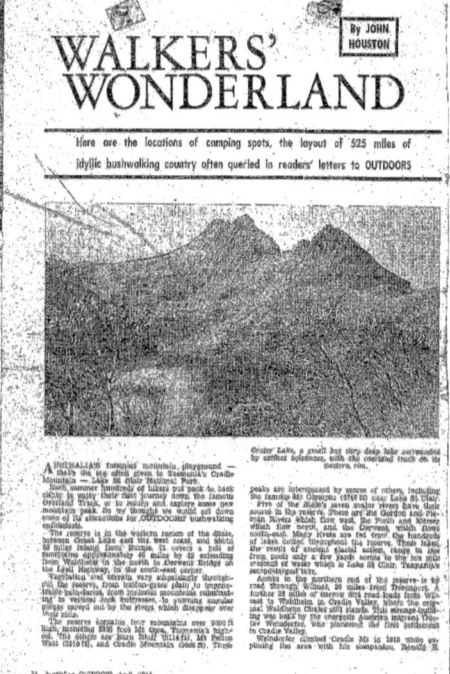

Cradle Mt, discovered, Outdoor Magazine 1964

Rest stop, Kitchen hut 1968

Barn Bluff

Mt Pelion West

JD on the summit, Pelion west

Waterfall Valley, Barn Bluff behind

The Acropolis, photo F Potts 1964

Mt Geryon, photo F Potts 1964

Looking past Geryon to Mt Gould

Early Tasmania Walk 2

Southwest Tasmania: Lake Pedder and the Frankland Range

The walk through the Cradle Mountain and Lake St Clair National Park in 1968 was the first time I had done any serious walking in Tasmania. At that time there was much controversy building surrounding the activities of the Hydro Electric Commission (HEC) in Tasmania and the threat to flood the natural lake in its SW by the name of Lake Pedder. I had seen pictures of the Lake and there was no doubt in my mind as to its attraction. So naturally I was keen to go down there as soon as possible and to see it with my own eyes. The notes which follow were written at the time now more than 50 years ago, and before the Lake itself was in fact flooded. All of this took place long before the controversy around the proposed dam on the Franklin River and the activities of then conservationist Bob Brown. Looking back on it now, I cannot help thinking that the tragedy surrounding the flooding of Lake Pedder greatly influenced the federal government which eventually intervened with the then prime minister Bob Hawke halting plans to develop the dam on the river. Many years later I completed a rafting descent of the Franklin, which is the subject of a separate diary.

This account however, describes the trip into the original Lake Pedder, the traverse of the Frankland range which rises on one side of the lake and our eventual departure by heading along the foot of the notorious Western Arthur range. I have edited and corrected the original text as little as possible to retain its original flavour. I do ask readers to keep in mind however that the writings are those of a precocious 20-year-old.

Back to Tasmania

Day 1: Friday 20 February 1970

It is quickly approaching the end of the day this 20th February 1970. We are camped way out on a windy Ridge on the Sentinels range, in the realm of Lake Pedder, Southwest Tasmania. The reason for this "turnout" (definitely a turnout) is that a party of five spirited and able men left to Melbourne early this morning on the usual delayed flight heading for two weeks of good hard hiking and back woodsman ship. The men include "Scutza" Sussex, John Humann, Lachie Creswell, David Hudson ("Huddo") and myself. The bus dropped us at the 31 mile post on the Gordon River Road and the trek south to the Lake started late in the afternoon. As usual for this area which receives at least 75 inches of rain per year, it was misty and raining. All the memories of the dark, boggy "lickholes" back at Cradle Mountain came back to me as we slogged along till about 6:30 pm. Behind us, down the valley of mist and cloud, you could just pick out Mount Wedge and Tim O'Shea and the Needles before darkness fell all around us.

Woe! What a miserable turnout. No flat ground and scrub thick and horizontal being mostly 2 feet deep. So we camped on a prickly sponge layer inclined at 10° the horizontal and 15° to the rain. The water fetching detail was almost as funny as the pitching of the tents, with clanking billies and water splashes and swear words from the thick jungle down in the galley where the creek gurgled invisibly. The evening meal was a beauty except it was too dark to see yourself eating it. Steak, mashed spuds, peas, plum pudding and cream – and also soup. We rounded all that off with a good hot cuppa and a Templer[17] and called a late adjournment.

In my little tent here, Huddo has quickly fallen off to sleep and as is in is so often the case I am left alone here with my thoughts with the gas lantern running low. Thank the gods its not too cold tonight. The tent in its present state of erection offers little protection from the icy blast coming up the Valley though there is some shelter in the scrub. I'm feeling rather tired and headachy after today. Our packs have all been near to 70 ponds

---

17   Temple Bar was a brand od cigarette in those days.

and, cranked up on one shoulder like this as I write, three pages is not a bad effort for today's recording of events. I'm glad to have made some opening remarks on this the end of our first day.

Day 2: Saturday 21 February 1970

We left in the morning and continued down the route from the Sentinels enjoying glimpses of Lake Pedder as we descended. We arrived at the lake late in the evening and found the moderately sized hut very cozy, with two nice fellows who welcomed us with a fire and a good store of yarns and smokes. The hut is lined with metal foil, the result being that in a shirt and denim jacket I'm quite warm here by the dying fire. Good to see an ample supply of racks, seats and shelves. They are what really make the difference. A large group of hikers dribbled in later in the evening in characteristic fashion, claiming clothes drying rights by our chops on the fire and the right to freeload our scarce supply of firewood. There were several women in their in the party who had the typical female hiker image – namely being dead set on nothing else but out doing their male companions in any and every manner conceivable. Terrible tomboys really and quite a bore. I couldn't help thinking it was a pity because some of them were quite nice looking.

Once again, the evening meal was agonisingly slow in both preparation and delivery although the sultana pudding with custard went down extremely well though I have a subsequent feeling that tomorrow soon after breakfast I will surely drop my guts. The track over here to the lake from the last campsite was rather poor – at least not as pleasant as it might have been. Huddo's kit was terribly wet from me rolling him out of the tent in my sleep. The rain really fixed him. The actual walk was made very boring due to the combined effects of strong wind and rain, very thick mud, very heavy packs and some nasty Hills. Huddo had a lot of trouble with cramp and many salt tablets were administered. The views were all spoiled by mist and cloud and there were few features of interest along the way. We reached Lake Pedder through the lickholes eventually. The scene was not as good as I had pictured but only due to the weather conditions. The pearly white shingle beach stretched a full 2 miles and it was as smooth as glass – it made me think and ponder over the shame of it all to condemn the whole area to a 40 foot watery grave. It appeared as if the little set Cessna aircraft had gone arse up halfway along the beach and was parked there, half way along the beach, awaiting a new propeller. I found out later that the front wheel assembly had fractured on landing two months ago and that spares had not yet arrived from the United States. What a turnout. Tomorrow weather permitting, we will try to reach the faces of the awesome coronation peak swayed in cloud at the other end of the Lake. If I arise at 6 to see clouds, we'll all be sleeping in. That's for sure. The walk dangerous as it could be would be tiring and pointless due to the poor visibility and extreme cold up there on those high crags.

I'm beginning to think my gas lantern is nearly out of gas – it's been hissing away gently for the last four hours. Come to think of it, it's got about as much staying power round the evening campfire as I have. We would have a hard day ahead tomorrow and in the fading light Huddo is watching me with a serious look on his face. We could not face the shithouse camp coffee and the Tolley's Hospital Brandy did go down rather better. There is intermittent snoring coming from the dark from the general direction of Scutza who really has had rather a hard day. I'm still a bit headachy but now with a sore back into the bargain. My socks are all wet, boots cold and hair a mess. I do hope the turnout over and above us improves. State Express roll your own is getting low. Sleep required; time 1:30 am Sunday. Zonk!

DAY 3: SUNDAY 22 FEBRUARY 1970

It just hasn't worked out today what with the inclement weather and all. Huddo, me and Lachie tried to do some fishing though this idea was quickly washed out with rain mostly going down our necks as well. All day the clouds covered the peaks that we have come here to climb. Scutza is still methodically attending to his stuff, his aptitude being somewhat increased with the decision to move out tomorrow rain snow or hail. Coronation peak must be climbed no matter what. On the subject of the lake, I still haven't the heart to describe it while in this weather as it's not as beautiful as it has shown it can be. It is evening again and we are around the fire drinking tea and yarning with some new arrivals – a group of Sydney University students. We have found a sense of harmony and compatibility common to all students.

DAY 4: MONDAY 23 FEBRUARY 1970

Yes folks, today was a day to delight all the multitudes and package deal preventers. In spite of our torrid night of damper and brandy, I awoke at 6 o'clock and aptly disturbed the crew right between the flaps. Our apprehension and misgivings over the weather speculation was rewarded as the day dawned clear sunny and altogether promising. Our boredom and disappointment disappeared just as the rain had the previous night even breakfast and clean up went quickly. It had been decided to make a round trip of the Frankland mountain chain so over half of our food had to be packed securely and buried in the form of a cache. A mock pirate treasure hunt followed after breakfast ending with the incorrigible Dylan[18] burying the sacks in a natural culvert quite near the Lake. Much spadework and camouflaging were used.

Goodbyes and so forth were wished to our new-found Uni mates and we set off for Coronation Peak and the rest of the Franklands. Our route initially saw us walking across the shores of the Lake. I must admit it as soon as the weather had cleared the true beauty and splendour of the area showed itself in one glorious array. Pedder assumed its famous, coloured tinge, smooth as glass and the surrounding crags and peaks emerged in a fanfare of coloured hues and wondrous palisades of rugged bush beauty. My earlier thoughts of the area were certainly changed and I do hope the record is set straight here and now. The very changeable character of the scene has me enthralled. All the way round the Lake the shores lapped at our feet as the warm sun pampered our shoulders, still cold from the icy evening. Even the swamps that followed became bearable. Our feet were wet but we walked in the lickholes with the characteristic togetherness of a herd of hippos. Huddo accused me of farting far less frequently and Scutza's technical level of bullshit[19] lessened to at least the level of a small bulldozer.

---

18   My nickname at the time.
19   He later became a respected surgical consultant at a major Canadian hospital.

The negotiation of the swamps and bog holes was a playful enterprise where, as Banjo Patterson once put it, any slip was death. We slithered and oozed our way across the floodplain to the realms of Timber Creek and the foothills of the Dome. An ascent was started and of course we will all soon hopelessly stuffed. I was still farting, Huddo wanted a mask, John, silently unamused with events, Scutza was relinquishing relentlessly and Lachie had disappeared in a cloud of smoke up his own backside. An auspicious start to the Franklands. In all 2600 feet were made in ascent when everyone unanimously dropped his pack and decided to camp. I have set out below the obvious reasons so that you can best understand the situation. Firstly, why walk after 5 o'clock in the evening? Secondly there was no hope of a pub meal. Thirdly me and Huddo had ripped the back of our pants. Fourthly the Road ahead was rather awe-inspiring. And finally, I needed to do something about whatever it was that was causing the flatulence. Anyway, on a slightly more serious note the day's hike was an extremely rewarding one. The peaks and surrounding arete looked as impressive and as anything I've seen. The views were so extensive that you could see well into the haze of distance and the whole panorama of inaccessible peaks like Mount Anne and the Turret emerged in full splendour. I just cannot recount the imposing and awesome front of the Citadel and its Turret, surrounded by the East and West buttress, surrounded way, way below by glacial moats and up surges of rugged relentless swamp and scrub.

So we are here at our first high camp, surrounded by clumps of alpine entanglement and the few meagre things of our establishment. The fire just won't burn too well and the ground is just too cold. These clear nights are alpine terror as far as temperature goes. Once again, the water patrol presented an evening episode common to us but not these bush gullies. You see, up here they just don't flow like creeks should and even if they did, they are so inaccessible with low scrub and "bastard bush[20]" that again the water patrol was faced with a challenge. Water gathering sortie number one turned out to be the first fiasco when scouts are left us splashing and cursing, heard muffled down the Valley in the direction of damp looking bogs. Later

---

20   Richea scoparia, very prickly and common in the Tassie SW.

that coffee billy tipped over so sortie number two got underway. Huddo and I went out to brave the elements of the ooze. I quickly went down in the mire with a triumphant slurp in mire and moss – the main culprits of the resulting three billies of water. The great, grey, green, greasy bogs had claimed again the same three victims. What a turnout!

I have just paused from my chain of thought only to realise that I have expired in a literary bolthole. I have sunk in so deep that further writing will be restricted until later on.

Day 5: Tuesday 20 February 1970

The day has ended long and hard. We are in the darkness at 3000 feet cooking an evening feed of soup, rice delight and stewed dried apples. Even though the fire glows warm and bright, and the food is piping hot, there is talk of an early night. I can't help feeling this is justified because we walked long and relentless from eight till eight.

The morning start was made from our high camp beneath the Dome. Right from the start the going was almost impossible. The scrub was so impenetrable and stout, that we almost broke down on the higher slopes with disappointment and exasperation. It took us till 2 o'clock to reach the Dome Summit. Immediately lunch was served up and some of us fell asleep before we had eaten, due to the warm clear sun bathing over our depleted bodies. The view from this peak was the first of many spectacular scenes in the area. So deep and extensive that you just held your breath. Lake Pedder by midday had assumed a deep blue hue of great beauty, already 10 miles distant.

Lunch over, we fell off the Dome down onto the high moor where tents were erected: the idea was to dash out to Oliver Twist and Double Peak returning in the dark to our pre-pitched tents. The journey was highly successful: the Western Franklands had been done all save Coronation Peak. We cut a fast pace all the way out along the razor ridge. Horrifyingly deep gorges with rushing streams fell away to each side of us falling thousands of feet. The crags, some of which were so steep they were un-climbable, were of fine a beautiful quartzite. The peaks were terrific and the views just too much. There seems little else to say. Today was so hard I could write much of what we did but little of what I felt. I'm too stuffed to collect my thoughts right now.

DAY 6: WEDNESDAY 25 FEBRUARY 1970

I awoke at 6 o'clock to hear someone yelling, "Get up Dylan it's late". This put a bit of a damper over the start of the day because firstly it was raining; secondly, I had been first up the previous two days; and thirdly I was just so warm and cozy at the time. So much for a miserable cold arousal. The morning meal was a rather cold, wet affair over which it was decided that a start to the day's walk could not be made until the weather improved. The traverse of the Eastern Franklands is quite out of the question in poor weather.

Needless to say, I returned to my sleeping bag and slept almost as soon as I got spudded in[21], only to find myself re-awoken 90 minutes later. Clouds up, mist cleared, some blue patches of sky, wind moderate. A start was to be made! We quickly got underway shoulders sore and feet a bit raw from the rocky trek to Double Peak late the previous day. I started off with a shirt, jumper and jacket which, after 30 minutes warranted stripping. Some of the going was easy – rocky with low grasses, however some parts of the traverse were precarious enough to inspire a freefall slip of 1200 feet. Vertical columns of rock reached upwards blending their starkness with the unsettled sky. It was an intellectual and stirring scene and thankfully I was not too tired to be able to appreciate what was some of the most incredible scenery to be found in Australia. I have travelled this big wonderful country of ours extensively and I can truly say at first hand that the rugged beauty of these Franklands could scarcely be surpassed. Somehow the peaks, valleys, scrub, domes and buttresses blend together in some fantastic array that only nature could provide. The views from some of the high camps and moors seemed somehow to belittle the man and put him back in his place. On these ranges, we are quite at the full terrifying mercy of the wilds.

So we pushed on. Ascents on the Buttresses, Citadel and Turret were rendered out of the question due to the state of the weather. All these peaks

---

21 An oil drilling term (from my time on the rigs); it refers to starting off a new well.

were shrouded in swirling mist and cloud despite our late start. It was indeed a terrible shame to the denied the chance to climb some of the best the area could offer but fitting in the respect that had the weather been just a little better, these climbs would have been perilous to say the least. The weather cheated us but through our own common sense, we were at least safe. The traverse continued. Some terrible cliff hanging scrub had to be negotiated as of old on the Dome. Terrible thoughts of another ordeal conjured up in our tired brains. Going was slow, painfully slow in fact, but fully justified by the state of the terrain. Once more the views were unsurpassed. It was unbelievable. We were hacking in and making hole[22] and soon found our way past the Citadel massive to the high slopes of the Grey Cap where we called a forced halt due to the fading light.

We have now got ourselves perched up on the high saddle just under the lee of the Grey Cap. Our altitude here is about 3000 feet with views East and West of about 100°. The skyline is jagged and clear amid the golden bath of a glorious sunset. The weather is clear and cold now and the promise of a good day seems now assured. Dinner is over and I now have time to enjoy a smoke and a brandy and reflect on the more humorous turns of the day's turnout. Firstly, our sleep in earlier in the day resulted in Huddo getting his blistered feet pinched in a rather morbid attempt by me to wake the lazy bastard up. Secondly Huddo and I quickly realised that the quickest way to a comfortable and noble bludge was just to smoke and generally "fuck the dog[23]" at the rear of the line. We even managed to force a reasonably early lunch adjournment, watching the mist and cloud swirl in and out of the perilous unseen chasms all around us the visibility was poor and the mist all pervading. Thirdly, Scutza got mixed up today over what he called "directional differentials" (whatever they are) and has recently let his logbook fall off the rock where he was sitting with a gentle clump and consequent curse. His disgust over lost tent pegs earlier today had to be heard to be believed. He was just so positive where he had put them but – well, the indomitable Scutza was wrong again.

I must try to record more of this later, but right now as I write, a beautiful golden 7/8s moon has edged its way up over Lloyd Jones down by the shores of

---

22 Another oil drilling term for making progress drilling the well.

23 Another oil drilling slang for avoiding assigned work.

Lake Pedder it is a truly beautiful sight and has us all enthralled. The lack of city smog makes the night sky a blazing and savage panorama of darkness watching over us relentlessly and with a sense of foreboding. I paused a few minutes ago to enjoy a drink, a smoke and a leak, and in doing so I took a quite impromptu gaze down the valley. Somehow the moon had matured in its aspect to cast at ghostly purple shadow of undertone told mysterious beauty away and below us. A haze of low wispy cloud fringed the higher peaks to the East and the dark deep abysses seemed to grope and a yawn with a damp gloom. The nearer peaks plummet into a dark gymnastic blackness[24] and fall away into obscurity. What a cold but memorable view. We are just so exposed up here on the high crags that our tents could easily be blown away, only to fall thousands of feet below. There are no trees whatsoever up here so the tents had to be pegged and staked face-to-face in a line and propped up and lined with Alpine button grass for warmth and insulation. This is ground where truly eagles fear to fly. If a man were to retreat into the darkness beyond the camp fire and lantern he could easily disappear dike roll and all to the land of the merry lickholes and bogs many feet below in the gloom.

I feel I must draw to a close now as the coldness of the clear alpine night takes hold of me and Huddo, alone here around the dying ashes of a faithful fire. The bag of salt is gripped with dew now and the water bottles are soon to freeze. I wonder if we will be able to sleep on a night so cold, unbelievably cold as this. Half our trouble is the time spent writing here in the open air. The body slows down and freezes over so much that body warmth, so necessary to outdoor sleep, finds difficulty in recovering enough to ensure a comfortable night's sleep[25]. So much for these things, and for the night. So much also for our most spectacular high camp yet, up here under the lee of the great Grey Cap.

DAY 7: THURSDAY 26 FEBRUARY 1970

It is evening, the culmination of a very long hard day. The party has just finished a really heavy evening meal and all the members have collapsed

---

24 Huddo and I argued that this language was verbose and a bit "over the top".
25 Readers are reminded that in 1970 outdoor equipment and clothing was far less specialised.

in a heap at the rear of the Lake Pedder HEC hut. Huddo is going through his final motions and poor old Scutza has fallen asleep without his sleeping bag. He just stirred, only to find his coffee cold; is now rummaging through his kit and has now found the sleeping bag. Once again, I'm alone here with my thoughts. What a day it has been! It all started around 6 to 8 in the morning as the fellows started piling out — I was last. As I mentioned earlier it had been a bitterly cold, clear night and few if any of us had slept well. There was little food left for the final run into the lake hut as had been anticipated. The plan was to include the following peaks: the Altar, the Throne, East peak and Lloyd Jones, so naturally there was little time to lose. A quick climb found us at the summit of the Cap and the day's walk was quickly underway. The weather was warm, following a spectacular sunrise, so a thick, oozing sweat quickly worked up. The Franklands just never seemed to end; there were some really gruelling hot climbs extending right through to lunch which was called at 2 pm. The day was fast running out on us. We made the summit of the Altar only to find the Eastern descent very tricky. We were faced with some nasty overhangs, with a path cleared by bulk boulder rolling from the summit. The descent was perfected successfully but only after some pack hauling, body manipulation, rock climbing and team encouragement. Time was now vital and a proposed immediate descent to the lake was put into operation. This too became very tricky. Huddo has trouble with the grip of his boots, and the Throne blocked our way — an overwhelming obstacle, sheer on all sides save the West. We circumnavigated, backtracked, probed our way down the perilous descent all in one terrible body straining episode. The rush was on. Night fell and darkness surrounded us in the swamps at the foot of the range. No time for idle admiration of the evening! We pressed on, on, until we were nearly all done in. Then the shores of the lake were reached 2 miles from the hut. Sheer collapse, physical exhaustion took hold of us all from thereon and after the hut was reached, food cash dug up, fire lit and the evening meal finished at 11:30 pm, total collapse was very clear. Personally, I feel that only the long nights of overtime on the oil rig left me with enough strength and stamina to record these events first hand. So, there you have it! I must pause now to brew up some warm coffee.

Who! It's warm and brown as the second-hand water it was made from — thin milk powder, cheap coffee, frozen sugar lumps and warm brown lake water. Real camp coffee with a Temple Bar to go with it. It is quiet now. Only the snores and deep breathing of my companions interrupt the warm glow of my lantern and smoke. Outside I can vaguely hear the odd cricket. Yes, life's rich pageant of colour and beauty unfolded itself before our eyes today — the views from the high peaks of the Eastern Franklands were even surpassed by the exquisite perfection of the glacier lakes and the towering quartzite crags. The Franklands are now finished. Fully traversed and in a blaze of beauty and colour, ruggedness as well is glory. What can I say now that it is over? Even my admiration of the range shines through my dull and motley exhaustion. They are still out there now just waiting for the next group of intrepid explorers, swathed in the mist and the cruel, cold realm of nature's wonderful ways. Yes, it is over for us now but will I forget those mountains? The days of sweat and toil, the nights of stark beauty and bitter cold, the high exposed camps, the impenetrable valley scrub. These are the Franklands -Coronation peak to Mount Lloyd Jones — always alive and relived safely in my reminiscence. And so as I conclude, the night must swallow me up, a mere extra victim of this our hardest day so far.

DAY 8: FRIDAY 27 FEBRUARY 1970

The day dawned here in the Pedder hut very late for five tired wanderers, presently fast asleep still nursing the rigours of the previous day. One by one we stirred — I was last again. I wiped sleep from my eyes stretched my back and picked my nose while the others were buggering about and generally making a good effort at doing fuck all. Breakfast wasted on past midday, the afternoon focussing on the playing "red dog" and gambling. Naturally enough, I was first to go out the back door — cleaned up. The time has come to recoup my losses and retaliate. Much should be said of the heroes who have beaten me into the ground — in particular their most recent examples of quite sorted behaviour. First there was Humannistic John who has now become so corrupted by rationing by Scutza that he mumbles Rice a Riso and Deb in his sleep. Then there is Lauchie who having most recently disappeared up his own arsehole, has now left the hut to clean it. Then there is the indomitable Scutza, who recently has proved himself expert at naming colourful vicious snakes, falling asleep on the floor, falling off rocks, pinpointing positions on maps and making sure that sugar coffee and milk powder don't run out. I recommend that he take-up rationing for the stricken millions in Asia. And as for Huddo the man who is determined to ruin my finances for 1970 (but for my profound proposed crackdown), he has spent the last day and a half falling on his arse, cursing his boots, sewing up his pants, pulling out his falling hair and also having a crack at snake identification. Still, they are all far better gamblers than me. Nobody loves me (when I complain at losing), and they all refuse to break violin strings over me. How my heart bleeds. Meanwhile as the gambling comes to an end "Fartza" are has cleaned us all out.

DAY 9: SATURDAY 28 FEBRUARY 1970

The day dawned clear and sunny and our late arousal was not warranted. All the gear for the hike over to Junction Creek was compiled so slowly that we really should have been ashamed of ourselves. I was elected to go and fetch the breakfast water down by the shores of the lake so, with warm sun on my shoulders and tattered shirt I padded my way down to the water. The silence and serenity were idyllic and drew me to singing to my heart's content top of my voice. The Franklands were mirrored to perfection in the shallows, and sand was gold and smooth. A gentle breeze blew wispy clouds or way into the distance and all was still. Here it was all laid out before my eyes. Here was life being lived to the full and all it has to offer. I paused to absorb this wonderful moment, turned abruptly, filled the billies and quickly returned to the more mundane things of camp life.

Back at the hut breakfast was underway and likes were remarking about lack of sleep the previous not due to John's (John Humann that is) loud snoring. There was a pile of diverse objects all around his sleeping bag which denoted articles thrown at him during the night. Breakfast was followed with a pleasant bog in the outhouse, situated 50 yards NW of the hut. I remember how pleasant it was sitting there in a three-sided commode, with the sun bathing my tired body.

The day's walk began in earnest around midday. It really was a terrible ordeal, the track going on and on to the horizon. The spirits of the party deteriorated with each boghole and culvert we fell into. Packs broke, shoelaces snapped, smokes were mislaid and in general the day went poorly. I had the misfortune to receive two jolts to the "knackers" by midday – things could not be worse! The pleasantness of the morning stroll by the lake was forgotten in a haze of button grass slosh and wooded gullies. It was well after the sun dropped under the western end of the Arthur range that we hauled into Junction Creek. A graded form of exhaustion existed right through the group, with Huddo confessing he was quite rooted. Almost immediately upon arrival it became evident that the shelter quoted on the map was more of a three-sided bus shelter than a hut but after 11 grinding miles along the narrow sloppy track across the button grass we were hardly disappointed. Wood and water sorties were sent out quickly and a huge fire heralded the arrival of a quick and hearty meal. The water ran out far before the fire wood so off I went stumping down the track behind the shelter with Huddo. I had to rinse out the rice billy and fill it for coffee when, of course, disaster struck. I dropped the billy[26] into the creek and the rotten, rusty little bastard of a thing went gaily bobbing downstream into the darkness. In I went after it and came out cold and very wet of foot. The only remaining testimonial to my brave action is our array of wet socks and footwear draped around the fire in cauliflower fashion.

The evening meal is long over in the camp fire embers of warm my feet as the coldness of the clear sky and austere moonlight ensures that the rest of me freezes. A smoke and some chocolate keep me going. John has promised retaliation if his snoring tactics meet with disapproval again tonight. I do hope to do some fishing and reminiscing tomorrow down by the Huon River and Cracroft crossing. For the nights of late have been too cold to do justice to

---

26 Critical piece of camp equipment.

my intensions. It has been great and much more must be said of our daring expedition into Tasmania is South West.

DAY 10: SUNDAY 1 MARCH 1970

Today we slipped up and failed to attend church! Instead, I suggested that it was Scutza's father who was second in the father of the year award and got hit in the teeth. After breakfast I was last up again – it's becoming a habit – I have found the airdrop tins[27] very handy thunderboxes[28]. The incorrigible Scutza followed and even had the tenacity and application to use the same tin as me. It had a re-sealable lid so we did the only fair thing and left it there for others to follow up. Not a bad idea as the scrub at the back of the bus shelter was strewn with used dike paper. It was a disgusting sight to behold. Come to think of it, it's so bad here that it blows about in the wind. Anyway, where was I, oh yes, the first day of autumn was a ripper-warm to hot and highly enjoyable. It was good to see the old shorts come out at last and to feel the warm sun on my shoulders, though as a result of 10 days sweating my shirt has finally fallen to bits.

So we left Junction Creek for Cracroft Crossing. We performed the 13 mile walk in one hour bursts, stopping for lunch at Seven Mile creek. What a beautiful setting it was there, too. The golden brown, sparkling water bubbled and barbled over smooth, cold pebbles in a cool, green setting just under the Western Arthur range. We were sweating heavily from a long morning's work so the fresh cold stream and wash there was excellently received by all. We left two hours later feeling refreshed and ready for the afternoon's walk. We virtually shot through to Cracroft Crossing after lunch. On top of the Razorback saddle we could see the next bus stop still 2 miles away, way down below by the riverside forest. The track (there was one for a change), was firm and the absence of lickholes and ankle twisters was early being noticed. Even in shorts the scrub was not too bad on my legs. As a matter of fact, the shorts made all the difference today, giving me a cool and

---

27 These were 20 litre kerosene tins painted orange and contained our food drops, thrown out of a low flying aircraft. We pioneered this practice, which was later banned.

28 A makeshift toilet.

ventilated run resulting in a change of pace which was noticed by the others on this reasonably hot day.

And so we arrived at the crossing. I quickly tried out the fishing gear[29] after a short but efficient inspection of the rock pools. The results were negative though the fish were rising. We should have some luck tomorrow if I can recover my snagged spinner! In the meantime, old Huddo managed to track down a very tame little wallaby who responded well to feeding – he is quite a pleasing little creature with all the familiar cuddly traits. A considerable quantity of food was left here at the heart so that evening meal was literally a Buster-rice stew with curry, beef mince stew, thick soup, Mellor and custard. Camp coffee never tasted so good. Tomorrow, we intend to take a day off, fish, sunbake and read. I hope to collect my thoughts and then in some cozy nook and continue writing then. In the next few minutes, I may read a Billy Borker yarn while Scutza finishes up his doodling in the gaslight. I suppose in a comical way it's back to "gaslight follies". John continues to snore night after night, except that now, as if to add insult to the injury of insomnia, Scutza has also caught hold of the snoring technique. Soon this will become a fashion in the group which I must learn. Before I do go to sleep tonight, however, I must check that all the gear is secure and possum proof. The large brown predators have shown signs this evening of performing a moonlight grade on our stores, so all the dirty billies have been strung out on the roof and the food housed securely. We must wait and see.

DAY 11: MONDAY 2 MARCH 1970

I am sitting by the evening campfire picking and cleaning my fingernails. The smoke is curling upwards towards the gaslight and clear sky, making my eyes runny and painful. The golden midnight pancakes reek of camp dirt but delight. The dark clouds of blowflies and sandflies have ceased their incessant drumming and buzzing for yet another day and for the while at least all is still. It was a strange day. Eventful but somehow not eventful – and in all it drew to a close with the dignity of a day of not much

---

29   I carried a two piece rod and a spinning reel.

consequence. A day when time stood still but somehow also wasted away as we lazed down by the cool bends of the Craycroft River.

Before we really got started, we found ourselves staggering after great quantities of porridge, pancakes and steaming camp coffee. The sun was already beating down warm and clear over the shelter and cooking area, and the flies descended upon us. By 11 o'clock they had reached impossible proportions. Although their bites were infrequent, their relentless buzzing and zooming was unbearable. It became more and more intolerable. We had the whole day to ourselves, with nothing at all to worry about, and yet the flies managed to spoil everything. And so, after an argumentative start to the day Huddo and I headed off to try our luck at the trout fishing. From the start it was a real let down partly because our efforts were not rewarded with success but also because we had such good equipment which we had lugged such a long way. Sometimes the fish rose but all we could rate was a snag. Spinners were lost in regular procession until the decision to revert to bait was agreed upon. Needless to say, the fly swatting (for bait) was a simple process although the aerial brigade seemed to become even more tenacious as we plunged through their numbers with relentless accuracy. The failure to hook anything with a fin on it was still unanimous till 3 o'clock, when a late lunch was called. In keeping with most of our lunches on this trip, the meal was indescribably pleasant. We just lazed on a large log by the rapids and chewed our dates, cheese and sausage with the silence that stems purely of bush contentment. Way above us on each side of the river the soaring amount and ashes showered their autumn leaves from the as it is your blue overhead down to the golden meandering waters below. It was as if the beauty of this outdoor setting was shedding its ornaments in one system at and somehow snowballing ceremony. It was a glorious rainstorm of dryness and perfection. I felt unsettled and could not explain it within myself. I had no excuse for feeling hungry or lonely, but somehow, I felt so. I felt sated but then again discontented. Returning to the camp, I tried reading an old Sydney paper I had uncovered, but the flies made that an impossibility. Things just weren't going well, but even as this was so I pulled myself out of this inexplicable rut without any seeming effort. I imagine the sun drove me to listlessness at a time and place when I had no excuse.

Nevertheless, let me think of the present for it is now that I'm most likely to remember the details. Airdrop tins are all around us here – empty here, full one there, new clean, now rusty, the food is sprawled around in and in discriminant array, merging with the fire blackened billies. Beside me, the spoons and forks are sticky with milk powder and pancake mix and the scouring pads a cold to touch in the night air. The fire dies slowly and each re-kindle results in clouds of ash which settle on everything in a powdery disarray. The shelter is cold now and its tin construction is more felt than ever what with its rust and its cobwebs. It's interesting to see the things here which are typical of bush shelters – the tattered old ropes strung out to dry the well worked, tired pieces of damp clothing, the rusty skyhooks which just hang and seem to have no purpose until you find them handy, the candle wax on the lower frame work, the initials left by countless rough predecessors, the cheap articles of gear left to waste away as part of the surroundings, the large logs of unchoppable wood, the broken down sloping fireplace and the traces of tinfoil and food wrappers well trampled into the dirt, in and around the paths around the camp. It is all here for you to see: the disorder, the dirt, the coldness, the dankness, the wafting smoke and the wayward wind. The glowing coals, the trampled bracken, the dirty feet and rotten stumps. The creeping mystery of the dark damp gullies, the unseen eyes that look and the untold yarns that are spun. The plans that are made, the achievements that are discussed and of course the feeling of being one with yourself and the outdoors.

Yes, it is all here and as I stir and pause, the chatter of well- chosen phrases amongst my mates rings true as always when away from it all. Still enough of these things – I would like to continue this description later in a different frame of mind, in an effort to give some sense of finality and completeness to these recorded thoughts. I think tomorrow some time maybe the thing.

To dwell on matters more of the present, there is within the confines of our group a mild crisis at the moment. You see, at the rear of the shelter are some un-opened airdrop tins marked "do not open till March 1971". A moral question is raging, namely, "Do we open the tin?" Scutza has determined that the ethics are definitely against the suggestion. "I would never do it – unless there was drink in there!" Huddo responded by saying, "Fuck the ethics…let's open it up!" Dylan to Scutza, "Well son, how about we engineer a swap: their drink for our curry powder?" From the rear of the shelter comes the remark "I've got the curry when you want it, plus there might even be a dehydrated woman in there. No, the morals are definitely not with it…oh alright then but only open one of them." All in all, it seems certain that in one year's time several members of the Monash Bushwalking Club will sense disappointment in the effectiveness of their airdrop – to say the least. Soon the encroachment will begin and it promises to be rather a dramatic and controversial little pageant. "Hey!" says Lauchie, "Got a mattock? I've got a root here." And yet here at Cracroft Crossing a play within a play, for as Lauchie is busy digging himself a hip hole to sleep with at 1.30 in the morning Tuesday, the intrepid four-legged creatures were beginning their midnight creep. However, their highly timely visitation has been upstaged by the opening of the tins. Much to our disappointment, the lack of beer was made up for by the presence of "strawberry happy ade". "Well fellows, one down two to go. Miserable bastards – only lolly water -they'll get no curry powder for that." Terrible, isn't it? Still nothing has been stolen as yet anyway. The tension is terrific – in our first true drama for two weeks. Deprivation has taken hold of us although it's not quite all in as yet. Here comes number three. The smell of sacking[30] is heavy in the air as I fade out. Zounds! It was the third tin which nearly wasn't opened. The cheer went up. Even Scutza sat up, as two large cans of Fosters beer emerged hot from their long useless slumber at the base of the tin. And of course, tomorrow we are off.

DAY 12: TUESDAY 3 MARCH 1970

Another long day, the fault of which was all ours due to our ridiculously late start. We lazed the whole morning away until the flies made life unbearable and the heat sent us dizzy. The prospect of washing up sickened us and we soon tired of Craycroft crossing. The walk to Blake's opening was quoted

---

30   The air drops were usually bagged in sack cloth.

as being 5 ½ hours but we were so tired and bloated after a two-hour lunch at 4 o'clock that the trip took eight hours and ended at 9.30 in the evening in complete darkness. We crawled into the cattleman's shelter by gaslight, so tired and weary that after a quick meal we are now all rolling over and dying one by one in our sleeping bags. I have summoned up the strength to write but this is soon to be no more. Aspersions have been cast on my ability to get up tomorrow in time to get the others out to the road. I got very touchy and angry and they all think I'm a shit[31]. So understandably I feel a bit injured, crapped off and not feeling much like writing. It might account for the way the moods of my writing change day today. Anyway, as I said, I am upset and cheesed off tonight and will try to attack the descriptions and character of the place with a clean slate tomorrow. Fatigue has got the best to me this evening and possibly the others as well.

DAY 13: WEDNESDAY 4 MARCH 1970

There was no doubting the happenings of yesterday. It was a hard hot day well spoilt by a late start which was directly responsible for the lantern walk in the darkness and the ear bashing I got from Scutza over his housewife tactics. But after all, that was yesterday and it's better to act on the present – Wednesday. For some strange reason Scutza decided we should rise at 5 am so that we could breakfast and get away to the art of road before the last timber jinker left us without a ride to Geeveston. It was pure conjecture (and by no means certain) on his part. So, his idea was taken with a bucket of salt by the rest and we drew porridge and pancakes out as long as possible. The walk from Blake's opening to the Arve road was gentle and scenic, and I couldn't help but think that those in the group that hurried, missed some of the changing bush, such as the rising splendour of the mountain ashes and the waterways widened out to display some impressive and ingenious river crossings of well-placed fords and swing bridges.

We eventually crossed the Picton River near its confluence with the Huon River and took the last steps in the hike. These last moments were

---

31   We were all pretty exhausted. Scutza joined me again on a trip the following year, as did John Humann.

not wasted – Huddo and myself walking and smoking together as of old. We honestly believed we had enjoyed (and derived) more from the journey than anyone else in the group. Things came to an end on the Arve of road with a snooze in the sun by an old "jumping off" shack[32] with an old coat and a kerosene tin inside. The roar of a 1000 m³ timber jinker drawn by a by Leyland prime mover woke us up. The driver pulled up and leaned out of the cab, "So yez are from the mainland, eh?" We knew we were back in the heart Tassie from that very remark which is typical of the warmth of these people.

As you might imagine, the group realised its divisions when it reached Geeveston for the only thing holding it together at that point was the love of the bush – something which then was left back in those great hills behind us. So, it was all for yourself and make your own way to Hobart. Things went very smoothly for Huddo and I. We managed to flag down some remarkably kind and friendly people on the route. I must record the ride with the snowy haired old codger with the characteristic pensioners stop sign. He was proud of his innings of 75 not out and was heard to say, "I am as energetic as a two-year-old" as he passed us round some juicy, red home-grown apples in a brown paper bag. Needless to say, he dropped us off at the Huonville pub. Later, a highly relaxing ride in a Mercedes landed us at the plane terminal in Hobart, where we found to our delight that we cut a very grimy image.

Not long after that Mrs Piggott[33] of Lyme Regis[34] was on hand insisting that we stay the night at her family home. Our decision on that issue went without saying, having already commented on the hospitality of the Taswegians. Nothing could have been more pleasant and I do hope this feeling is justly recorded here. It is all over now. Nothing is left save the departure for Melbourne at 7:15 am tomorrow. I think it would be fitting here to leave off and form some kind of epilogue tomorrow while flying across Bass Strait.

---

32 Often, major walking routes off formed roads have such a shack where your can set off or crash when you come back. Good place to wait for a lift.

33 Her husband, Russell was a friend of my father's.

34 The Piggott home in Sandy Bay.

Epilogue

WRITTEN EN ROUTE TO MELBOURNE FROM HOBART

It is morning and we are bounding across the layer of white clouds which stretch from here to eternity and from there to the inner mind. Looking out the cabin window the mind wanders back to the toils and joys of the last two weeks. There was Scutza, who for all his household ways greased his knackers daily during the evening water sorties. There was John who just thought it was all "no worries". There was Lauchie who became an expert at pack manipulation and lightening. And of course there was Huddo who burnt stews, developed blisters, knew who were his friends and couldn't catch of fish – and who blamed me frequently for farting. We are sitting here over the map we used throughout the hike and all the places and memories flood back the Swampy Creek, the shores of Lake Pedder, the mist over the Franklands, the Lake Pedder hut, the button grass, lickholes, the bus shelters of Junction Creek and Craycroft Crossing, the track to Blake's Opening and the Arve road. All of these places ring true now as they will forever. They are history now and will be affectionately remembered by me for sure[35].

Vale Lake Pedder
Thursday 5 March 1970

---

35 Some of this group returned to the SW a later in 1970 and probably marked the contiuing of my many return trips.

Lake Pedder in 1970

Huddo on the shore of Lake Pedder

The plane on the beach, Lake Pedder 1970

Lunch and a kip, The Dome, Frankland Range

On the Franklands traverse, day 5

High camp on Grey Cap

Looking through a chasm near the Altar summit

A precarious route, in places

The arrival at Junction Creek

The Cracroft Crossing

Tired bodies...

Arve Rd reached at last...

Journey's end at the Huon River

The route as it looks today

Another more recent view

Early Tasmania Walk 3

The southwest coast to the eastern and western Arthur Ranges, 1970

INTRODUCTION – WRITTEN AFTER DIGITISATION
OF THE DIARY TEXT

This was the hardest extended cross-country journey that I have undertaken at any time outside of the Himalayas. It took slightly more than two weeks and extended a bit less than 100 km though at times the going was so severe that we advanced as little as three kilometres. The journey took a great deal out of our party in a physical sense, though we completed it without accident.

It remains, to me at least, the finest, longest and toughest wilderness walk in the country. Highly recommended, but perhaps not for the less agile, or if time is more pressing. I have returned many times to Pine Valley in the Cradle Mountain Lake St Clair National Park. These shorter, less arduous trips are the subject of separate diary accounts as later chapters of this book.

The route can be seen on the Tasmania 1:100,000 topographic map published by Tasmap as Old River Sheet Number 8111. Access was gained by landing by light plane on the beach at Cox's Bight on the south coast of Tasmania. From there the route headed roughly northwest past the historic Melaleuca Kings Memorial area and further north to the Crossing River where access can be gained to the Arthur range at its northern end.

On reaching the crestline of the range the route follows the following peaks or lakes: Hesperus, Lake Fortuna, Lake Cygnus, Hayes, Procyon,

Square Lake, Orion, Sirius, Lake Oberon, Pegasus, Uranus, Capricorn, High moor, Buggery Bumps, Taurus, Haven Lake, Scorpio, Promontory Lake, Canopus, Phoenix, Centaur, Andromeda crags, Portal, Lake Rosanne, Lucifer Ridge, Pass Creek, Luckman's Lead, Boilerplate's, Stuart Saddle, Goon Moor, Bechervaise Plateau, Hanging Lake, returning to Cracroft Junction (or Blakes Opening via the Picton Range).

After reading the following day to day account, I added an epilogue which may answer some of your questions. Keep in mind, this was more than fifty years ago.

DAY 1: SATURDAY 26 DECEMBER 1970

It is 1.30 pm at Cox's Bight on the southern tip of Tasmania. We are basking on the white sand in the warm sun which has been improving ever since we left Melbourne at six o'clock this morning. Strong, hot gusts of wind made our Cessna aircraft pitch and roll as we hovered in an hour ago to land on the pristine, beach and we're wondering if John Humann will make it in on the next flight.

This place is very similar to Wilson's Promontory in Victoria [36] with its jagged peaks surrounding unbelievably picturesque bays of gold and blue. We had one of those great beach cricket stints with driftwood as a bat, an old rubber ball and a fruit box off some ship or other and soon found ourselves running and shrieking, and dancing in the warm sun.

The weather is perfect. During our inward flight we saw Federation Peak and all of the Arthur ranges, an awe-inspiring sight to say the least. The towering jagged crags are only fit for eagles and the yawning chasms and lakes have to be seen to be believed. Even at this early stage, I think this is going to be the hike to end all hikes. This morning's the little plane trip was fairly rough we all got out on to the beach looking pretty pale and feeling mighty chunderous. Pilot Jim England [37] struggled to put us down safely due to the severe turbulence around these incredible peaks. But now that we are here it is ever so pleasant – the surf is up, the water is quite clear save for a

---

36   My first camping experience as a 'tenderfoot' scout in the 1960s.

37   Jim also did a number of food drops for us ahead of our embarkation.

little seaweed, no rocks or stones. I'm feeling hungry so am wishing John [38] will soon arrive on the second flight with the other half of our food supplies, which includes lunch.

Later, after moving inland, we set up camp in sweat and mosquitoes at Kings Memorial hut, Melaleuca Lagoon. We had a sumptuous meal of grilled steak and onions with trimmings and I rounded it off with tea and brandy.

Christ, it's warm. I never dreamt I'd be sweating after dark in southwest Tasmania. Actually, this is a rather dreadful place surrounded by swamps, mud and with no firewood. Apparently there are two real characters [39] living in obscurity somewhere around here. We may see something of them tomorrow. The word is that tomorrow promises to be a long hard day in the mud. This worries me a bit because I have two trouble spots – feet and back – due to the fact that my shoes and pack are new and showing teething troubles. I hope everything goes well because we're nowhere near the high realms of the Arthur Range as yet which is still two day's walk distant. To summarise the first day – typical southern Tasmania bog country, terrible underfoot and altogether hard to take. But spirits are high. Here's to you all – Merry Christmas and have a brandy! Cheers!

A historical note on the history of the area

The longest lasting European involvement in this area was associated with small-scale alluvial tin mining following the discovery of deposits near Point Eric at Cox Bight in 1891. The mining activities continued until the 1940s, followed by sporadic use until the 1970s. Mining activities in Cox Bight were made difficult by the isolated location, high cost of transport and harsh winter conditions.

Relatively widespread remnants of the mine workings can still be seen in the area, including races, retaining walls, tailings and artefacts related to mining. The remains are significant as they are generally well preserved and are from what is thought to have been the most isolated mining field in

---

38 John Humann, who was a party member on the trip to Lake Pedder (Trip 2) earlier in the same year.

39 We met Charles Denison 'Deny' King, who offered us his guest hut for the night. His wind turbine stood out as we approached the area.

Tasmania and the first in southwest Tasmania. The artefacts demonstrate lifestyle and work practices associated with historic alluvial tin mining enterprises in remote areas.

The following Cox Bight sites are listed on the Tasmanian Heritage Places Inventory (THPI): Cox Bight Camp; Cox Bight Hut; and Cox Bight Tin Field. The Cox Bight Hut has gradually collapsed over time. Tin mining began at Melaleuca in the 1930s when the New Harbour Tin Company started mining operations (King and Fenton 1979). Many different miners worked at Melaleuca and there is visible evidence of various mining operations from the 1930s. 1941 marked the start of the King family's long association with Melaleuca when Charles King moved from workings at Cox Bight to start mining at Melaleuca. His son, Deny King, mined the area from 1945 until 1985.

Charles Denison 'Deny' King, a notable resident of the isolated area, lived at Melaleuca with his wife Margaret and their children Mary and Janet. They built a house at Moth Creek, as well as a garden and several structures associated with their tin mining activity. Deny King also constructed the airstrip and led the building of the two historic walkers' huts. Deny was a popular figure and is the main focus of historic interest in the area. His home and mine, the bushwalker huts he constructed with volunteers from bushwalking clubs, and other associated items are significant due to their association with his isolated pioneer way of life.

Deny lived at Melaleuca for fifty-five years until his death in 1991. His descendants continue to have an important connection with the area and hold a residential lease over the house and outbuildings associated with the King residence. They undertake essential maintenance activities with other long-time friends and visitors who formed the Friends of Melaleuca (Wildcare Inc.) in 2009. The Melaleuca Historic Tin Mining Area is listed on the Tasmanian Heritage Register under the Historic Cultural Heritage Act 1995 and covers parts of the former King mining lease, homestead and garden.

Peter and Barbara Willson also undertook small-scale mining from the mid-1970s until the lease was relinquished in 2011. The Willsons used ingenious methods to process the mined materials on site and undertook extensive rehabilitation of the worked areas as the mining progressed. In recognition of the Willsons' forty-year association with Melaleuca, Mrs Barbara Willson retains a residential lease within the former Rallinga mining leasehold. The smelter and processing plant components of the Rallinga Mine are considered to have heritage value[40].

DAY 2: SUNDAY 27 DECEMBER 1970

The day was eventful in that it rained without respite. Water dripped down our collars, ran up our sleeves and dripped off our hair, over our foreheads and into our eyes. It makes for hard walking – slippery underfoot and sweaty under the parka. Consequently, I despised the day; one filled with button grass and mud. And rain.

The crossing of the isthmus at Bathurst Harbour[41] was rather amusing. It featured the old mathematical problem: you are to cross the river and there is a boat on each side. After crossing, one boat must end up on each side and so on. It was made more complicated by the fact that there was a severe rip passing through the channel and one boat had no oars. It was so funny if you could have seen us, threading a zigzag course back and forth under the lee of a very impressive Mount Rugby. I remember playing captain, shouting various trumped up nautical expressions from the helm whilst Scutza[42] supplied us all with a pitiful exhibition of rowing. There was no evidence of seasickness.

We were now eighteen miles from our starting point at Cox's Bight, camped on a cliff with no water save for rain, mist and dew. We would have been very thirsty but for ample supplies of Chatelle brandy and Beenleigh's legendary rum. My throat is not dry – it is burnt as I lie here in the muddy lick holes with Scutza. The canvas is pretty dry and I'm warm as toast in my two sleeping bags but as usual I've copped a large sharp root or something to sleep on – right in the middle of my mud patch. You don't have to look

---

40 Melaleuca–Cox Bight Management Statement, Tasmanian Parks and Wildlife Service, Department of Primary Industries, Parks, Water and Environment GPO Box 1751 Hobart Tasmania 7001.

41 There is now a hut there on the north side of the crossing – not when we passed!

42 Bruce Sussex, another party member from the earlier trip to Lake Pedder (Trip 2).

for mud and bog round here, and if you mind your own business you still fall in when you least expect it – black and leech infested.

We have two days at the outside to get up on to the Arthur range to our food drop so we had better kick along tomorrow down to the Spring River, up over the Lost World Plateau and on over a further ten miles of bog plain. These early stages of a hike can really turn you right off especially when your only footwear is too small and pinches your feet[43.] But enough of these things. Tomorrow I'll write more if the day presents us with more and if I'm in good spirits. I tend to find this situation always exists when I write in a mood entirely consistent with the current turn of events. The brandy is going to my head… see you tomorrow.

DAY 3: MONDAY 28 DECEMBER

The day got off to a bad start due to the fact that we woke late at 9 o'clock only to see rain drizzling down. We saddled up nonetheless and moved out, saving our breakfast for lunch later on. The track was as relentless and muddy as ever, winding, turning and rising and falling, oozing and greasing, hour after bloody hour. Once again, the day leaves me with little to comment on.

The going is so slow that the Arthurs are still at least a day's walk hence. That puts us one and a half days from our first airdrop as our food runs low. Our spirits are high; the persistent rain does nothing to dampen them – only our clothes. We are now walking faster, stopping less, coping better with the lack of running water and becoming more and more skilled at lighting fires in the wet with no dry wood. A little hexamine[44] goes a long way. My feet are holding out pretty well and are now no more sore than anyone else's. That silly pair of gym boots[45] I brought may yet hold out.

Late in the afternoon we crossed the Spring River along a greasy narrow pole (we nearly lost Hector[46]) and pressed on up to the Lost World Plateau

---

43   More on this as trip goes on.
44   Kerosene impregnated firelighters were available even then.
45   Canvas basketball shoes were a poor choice.
46   The late Hector Maclean, our fourth party member, who became a distinguished ophthalmologist.

where we are camped at present. The surroundings are dull, the track is poor and ill-defined, the mud is shocking and it rains incessantly. Things must improve. Take tonight for example – no shelter whatever, very little water, little or no wood, rain while you cook and incredibly wet and muddy undergrowth. This is what makes the Arthurs so inaccessible and infamous.

Oh! Did I mention the leeches? Well, there's plenty of them around to keep you interested as you squelch along during the day. You wonder if that noise in your boots is water or blood. Luckily it is usually water because we keep a sharp lookout.

The only really humorous events of late are our fire lighting efforts. This evening, we were lucky – we found three or four pieces of choice log under three inches of water and eight feet of wet scrub and still managed to make a great fire out of it. Its peculiar having not only to find the wood but then split and dry it before attempting to burn it. This ritual is usually successful, resulting in food being eaten and tidy bundles being dropped in dark gullies.

During the day, we met two other groups going the other way. How is it that these inimitable fuckwits are so consistent in giving you poor directions and distances? They'd do us a splendid favour if they all walked off one of the many cliffs around here or disappeared in some of the deeper lick holes. I've developed a theory for hiking in this type of country which is completely dependent on what I have called Dylan's automotive analogy:

The machine consists of a robust motor with rough upholstered and medium quality tyres.

At high revs under full load the motor needs to stop and have radiator topped up.

Petrol is required two to three times a day.

An oil change is required once a day and hands should be washed afterwards.

The vehicle is a good performer in all types of country even on poor roads, but like any other mechanical device it sometimes fucks up for no apparent reason.

If mechanical breakdown occurs, the makers recommend

stripping down and complete rest. Only genuine recommended spare parts should be used.

Panel beating is costly and time-consuming so uncontrolled skids should be avoided. Check nuts and cranks at intervals for tightening.

Above all else, avoid shifty second-hand dealers and select a carefully run in restored model.

DAY 4: TUESDAY 29 DECEMBER 1970

A great day depending on how much you fancy being up to your knees in mud for ten hours. At last we have reached the ford over the Crossing River and are at the foot of the Western Arthur range.

Tomorrow the hike really begins in earnest, starting from peak one through to peak thirty or so. We've been hoping the traverse won't take longer than seven days and even that is allowing for weather which is incessantly bad. It is rather exciting perched here right under peaks one to three and Hesperus, with our first ascent only hours off. It sure will bring a fresh change to get out of our four days in the swamps with the leeches and unpleasant undergrowth[47]. Scutza and I are crouched in our tent illicitly munching rye bread and cheese. I say illicitly because we shouldn't be gorging ourselves on camp food. It was not without some reluctance that I convinced Scutza that cheese would be required. We have succumbed! But really there is plenty. The trouble right now is that I feel like a piss and it's too cold to get out of the tent and do something about it. Sheer laziness after a long day but my feet are dry for the first time in ten hours. Oh shit! Forgive me for I have urinated on Scutza's side of the tent flap. No chance of rusting hubcaps here.

Late this evening after a good meal of onion soup, Vesta chicken curry, Deb mashed potato and stewed apples, we had a sock washing brigade down at the river. Can you imagine four guys all washing two or three pairs of socks and all hanging them over the fire? The place looked like a continental

---

47 This point is about 45 km from the beach at Cox's Bight – a muddy slog all the way. Probably better today.

adobe yard, with special flavour added by the cabana sausage, strung up from the tree out of the range of four-legged wildlife.

Summary first four days: a very poor walk by Tassie standards, shocking weather, swampy, poor camping and very slow. Inevitable however in order to reach the foot of the Arthur range as it is the only viable approach from the south coast[48].

DAY 5: WEDNESDAY 30 DECEMBER

This note concludes the epic fifth day — surely the hardest and coldest and wettest yet. Today began raining as usual with a good breakfast by the steadily rising Crossing River. The weather was so poor that we hesitated over whether to break camp at all. But we decided to move mostly due to the fact that food was low and we needed the Hesperus food drop above us on the range proper.

We must've looked rather absurd, completely naked and up to our privates in the freezing floodwater of the Crossing River ford. If much more rain had fallen, our crossing would have been impossible and the journey would have ended there. We used our climbing rope rigged across with a handy billy[49] and belayed the last man, Scutza, across. His fall was inevitable and we ended up hauling him in like a cold fish. The day continued and the rain kept up, heading for a twenty-four hour non-stop drench. The track was impossible. It seemed as if the plains surrounding the Arthurs had deteriorated into one huge floodplain with a water mud coverage from six inches to a foot deep. The swirling mist and clouds made finding our moraine ascent very difficult. The biting wind and sleet made it unbearable to turn the head into the wind. Within an hour and a half we completed a good ascent reaching the foot of moraine A, arriving quite drenched.

We hesitated. A short conference was held in the mud like a half time football talk which revealed one thing, namely the climb was inadvisable due to the state of the weather but we had no choice since we were out of

---

48 This could be shortened by chartering a float plane and landing in Bathurst Harbour, under Mount Rugby at the isthmus.

49 A term used to describe a pulley arranged to draw the rope taught.

food. The climb began with our food drop an estimated three hours hence, somewhere up in the swirling mist and sleet. I was very sceptical indeed. The climb was about 2000 feet, very steep, very exposed and terribly wet and the visibility was so poor that the ascent appeared very tricky and dangerous. However, the climb had to begin and pitiful conditions soon made the going very strenuous. We rested after an hour at which time we found ourselves already in shrouded in mist and driving sleet. This first pitch left us on a bad looking ridge with dead-end crags all around us. Water run-off from these sheer faces made the finding of footholds very nerve racking and tiring. The ground surface was unsafe and slippery in places though we all climbed well together.

The next pitch of the climb was vital from my point of view. There appeared in the limited visibility to be limited access to the summit ridge and this was made worse by the weather which was deteriorating even more. A piercing southerly was running and the temperature falling even further. Scutza and John had their over pants on (as opposed to Hector and I) but we were all pretty well knocked up and freezing with wet and cold. I led this second pitch further up the moraine bearing left; after another hour we were near the top. But the top of what? At this stage we should certainly not have been climbing but there was no shelter or flat ground on which to stop. We pressed on and made the summit ridge of the main Arthur range on good ground in what must surely be recorded as the worst possible conditions. Few people would ever have climbed on such a day.

We found ourselves perched on a peak the size of a tennis court with visibility virtually zero in all directions. If I'd had my log out then I would have written 'position serious; party knocked up and frozen weather; shocking blizzard conditions; pinned down'. Our situation stressed the reality that the weather here cannot be taken lightly. Our wellbeing very much depended on our next steps and our safety was in the balance. We could not camp where we were because there was no shelter or tent poles[50] for our tents. We were far too exposed. We had to move since the weather

---

50   This was before modern tents with flexible, shock corded aluminium poles became the standard.

was very quickly ironing us right out – our legs and hands were turning blue in the driving snow and sleet.

We had an approximate fix on our position and knew that Lake Fortuna was only our only hope for a camp. A rough direction was chosen and we moved off with cliffs and vertical faces all around us, yards away through the blizzard and mist. Struggling and stumbling we found the summit of Mount Hesperus and thus fixed our position and located our airdrop intact. This put us in a much better position. We now had our food and only needed to march on to a known bearing to find shelter.

No time could be lost. It was already 6.30 and Hector was showing all the signs of exposure: frozen, fidgety, anxious, shivering and upset. Food was divided up quickly – some of the plastic bags had been broken by the impact of the airdrop so preventative measures were taken as good as could be expected to save the contents. Brandy was passed round and some of us tried to smoke. It was interesting to see two other tins there for other parties presumably still to come.

Lake Fortuna could not have been more than a mile off but we had no chance of seeing it. Our bearing was true however and soon we broke out on to an exposed low saddle under which the lake was finally sighted. I remember how we struggled in fading light, scrambling over rocks and bushes with our faces cut to ribbons by the piercing southerly. The ground was flat and spongy, under two inches of water with no hope of a fire. The two tents went up very rapidly and we bagged ourselves in what dry clothing some of us had. It was bitterly cold and as no lunch had been taken a meal was turned out over the stove inside our tent. Soup, canned tomatoes, boiled dried apricots and coffee. Gradually we recovered from our ordeal – a cold wet and miserable one indeed.

It's 11.30 in our tent here at Fortuna. The weather has eased off and the flaps of the tent are quite still. I can hear John snoring over in the other tent. Today we learnt what we're up against on these Arthurs. We certainly can't afford to take them at all lightly. Tomorrow we won't lift a finger (let alone a pack) until the weather looks entirely stable and safe. This is because Lake Cygnus (the Capella Crags separating us from Lake Fortuna) is two hours away, after which point the only feasible camp is seven hours away, at Square Lake on the north side of Mt Hayes. The whole route is almost completely cliff bound. You might say you can't mess around here but given one good day and the country will unfold before us – unbelievably spectacular and these risks have to be taken in order to see these sights.

It's so cold that rather than leave the tent to pee I leaked in a can and hurled it out the tent flap. Scouts should be more polite. Tomorrow our spirits will rise, particularly if the weather improves so I hope I can say the best is yet to come.

A summary of the fifth day: an epic climb from Crossing River up Moraine A to reach our airdrop below Mount Hayes and finally camp at Lake Fortuna. Very poor weather conditions reaching blizzard proportions with zero visibility. Careful navigation and route finding kept us safe and we reached our objective. A lesson learned.

DAY 6: THURSDAY 31 DECEMBER 1970, NEW YEAR'S EVE ON THE ARTHURS

As I write we are celebrating New Year's Eve at Lake Oberon sheltered high up in the central West Arthur range; the wind is icy cold and gusty and rain was falling heavily an hour ago. We are turned out on a miserable mud patch just down from the lake – too buggered to do anything.

The day dawned clear (of all things) for the first time for six days and a late start was made for Lake Oberon. Along the way we missed much of the scenery due to mist and general party exhaustion from the previous day but much was there before our eyes. It was too fantastic, rugged and beautiful to describe – but perhaps I'm too dog-tired to do so. Along the way to Lake Oberon we climbed the following peaks in all their glory: mounts Hayes, Sirius and traversed Orion and Procyon, and visiting Square Lake and Cygnus on the way. It was almost too much – the best I've seen and modestly speaking that says a lot for the mountains here. The peaks must be seen to be believed.

We spent most of the day crag bound on muddy, precipitous crags which held us up on Mount Hayes and much of the rest of the day was composed of some of the hardest climbing and bush bashing I have ever encountered. Right now, I'm too buggered to say more. I'll write more tomorrow. Happy New Year to my dear wife Heather whom I do miss very much. There is no wood here and a heavy meal put together on the stove in the tent is sending me off to sleep[51].

DAY 7: 1 JANUARY 1971, NEW YEAR'S DAY ON THE ARTHURS

According to our climbing guide today would be 'a very long hard day on very rough terrain approximately seven hours with no intermediate camp site'. That's a pretty accurate description of our climb from Lake Oberon to High Moor where we are now camped – very exposed and with cliffs all around us. Since I am not so tired tonight, I thought I might describe in some detail not so much the incidents of the day but rather the very technical day's climb.

We started late after joining up with a couple we met earlier in the morning and climbed out of Oberon and started an ascent of Mount Pegasus. This climb was quite difficult because the peak is composed of precipitous blocky slabs and engulfed by intolerably sharp, thick pandanus and scoparia[52]. The trace of an earlier ascent was followed, but success could not be achieved before resorting to some elementary rock climbing and pack hauling. Technically the climb was okay but physically it was tough and much skin was taken off our legs by the terrible scrub. Time taken about two hours. The descent of Pegasus on the western side was very tricky indeed. It involved a wide and very exposed traverse inching our way over lakes Uranus and Miranda way below us. We swung around across the lower scree to the saddle leading up to Mount Capricorn. Total time three and a half hours. In the saddle the sun was quite warm at times so we had one of those typical hike lunches, the only memorable feature being a really beaut cup of tea.

The ascent of Capricorn was fairly easy. Scrub cover was mild and there was a bit of a track to follow. As is typical of all the peaks in the Arthurs,

---

51 Stove fumes can have this effect in confined spaces.

52 Richea scoparia, very nasty on bare skin.

the view was absolutely marvellous. We could see Cox's Bight[53] where our journey began and also see Federation peak where our journey would near its completion. You sit up there on top of the world as your sweat dries off your body in the chilly rarefied air. At this stage all we had to do was to descend Capricorn to a saddle leading up to the High Moor in order to complete the day.

This would seem very simple in view of the fact that the whole day's walk so far was only three miles. But let me set the record straight – the three miles we did today were almost entirely over quite sheer and perfectly terrifying, very exposed cliffs and crags – that's the only true way I can put it.

The descent of Capricorn was as near to vertical as makes no difference. I can't for one minute understand how the scrub and moss hangs on such steep and exposed country. But for some reason it does and this made the descent viable but only just. If we'd had enough rope we could have abseiled a full thousand feet. And not only that, the moss and scrub is so unsure that an ascent here would be even harder than on pure rock. What I am suggesting is that a traverse of the Arthurs East West instead of West East would be impracticable to say the very least. Very few have ever done it[54]. It was just too much to come off Capricorn, making a route down towards High Moor and to see the cliffs and sheer faces open out and fall away all around us. A powerful experience. A good slip here and you'd be peeled off the saddle floor below in pieces – that's if the others could get to you!

The saddle between Capricorn and High Moor at the base of Capricorn was reached five hours after starting. This left one more climb for the day, up to the Moor itself. It started to rain as we ran into really bad scrub. Time after time we turned back and re-climbed. It would have been easy but for the scrub. Luck turned our way and we found a faint track up to the top and reached the moor after seven hours with an extra hour or so for lunch. It was about 8 pm and the mist and rain had set in.

The site is extremely exposed and very high, there is no wood and the place is littered with airdrop tins, new and old. Our second drop was located

---

53 At this point. fifty to sixty km to the south

54 This is probably not so now, provided this section has been marked out and made safe.

and found to be intact. Incredible as it may seem, there was so little dead stick here that we were very hard pressed to even pitch a tent. Such is life on the Arthurs-we had haven't been able to light a fire for three days and twelve meals. It's putting a heavy strain on our gas supply.

Tomorrow is another seven hours of technical climbing which should well and truly break the back of the hardest part of the traverse. The party's in good shape but we're finding a great strain is being placed on our gear. Any weak points become really emphasised – for example my gym boots – are guaranteed to wreck my feet and not last the distance anyway. Also Hector, who carries a light pack but is really in trouble in a blizzard. Then there is John whose pack is too small and too old and has small breakages and faults all the time. I could go on but the final analysis reveals that you need plenty of experience, good equipment and a mending kit before tackling this very difficult Arthur range.

Overall, a very tough and very tricky day as expected, moving from Lake Oberon to High Moor. The hardest New Year's Day on record.

DAY 8: SATURDAY 2 JANUARY 1971

Today sees the end of the worst day yet on the traverse – High Moor to Haven Lake, via the Buggery Bumps and the Tilted Chasm, followed by Lovers Leap[55]. I can only look back on the day with amusement as it was too shithouse for words. Everything went wrong at once – my shoes continued to pack up, my legs and hands were cut to ribbons in the scrub., I was loaded down like a pack mule and of course it rained. It all started late at High Moor when we all arose late, almost as if we knew that the horrors of the scrub awaited us.

Nobody really seemed to want to set off and in consequence the morning very quickly slipped by until at noon we decided to pack and leave. The army had dropped in quite a large quantity of food and, true to form, we never made it up to the Moor to get it – so needless to say it was all in. This is why I left High Moor loaded down like a pack mule.

---

55 These were local names on our Hobart Walking Club track guide – they don't appear on the Tasmap Old River sheet 8111.

We had not been gone long when the track dropped off a cliff (what better way to descend) and it started to rain into the bargain. Loose rock and moss accumulated badly and soon we were falling all over the crags rather dangerously called the Tilted Chasm which was negotiated amid falling rocks, flying bodies and moss strewn with pandanus, scoparia and dripping water. Round, over and down. Round over and down. One Buggery Bump after another[56]. The scrub was so bad that it was rather pathetic. You'd push and pull your way but the growth was so thick and the ground so steep and muddy that you didn't have a chance.

Here is a typical scene from the day's pantomime – you're moving down, front first. You grab a bush as you slip – your pack over balances you – you fall uncontrollably – you grab for a bush-pandanus – your hands are slashed – thump – you connect with the gulley – your pants ooze with mud – you swear 'fuck that bush'!

You may find it hard to believe but the ridiculous and really sordid scrub bashing on the greater and lesser Buggery Bumps took from noon until six by which time we were at our proverbial wits' end and knew not where we were. Somebody made a sensible suggestion that we get a move on as camping on the cliff face at seventy to eighty degrees covered in four to six feet of rock and scrub in the rain with no water might just possibly present a problem. So we tightened up our straps and proceeded to go mad on the next peak (the name of which then eluded us), climbing, slipping, sliding, falling and swearing all over the place, trying to find a route down to this mythical open saddle at the base of the cliffs below. It was so tough, so unbelievably frustrating that you felt like letting go of your pandanus bush and rolling down the cliffs to the mossy, muddy and mashed up final solution.

Hector lost his cool and told Scutza to get fucked and disappeared down a cliff not to be seen for ninety minutes, luckily safe at the bottom. The rest of us took a few precarious false leads and got 'crag bound in dense pandanus forest' to quote the guide. As Scutza said, it was a comedy of errors – the peak turned out to be Mount Taurus and the lake on the other side at which

---

56 These were bumps along the crest of the route, which had to be traversed a little below the crest line.

we decided to adjourn for the evening turned out to be of all things Haven Lake! A bit of a surprise, as we were originally heading for this lake anyway. It was rather like winning one of those Darwin raffles when you never had a ticket in the hat.

Of course, the campsite at the lake was under water and with the time approaching 10 pm tents were hung as opposed to pitched between the tufts of pandanus and scoparia in the swamps. It was now five days since we had been able to light a fire[57] – this showing how hard fires are to put together on the Arthurs. The result of this was that food was piling up (gas supplies were low) as we hiked from drop zone to drop zone and the weight of our packs was increasing to ridiculous proportions. Accordingly we decided to have a rest day soon, during which we planned to conduct a feast. At least it will give our blistered and torn feet a chance to recover from the rigours of rock and 'cuntiferous' scrub. Tonight is not so cold as I write with my least cut up hand. The ground is oozing with mud, the frogs and crickets are croaking at the lake five feet away, lapping at the tent. Further off, the shores of the lake give way to soaring gullies of dense scrub reaching up to the jagged crags all around us. Gusts of wind are filling the tent like a sail but the weather is okay for a change. Our 8 o'clock shower came right on time.

Tomorrow we head for Promontory Lake and two air drops. The focal point of the moment is not how much food is in them but rather how much beer and brandy. We plan to make a late start after trying to light our first fire on the Arthurs for cooking breakfast. Honestly, you'd need a bullock driven with a long whip to get me going tomorrow for today was the crux of the Arthurs traverse and we did it. The rest is not so hard, relatively speaking. Only by the kindness of the weather and our own tenacity have we made it this far.

Summary of the eighth day: traverse from High Moor to Lake Haven via Buggery Bumps and Mt Taurus – very tough indeed. I don't believe there is any more difficult terrain anywhere in Australia.

---

57 Now no longer allowed.

DAY 9: SUNDAY 3 JANUARY 1971

Today we dangled ourselves on and around the cliffs from Haven Lake to Promontory Lake. Once again, an easy day was made hard, but we had an excuse. It was so pretty this morning at Haven Lake that virtually nothing concrete was done. We took hours over a leisurely breakfast in warm sun and never got hiking until 2 o'clock. It was an incredible campsite circled by sponge moss, flowing water and prickly bushes.

Having finally left, we ascended to the first saddle above the lake where I had a disaster – first I lost one of the batteries for my flash gun which annoyed me no end and second, I slipped and fell heavily on a sharp rock landing right on my arse. My left arse cheek is so sore I can't sit down – it's rather like the after-effects of a really solid rugby match[58]. Feeling rather slack after an effort like that we buggered around the peaks until Mount Scorpio was finally climbed. A tricky descent to lakes Juno and Vesta resulted in the taking of two false leads which left us crag bound. At this stage Scutza slipped and fell in a steep gully and wrecked his knee, so the going was pretty slow from there on to Promontory Lake, where our two airdrop tins were found safe and undamaged.

It's really very pretty here with monstrous crags towering over tranquil water. Tonight we managed to light a fire and the meal we finished was correspondingly excellent-soup, egg omelettes, chocolate cake with cream and custard. The evening was so cool that we sat and yarned round the fire for a while.

So much for today. I'm really too tired to write at a stage where the Western Arthurs traverse is nearly completed. My new gym boots[59] are almost ready to be thrown away and my feet are as sore as ever they've been on any hike on record. There it is: too tired to record any further thoughts – too many cliffs, too many peaks and gullies. I fell asleep at this point and slept well all night. We were all exhausted.

---

58 I once got kicked in the base of the spine by some Queensland Reds and was called 'tail shaft' in the university rugby club after that, in reference to my fractured coccyx.

59 Totally unsuited to this walk. I should have worn light mountain boots which were still leather at that time.

DAY 10: MONDAY 4 JANUARY 1971

I vaguely remember dozing off amid three other snoring bodies as a possum descended upon our cooking billies. This morning, I woke hot and sweaty – the sun was already well up and the day well on the way to being warm and sunny. John and I scrambled up, made a quick fire and amassed tea and porridge with flies (of all things at this altitude) buzzing all around us. I couldn't understand why they were so interested in our efforts until I found the source of their activity – the possum had left a turd behind the fire, lying there small and distended in the warm sun (watch out for your feet). The custard and cake billies were clean and shiny – obviously animal cleaned, which accounted for the metallic clanking in the warm air of the previous evening. We realised that we are all pretty well knackered, so a day off, resting, was proclaimed here at Promontory Lake. All the extra food is to be eaten and much sunbaking, swimming and card playing would soon begin.

It is evening now and the long shadows of twilight have thrust across the still waters of the lake and over the steep crags above and beyond. The clouds slowly lowered and Scorpio above us was first to be obscured, heralding the onset of darkness. We sat around the fire yarning after dinner and in our lazy lack of attention failed to notice the falling of a thick mist all around the campsite. Soon our hair was quite wet with it and with time the conversation dwindled as did the glowing fire embers. So we all peeled off, urinated and headed into our tents, the time being about ten.

The possum again began his nightly creep as I lay there with a headache from falling asleep in the sun. The day had done us good. All our clothes were washed adobe style in the lake and dried in a similar fashion on bushes in the sun – a successful day of bush laundry. Moreover, we were all able to have our first good wash for ten days which had a really exceptionally refreshing effect. I felt a tremendous improvement mentally and physically.

Tomorrow we leave the Western Arthurs and head for Federation peak and the Eastern Arthurs range. All is in readiness for an early start to a long haul over to Luckman's Lead – the base of Federation peak. Scutza is six inches away busily mending his feet for tomorrow's ordeal. They look rather battle scarred and cut up. I hope they (and to the same extent all of us) hold out in this incredibly rough country. There are other goings on in the air; muffled talk from the other tent, crickets and frogs nearby in the dark, the flap of the tent in a gentle breeze, the scratch of the biro and the curl of the cigarette smoke, the curious drip from the end of Scutza's nose, the hiss of the lantern.

A great piece of mind has come over me and though a little headachy, I feel genuinely good and warm inside which is the real essence of a good journey. Of course, one misses one's wife, girlfriend, pub or other comforts of home – but you can't deny the value of spending some time out where the sky stretches before you right down to your boots and you live with the wilderness all around you.

So much for the idle thoughts of the two-bob bushman. Tomorrow, we strike out for 'Fedder' and more climbing. So let's leave it there for another day – we've had a great stopover at Prom Lake.

DAY 11: TUESDAY 5 JANUARY 1971

I am lying here in our tent at Lake Rosanne, camped under a huge boulder problem, as the rock climbers would say. It stands out like a miniature Ayers Rock (renamed in 1993 as Uluru) on the open slopes of the lake and looks very quaint with two tents underneath it. Once again, I am completely buggered after a hard day and again have the consequent problem of trying to get my feelings down on paper. But what a day.

We left Promontory Lake, traversed Mount Canopus, climbed the Phoenix, traversed the ridge of the Centaur and climbed one peak, climbed on to the West Portal and Andromeda's crags and descended to Lake Rosanne. We finished the Western Arthurs but not before they had one last go at us today.

The day was hot and water absent, the views often obscured by mist, the uphill hauls gruelling, the falls numerous and the scoparia at its worst. I neglected to leave Promontory Lake with water this morning and consequently paid for my mistake by getting my next drink from the rock pool at 5 pm! The day also took a toll on my feet and boots. I am now sure the gym boots won't last out this journey and I'm hoping to get something off the others. Trouble is I have the biggest feet, so I'm really in for trouble – more on this later though at the moment it looks like bare feet in Hobart.

Tomorrow John leaves us as planned. He returns to Melbourne and the remaining three of us hope to reach the Goon Moor high up on the Eastern Arthurs. Another long day – it concerns me a bit when we endure one long day after another because the routine is pretty rough on the group, taxing body and soul, the result being that we tend to get a bit on each other's nerves. This is a problem that one should be able overcome with a little intelligence and understanding, but then it is difficult when Scutza has bad feet and a wrenched knee, John has a pulled leg muscle, Hector is rather deaf and I have feet problems and disintegrating footwear. We slow each other up at the different times of the day but luckily we are getting on okay together overall.

I went out of the tent for a leak and couldn't fail to notice the blazing clear sky. A magnificent sight and rare for Southwest Tasmania. The frogs were croaking in their thousands over in the thickly forested side of the lake. They're making a huge din all in unison, singing their dank and muddy, monotonous songs to each other. Possums are out again and waging war against our food and dirty billies – guerrilla style. It's good to have a really great meal under your belt after a day like today – soup, Rice a Riso, stewed apples and custard and hot coffee – though I detest getting my bed clothes wet while wading in eight-foot scrub after dark, half a mile from camp getting firewood and falling in the mud when bringing it back!

It's 1.30 in the morning now and I'm enjoying one of my now scarce tailor-made cigarettes. Scutza and I have been quietly planning an ascent of Fedder with particular emphasis on keeping all party members in footwear. No wonder we feel so tired considering we walk, climb and haul from dawn till dusk and then talk most of the night away[60]. I must sign off now as our gas supply is very low and we will surely need all we have for cooking high up in the wood forsaken Eastern Arthurs. We'll leave it there with the first major phase of our journey completed very neatly and without major epic or drama.

---

60 I did add a footnote here that I did not sleep much anyway.

DAY 12: WEDNESDAY 6 JANUARY 1971

Today was notable for several reasons, not the least of which was that John left us at Lake Rosanne to head off for Melbourne and on to Perth for his conference. There are only three of us and our packs are correspondingly heavier, which could account for our exhaustion.

We left Lake Rosanne around 10 o'clock (an early start for us, shamefully) and left the Western Arthurs via Lucifer moraine. Through heavy scrub and tufty grass I fell seven times with my sixty-five pound load. We crossed Pass Creek and found Luckman's Lead – one of the few accesses to the Eastern Arthurs. From here till well after lunch it was climbing, gruelling climbing, climbing to exhaustion.

I remember the beads of sweat dripping from my nose and soaking my shoulders and back. Shit it was hot! Flies buzzed around my dizzy, tired head and the mud on the ground steamed. We staggered on upwards, ever upwards, until my legs throbbed and my feet felt so bad it didn't matter anymore period.

Federation Peak came into view soon after we reached the main ridge, all tinted in a purple hue in the hot shimmering air under a clear, deep blue sky. Exhaustion was complete as we traversed the Needles and Boilerplate in thick tearing scoparia and reached Stuart Saddle. We had hoped to press on to Goon Moor but we were too stuffed and an adjournment was called for, and taken at Stuart Saddle. Water was a problem until I dug a hole with (coloured brown) success. Wood was fairly plentiful, which kind of offset the displeasure of having no flat ground on which to pitch our tent. There was plenty of light left and setting up camp and cooking our evening meal was for once completed without gas stove or lantern. This is a far better way to do things –I even had enough time to mend my absolutely buggered feet before bed at ten o'clock.

We were sitting around the fire this evening having a beaut cup of tea up here on the crags, when the sun set in a blaze of real glory. It was one of the most glorious sights of the hike so far. The valleys were filled with white cotton wool cloud and the jagged peaks looked like islands in a fluffy sea. Above the darkening sky was still a rich blue, but tinged with cloud – streaky here, fluffy there, some pink, some red, some purple. As the golden sun finally sank all the vertical faces of the Needles turned a perfect pink and the overall effect was simply glorious. Our little camp up here seemed so high that it was as if we were above at all, looking down on it with admiration and warm tea.

Later the heavens gave way to the inevitable twilight and mist swirled in over Goon Moor and Fedder – quickly, all too quickly, the beauty was gone and darkness enshrouded our tired selves so we crept off to the tent, sloping down this sloping saddle, the temperature falling as rapidly as the pervading dew. The stars were all ablaze like last night. I wonder if tomorrow will bring weather as good as today as we finally get within striking distance of the peak – only eight hours and one mile from us[61]. It's not too cold as I write but I'm feeling thirsty and my lantern is not working properly. In direct contrast to last night, it's deadly quiet here – no frogs or crickets but plenty of rock. Plenty of climbing and truly incredible scenery.

Tomorrow will see us traverse to Goon Moor and then on to either Bechervaise Plateau[62] or Hanging Lake. I hope everything goes well. There is much I could say tonight, plenty I should say, but I'm feeling rather slack, tired and sore or something – the tone of my writing every night directly relates to the way the day knocks you about physically.

As usual darkness has brought the desire to sleep, so with tomato soup, spaghetti and 'mellah' in my belly I bid you goodnight from this marvellous and totally memorable place.

DAY 13: THURSDAY 7 JANUARY 1971

Scutza summarised the day well when he said, 'One of those days when you get up very late, get away even later, dawdle all day, take plenty of time and think you've done well'. It's so true of today. It had to happen because we were so exhausted after the two very hard previous days that our energy had to run low. And so it was that we made a two and a half hour traverse from

---

61   It was actually 4.5 km as the crow flies.
62   Named after John Bechervaise, a member of the first climbing party. Later a teacher at Gelong Grammar in Victoria.

Stuart Saddle to Goon Moor via the Needles and let that take up the whole day. I don't think we even left our beautiful camp at the Saddle till near 1 pm we did so much yarning and tea drinking in the warm sun. It was worth it.

We finally hobbled off along the cliffs and had a breathtaking lunch stop perched midway across the Needles in full view of the whole eastern and western Arthurs and Pictons. The warm sun and clear sky were ideal and we sunbaked and further wasted time with very little encouragement. We had a couple of nice cups of tea up there too. We climbed down off the last needle and sidled around through some thick scoparia to Goon Moor. Some people say the 13th is unlucky —after looking for two hours for our second airdrop tin without success we were inclined to agree. Just think of it. Miles from nowhere, depending on our airdrops and we only get one tin out of the two that were thrown out of the plane. This means half our milk, half our rice, half our beer, half our chocolate etc half of bloody everything. So now we may be forced to go on half rations. Luckily our new stash of brandy was in the tin we found. A lesson to be learnt by anyone making a similar trip.

We've got a good campsite just below Goon Moor with flat ground for a change, water and even a little wood. All very sophisticated for this area, and all very much in keeping with the group enthusiasm of the moment. We've had a great day's food and an incredible amount of tea and urination, except for my losing a few votes for buggering up the sponge cake and custard preparation. It's not too cold and I'm not so tired tonight so it's a good time for reflection and letting your feelings flow from the pen to paper.

I thought I'd let my mind open out on paper for a while and see what happens. We should make Federation Peak tomorrow, weather may hold out; gas running low, will probably have lighting and cooking problems; feet sore, really does hurt to walk now; got a good daily routine, but still find it hard to get started in the morning. I miss the comforts of home and Heather; finger feels sore, with a thorn of scoparia deeply embedded, feet very smelly, shirt stained yellow, running low on film but incredible scenery. I hope the rat outside doesn't chew a hole in my pack – rather an uncomfortable writing position and I'm starting to feel a little tired. Hector is asleep, Scutza is scribbling away in bursts, very little wind, my writing pen casting a shadow over the page in the lantern light; very soft here lying on all these airdrop sacks. It is Scutza's turn to go out and get some water. Ah yes, that feels better.

That about sums up what is on my mind at the moment. In summary, the group feeling is that we'd like to do Fedder now then get out of here as quickly as possible. It's been too long and too hard I suppose. Getting a bit tired of cliffs and scoparia – want to get home and see some cricket, drink some grog and catch up on some family life[63]. Bugger this writing, let's get some sleep. Scutza has finally gone out to get some water.

DAY 14: FRIDAY 8 JANUARY 1971, FEDERATION PEAK CLIMBED!

And so you've come to the southwest of Tasmania to take on the peaks. Did you know you were also taking on the natural elements of water wind fire and space? Did you know the mud in the valleys would ooze and the get going so hard you asked yourself if it was worth the effort? Or that the gullies would tire you until you flaked out? Did you know the scoparia would cut your arms and legs till they ached and bled, or that the rock would give way under your ankles and send you crashing painfully into a gully or chasm or more scoparia or pandanus? Did you know that the weather would freeze you to the core or boil you till the sweat dripped from your nose or that your feet would blister till you limped like a hobbled mule? Did you know that wood was so scarce that fire lighting would become a farce or that wood spars for tent poles just would not exist? Did you really know these things? But then did you know that you would crown the peaks and scan the country for miles around and feel your spirit soar? Did you know you would traverse the Arthurs and ascend Federation Peak? Did you know you would experience all the very best that Southwest Tasmania can offer?

A lot has been learned and a lot of ground has been covered. Many miles have been trudged[64], many cliffs and faces traversed, many gullies descended and lakes and rivers crossed. And then many peaks. We have taken full

---

63 It is perhaps not surprising that, at this point, our resolve was being challenged. Even today the east and west Arthurs are rarely traversed in one long, very hard trip.

64 The trip in total approached 100km with little or no track to follow with progress rarely exceeding 8km a day due to the severity of the terrain.

measure of this great rough wilderness and this has been the measure of our stay. Today, another long hard one, climaxed the whole journey. We completed the southern traverse and scaled Federation Peak. It was hard, it was great, and now we are wistfully turning our tails for home with a feeling of relief, satisfaction and exhaustion.

We left Goon Moor fairly early and made good time to Thwaits' Plateau via the four peaks and stopped there for lunch. An incredible exhibition of rock climbing, pack hauling and mud running left us absolutely parched under a very strong hot northerly. We met some climbers who advised us the best access of Federation was via the southern traverse and not the Forrest Chute. We found our way out along the ledges to the base of the final tower. The final ascent was easy and not expected, and correct belaying procedure was hardly worth the effort. We made the summit by seven o'clock in good light but severe wind from the north. We abseiled back down to the base of the climb proper like real professionals – just so our rope didn't go completely unused. We camped on lower Bechervaise Plateau at the base of the tower very late in the evening. Tent and campfire nearly blew away across the swampy ground.

Once again, I'm very relieved but absolutely buggered. It's good to be on the home run after these many days in the saddle as it were. Bloated with food, writing in stops and starts, dozing off slowly, I can't keep going. Cracroft Junction[65] tomorrow we hope.

DAY 15: SATURDAY 9 JANUARY 1971, FLOODED OUT!

I suppose we could record this as Black Saturday – a day in which we awoke tired in the late morning to hear the heavy pattering of rain on the tent flaps and surrounding puddles. We hardly even stirred. Under such circumstances we felt there was very little reason to do so. But being very soon substantially damp in body and clothing, we were forced to start bailing water out of the pools in, under and all around us. Still the rain poured down and as the water level rose so our spirits dwindled. Eventually,

---

65 This where our journey finished about 13 months earlier.

with Morale at a low ebb we disconsolately tried a few hands of 500 while munching dry biscuits which were no longer dry.

It was a cow of a day as we huddled together, cold and becoming wetter and wetter and progressively more pissed off. I slept soundly till late when I was rudely awakened by a troupe of Monash walkers who had made it up to Bechervaise in the rain, singing 'She'll be coming round the mountain … ' etc until I nearly had a case of the hot steaming flows.

Things began to look very grim. All we wanted to do was to get out, but the day was a write-off. Hunger finally impressed its needs upon us and we stirred ourselves to cook an evening meal on the stove. After porridge and hot pancakes and jam with some coffee we felt much improved. We began to feel less unhappy and got back to our normal selves. But the water from the heavens showed little signs of abating as we became pretty well flooded out. Only the most precious of items were kept dry during this irksome spell – basic clothes and smokes – all the rest went into wet packs: sleeping bags and food. What a wet cold dismal turnout!

Occasionally during our twenty-four hour stint in the puddle strewn tent, nature necessitated an exit and during such times the mist was often seen to clear in great swirling rushes. Boredom running rife, we decided come rain hail or snow that next day we would move out down Moss Ridge to Cracroft junction. Yes it was a bastard of a day – a day when you learn that being holed up in heavy rain and gale force winds in a less than adequate tent[66] really can wreck the morale of your group, no matter how many songs you sing to each other or how many jokes you tell. It's strange though how you can come to understand your mates and really try to get on well together under hard conditions – really try. We truly made the best of a very bad day: cold and yet warm, wet and yet dry, dismal and yet cheerful in the thought that tomorrow we would walk out for home.

DAY 16: SUNDAY 10 JANUARY

A day of some merit, partly because we were spurred on by the thought of heading rapidly out of the area after our day spent being tent bound.

---

[66] In those days flimsy cotton tents had no fly covers and usually leaked in the rain.

Keeping to the plan we had resolved the previous evening, we arose early with none of my early morning antics and breakfasted fairly rapidly, hitting the track at 9 am. The day had dawned stable and cold and we bashed our way down the slippery Moss Ridge for three and a half hours non-stop, which brought us to the foot of the range at Cutting Camp. From here the path to Cracroft Junction was an unsolved enigma and lunch was taken.

Later we found a sort of track leading out of the swamps but soon we were baffled, bamboozled and lost in the dead stick country, and bushed completely in the tangled jungle surrounding the West Cracroft River. As the going was hopelessly frustrating and tough we sloshed our way up the river as a last resort. You can't imagine how upset we were, trying every possible means of navigating a course and finding every pathway blocked by intolerably thick scrub. Late in the day we wearily crossed the Cracroft River and gradually cut a course to our airdrop at the junction. Some really bad bush bashing had to be negotiated and I mean really bad – up to three minutes for every yard of advance in terrible thorny scrub. Our legs were ruined. More sloshing up the river and we dragged our tired selves with our airdrop intact into the Cracroft Junction camp[67].

The area had been burnt out by a careless party some time before and so the whole turnout was black with charcoal and mud. Rather an uncomfortable and uninviting place. The junction of the West and South Cracroft River is at the foot of the Wills micro lead to the Picton range, via Baldy and Blandfordia Ridges.

The evening water sortie really rounded the long day write-off: up to the ankles in mud, freezing water and a fall into the bargain into the black charcoal and sharp sticks. Dinner on the other hand was great – those stewed apples and custard were so nice. Thankfully Hector really enjoyed his share at a time when he was getting pretty crapped off with this very long very hard walk and desperately wanting out quickly. He was not alone in this regard as were all openly talking of getting out as quickly as we could get our tired legs to move us.

---

67 From the bottom of Moss Ridge there is about 2 km of swamp to the Cracroft River, then about eight to ten kilometres down the river itself, heading north to the Junction.

Tomorrow is the vital day — if we strike out hard and put in a long day then we'll get out the next day. if not it'll take us another day so we should be out by the 12th or 13th.

This is a good time to pause and reflect on several aspects of our journey. We've seen some really superb country — the best that Australia can offer without a doubt. But the price has been high for it's been very long and very hard. Very taxing and very trying. Would I ever return? All I can say is that I simply don't know. All I do know is that I miss my wife and that the country is so rough that I often feel my love for the country, my spirit for it all is partly broken by its terribly rough bush and scrub which makes travelling from peak A to peak B so much misery. You have to love the country to be here yet I am here and frankly don't know where I stand. Perhaps the familiar humdrum city life will force me out here again — who knows? Tomorrow we strike out for a two-day exit. Will my cigarettes last the distance?

DAY 17: MONDAY 11 JANUARY 1971, ON THE WAY OUT

It's 4 pm somewhere on the Wills micro lead up to Mount Picton. Earlier, soon after having lunch a helicopter circled overhead and dropped a message which read, 'John Humann is missing — if you are the Melbourne Uni mountaineering club party, walk downhill; if not, walk uphill. We will try to land on a spur down further.'

We were shocked and worried as a few hours later we waited down the hill with our signals laid out on the ground, waiting for the search chopper to return. More later.

By evening of what was the end of a surprising and startling day a huge search and rescue operation was well under way searching for John who had left us five days earlier for a two-day walkout when he had to leave early to make Perth for a conference.

He was three days overdue and the rescue party were very quick to record him as missing. They had obviously checked the advance letters we had left with them and had acted accordingly. A large operation had swung well into effect. They imagined John had not left us but rather continued to walk with us, thus accounting for his late arrival, so they were anxious to locate the rest of us to see if he was still exiting with us. They were quick to see that there were only three of us so they wanted to pick us up and ask as where John left us.

We bashed our way down to a saddle halfway down the Wills micro lead where I thought we could be picked up. We laid out yellow overpants as a marker and very soon the whirring of the helicopter was heard again. The pilot made a very precarious touchdown on the tussocks of button grass and picked us up. The plan was to land us at Cracroft Crossing, the base for the search, and then ferry in the rescue party. The radio men were already stationed on surrounding peaks and a party was on its way from Federation Peak. Everyone was swinging into action as the news reached the national ABC network.

It was a return to flying in choppers for me after a year since working on the oil rigs and I quickly remembered the shudder and the roll in the wind as we towered over the gullies that took us days to traverse on foot. The pilot set a bearing for the Cracroft Crossing and we were about halfway there when by chance we saw some smoke. We banked and turned and there, by the Cracroft River surrounded by rolling hills and dense scrub was John, waving and waving by his tent. He looked okay and the messages went off as follows, 'Call it off – Humann located stop. Safe and well stop. Roger Roger Wilco'.

With that, the search was abandoned as quickly as it had started. The rescue party which had assembled at Cracroft Junction was lifted out and we were left at the junction shelter (with John, so now a party of four again) one day from home, passing round the brandy.

Personal thanks to Reg Williams, the number one bush rescue man in Tasmania, Jim England and others. What a fine operation under circumstances which last year resulted in a man being left lost and dying of exposure. It showed how the system can work and how important it is to lodge an intentions letter before you start your hike.

It's now late evening and getting dark. It's rather hard to write this as the news just came over the transistor radio, 'Bushwalker Humann found safe.' It's raining heavily on the tin roof and I'm saying to myself better here than under the rain upon the Pictons, fifteen hours walk hence. It's the end of a very eventful day and I'm wondering how worried everyone is in Melbourne. The way the media beat these things up, I could only imagine the worst.

Have sunk a very large cup of tea after which Scutza went out for a spew in the rain — he probably ate too much, drank too much tea and coffee and was unwinding. All safe and well — as if my friends didn't know. It's now too dark to write so I might get out a lantern soon.

The evening shadows have given way to a damp darkness which engulfs our little shelter surrounded by dark, awesome bush. Inside, we are settled down for the night amid the pitter patter of the rain on the rusty cobweb-strewn corrugated tin roof. John has told us of how one circumstance led to another and the events which ended with his eventual rescue. And now the company is quieting down. The inevitable sleep is near. Looking around me, the hut is much the same as it was when we left it eight months ago, last March — the cobwebs. the sacks. the airdrop tins, the candles, the flies and insects, the mozzies, the wire, the fishing line, the shoelaces and the inevitable large logs which are always too large and too wet to use. The whole place broods an air of familiarity and seems like an old acquaintance — an acquaintance rather than a friend in the true sense of the word, because the country can be very unfriendly if it wants to.

There is little else that I would really choose to add at this moment. Things have been rather tough and I'm rather worn out. There are perhaps so many things I should describe, things of value that I should record but there it is. But enough for now. In time, I may gather all the ends together and tidy up the rough edges to these notes.

Tomorrow we get out to Arve road and all that. We should make it okay but we are buggered physically for sure. It's been yet another day.

DAY 18: TUESDAY 12 JANUARY 1971

All our trials are over! The day has ended after we hiked long and hard from the junction to the Arve road in eight hours. We left at nine and from the start it was up one spur and down the next. We knocked them over in order — Mackay's Spur, Harrison's, Tea tree, Yoyo etc, one after the other, hour after hour, travelling in bursts of one to two hours and arriving at the

Arve road utterly stuffed. Somewhat by luck, we ran into the Holton family who have been very kind to us, opening up their house and giving us all that was theirs including their beds.

They picked us up, took us to their home in Geeveston, washed us, fed us and made sure we were comfortable. I'm sitting here in the living room setting all this down on paper while everyone is retiring for the night and I feel a somewhat rude to be writing here with Gerald Holton trying to get to sleep on the sofa. So I'll finish these notes tomorrow.

I never did.

Epilogue to the Arthurs

Written after digitising the diary notes for publication

As I lookback on this adventure after more than fifty years, readers will not be surprised if I admit that I cannot recall more details about the recovery of the lost John Humann than appears in the recorded diary.

Nor can I recall any more about the hospitality of Gerald Holton and his family who transferred us from Arve Road to their home in Geeveston. I suppose they helped us in some way to return to Hobart and to link up with our flights back to Melbourne. I have still to track down Jim England, who I know has been active in all forms of Tassie aviation until at least recently.

I did attempt to track down the three other party members to find out what they are doing now. With John Humann I was unsuccessful and if he is still alive he would be in his early seventies. As for Hector Maclean, I am pretty sure he became an ophthalmic surgeon at the University of Melbourne and passed away only a few years ago.

As for Scutza, as we called him, Bruce Sussex, as far as I can tell he is a consultant surgeon at a leading hospital, possibly in Montréal, Canada, though I have not received any response to messages seeking confirmation.

It will be evident particularly from the last few days of the journey, that this was an extremely tough and rather gruelling traverse of the Arthur ranges, to say nothing of the extensive swampy country which had to be crossed to reach them. This remains the hardest extended trip

I have made outside of the Himalayas. I completed a circumnavigation of Wilsons Promontory on one trip; on another I walked from Mount Buller in Victoria across to Mount Feathertop over a similar period of time; and in 1966 I formed a team and we walked from Licola in Victoria across the Snowy Mountains and Mount Kosciusko to Jindabyne in NSW.

These were all hard trips but none demanded the sustained difficulty of the Western Arthurs at a time when there were no established tracks to follow and all we had was a route guide published by the Hobart Walking Club.

While the total journey was not overly long at around 100 km, the difficulty of the terrain meant that at times we could only advance as little as three kilometres. This, coupled with the uncertainty of making progress, accounted for our use of the now discontinued practice of airdrops. These were simply kerosene drums thrown out of a light plane at specific locations where the terrain's which mostly dense cover offered an open space. Pilot Jim England, who also took part in the John Humann rescue, helped us by laying out our airdrops as well as flying us in and landing on the beach at Cox's Bight. We had airdrops at Lake Fortuna, High Moor, Goon Moor and Cracroft Junction.

Apart from the damage to our feet, which in my case took at least a month to fully heal, we managed to complete the trip without accident. It should also be noted that our equipment, whilst probably state-of-the-art at the time, was nowhere near the quality available today. For example, today's tents s are self-standing, usually with aluminium shock tubes, a fly cover and a waterproof floor. In addition, Gore-Tex clothing is now pretty much stock standard. Our rucksacks, or packs as we referred to them then, were crude H frame and canvas constructions which lacked breast or hip straps and were far less comfortable to carry. To do the trip today one would need to carry a gas or kerosene stove as fires are no longer permitted. It is also considered essential to carry a forty-five metre nine millimetre climbing rope be carried[68]. This is highly likely to be needed not just for pack hauling or abseiling, but also for dangerous river crossings.

---

68 Waist harness and minimal climbing gear optional.

It also goes without saying that for an extended trip, a comprehensive mending kit will be needed at some point as well as a first-aid kit with plenty of tape. We did not have walking sticks but I would not recommend using two as most of the time you will need at least one hand free.

I only took black-and-white film with me, together with a very small amount of colour film. Over the years, the quality of the negatives or slides, as the case may be, has been adversely affected by time and moisture. For this reason, I have included a mixture of reproductions of the original photos as well as some borrowed images to give a clearer image of some of the route in more recent times.

Looking at the internet I see that the route we followed can be taken on a guided basis, and in most cases has been divided into sections of a shorter duration.

Flights were cheap back then!

Federation Peak, seen from the air flying in

On the beach Cox Bight 1970

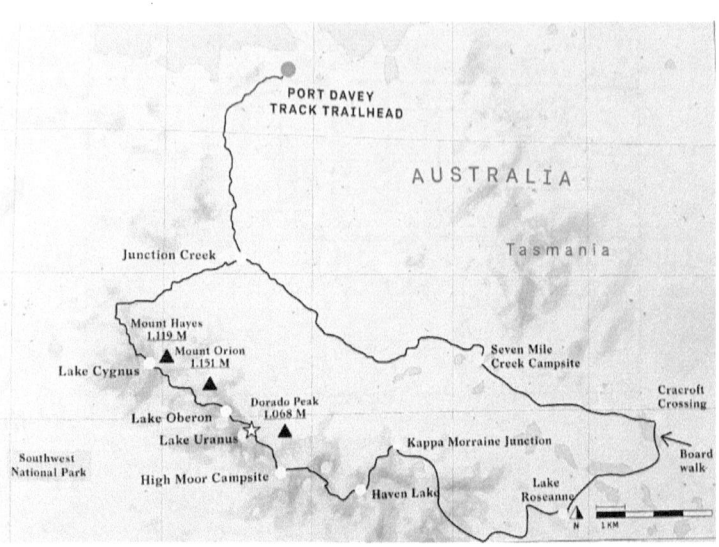

The route taken

A wet camp at Crossing River

Onto the main ridge of the Arthurs at last

The route stretched out before us

There was no track to follow back then

Scutza on the Pegasus climb

Looking back at Mt Hayes

Lake Geeves from Federation Peak

Photo courtesy Hiking Life

Towards Pagasus, the travers continues...

Photo courtesy Viktor Posnov

Photo courtesy Viktor Posnov

Hardy souls on the summit of Federation

Hector and I on the summit

Hector abseils off – note the "Dulfer" rope technique before descenders came into use

Early Tasmanian Walks 3a – Frenchman's Cap 1971

Franklin Gordon Wild Rivers National Park – Frenchman's Cap

A Retrospective

It was 1971 and I had graduated in mining engineering from the University of Melbourne. After a short spell working at the A1 mine near Woods Point in Victoria, I was recruited along with some other young graduates to work with the Electrolytic Zinc Company at its Rosebery mine on the west coast of Tasmania. I remember being quite excited by this appointment because the mine offered an excellent internship or training program for newly graduated mining engineers and geologists, but it also offered the opportunity to continue taking adventurous bushwalks to remote parts of Tasmania which were, even then, becoming very popular with ardent bushwalkers.

By the time I took up my position at the mine, I had already walked the Cradle Mountain Overland track and had spent time at Pine Valley as well. So it's easy to understand that by the time I had settled in at the mine with my young family, I was keen to add to my Tasmanian walking experience. After taking my young family back to Waldheim at Cradle Mountain, my sight became set on walking out to Frenchman's Cap. In this regard I was not alone. Amongst the other new recruits was a young geologist by the name of Ron Furnell who shared my enthusiasm so it was agreed that as soon as we had a window available in our work schedules we would form a two-man team and head out there.

In those days there was no guidebook or detailed maps as there are today[69] and the definitive *Guide to South West Tasmania*[70] written by John Chapman[71] did not appear until 1979. The track was poorly defined and very overgrown. There were no boardwalks or graded sections. There were no swing bridges as there are now. And of course there were no established huts anywhere along the route. There was simply a car park and a signpost on the Lyell Highway near the Franklin River crossing simply indicating Frenchman's Cap. My own images of this trip have degraded over the years to the point where they are mostly hardly worth reproducing so I have used some images from the internet which are gratefully acknowledged where possible. I have also included notes from John Chapman's guidebook which gives a pretty good outline of the three to four day trip and also mentions the alternative exit route via a descent to the Franklin River, camping at Irenabyss[72] and walking out from there. Chapman writes:

> This outstanding park dominates the Franklin River area and is extremely popular with bushwalkers. Its white quartzite dome is flanked by Tasmania's highest cliffs which reach 500 m on its southeast face. The mountain and surrounding jagged ridges are composed of brilliant white quartzite which give the impression that the surrounding region provides excellent views over much of Tasmania in fine weather.
>
> The peak is located south of the Lyell Highway not far from Queenstown. The Lyell Highway (Hobart to Queenstown) provides access to the now well used track. A full day's walk is required to reach the peak and most parties return along the same track. A

---

69 Go to Frenchman's Cap on the internet for details and images.
70 South West Tasmania , John Chapman, third edition 1990, published by the author and printed by Globe Press, page 182.
71 I knew John from the Melbourne Uni Mountaineering Club and we rock-climbed at Mount Arapiles in Victoria. John also walked with Mike Rheinberger, who climbed with me later in the Himalayas.
72 See my later account of the descent of the Franklin to the lower Gordon River in 2022.

circuit can be made by following rougher tracks crossing the Franklin River at Irenabyss then north to meet the Highway. Fuel stoves must be carried as the entire track has been declared a fuel stove only area.

Standard: a good track exists from the Lyell Highway to Lake Tahune hut providing good access in all seasons. The route from the hut to the peak is well cairned and requires some easy scrambling. The track down into the Irenabyss is a rough reasonably defined track. The continuation from the Irenabyss to the highway is poorly defined and suggested only for parties experienced with navigation.

Also included with these notes is a topographical diagram showing the route to the and the drop-off point from Lake Tahune down to Irenabyss.

Returning to our journey back in 1972, Ron and I snatched a four-day window and drove down past Queenstown to the Frenchman's Cap car park where we left my old 1956 Holden FC blue and white sedan locked up until our return. Allowing for the drive down to the turnoff from Rosebery, we were on our way as soon as possible, dropping down from the Lyell Highway to cross the upper reaches of the Franklin River, then passing over the lowly Mount Mullens before dropping down on to the Loddon plains, beginning with a crossing of the Loddon River. What followed was an interminable scrub bash as the track was fairly heavily eroded with the result that the ground cover was very hard on the lower and upper legs and also tore at our chests in places. Eventually we climbed up out of what we called the 'sodden Loddon' and reached a small pass which that us to sidle across to Lake Vera, which was reached at the end of the first day.

I don't recall any detail of our camp overnight at Lake Vera, but I do remember the following day we walked along what I recall as the northern shore of the lake to reach the foot of a steep climb up to what is now called Barron Pass. We left pretty early and the climb up to the pass was steep. By the time we reached the top I was surprised to see the morning mist still shrouding White's Needle and some of the surrounding quartzite peaks. We stopped here for a short rest and to admire the beautiful morning panorama[73]. We could see Frenchman's Cap, close now, away to our right and Lake Tahune at its foot, our objective for the second night.

Continuing from John Chapman's guidebook,

> From Barron pass descend west into the edge of the forest then traverse the slopes of Sharland's peak crossing some scree slopes. The track meets an open ridge which is followed down to Artichoke Valley, a green swamp of pineapple grass. At the end of the valley the track climbs a gully and then traverses rough slopes to Lake Tahune itself.

There is now a hut there with accommodation for twelve people, and additional tent sites nearby. We spent the night more or less in the location of the current hut and noted the turnoff down to the Franklin River, more or less onwards and upwards to the start of the climb on Frenchman's Cap itself, referred to as the North Col.

The morning dawned clear for our climb and the topography attached to the images gives an idea of the route itself, which I would describe as a rock scramble with a fair degree of exposure. It would not be a nice place if the wind got up and the weather turned foul. I recall the summit area as being broader and flatter than I expected, with a very large cairn. The southeast face drops vertically for about 500 m and has been the scene of base jumps (long after our visit, of course) and the view is expansive in all directions.

Continuing from John's description,

> From the hut follow the tracks across the outlet creek then west up the scree slopes to the saddle above known as the North Col. Turn south following the ridge to the cliffs. The track climbs a chimney above Lake Tahune and then ascends a series of ledges to the slopes leading to the summit cairn. In fine weather the views are tremendous and well worth the effort.

---

73 Great views of Philip's and Sharland Peaks on each side of the pass.

We were pleased with our summit day and grateful for sufficiently fine weather to take in the magnificent views from the top. To this day I cannot recall whether we spent a second night down at Lake Tahune, or whether we backtracked over Barron pass and spent a third night down at Lake Vera. Whichever was the case, we trudged back over the sodden Loddon and got back to the car park pretty much exhausted the following day.

This trip did not it present the extreme challenges of the eastern and western Arthurs, nor was it anything like as sustained. Nonetheless it remains in my memory as a high-quality short walk and it is clear that a great deal of work has been put into improving the track and positioning some huts along the way. Every time I go to Tasmania and glimpse the Cap in the distance from wherever I happen to be, I look back on this trip as a very special one, imbued with pleasant memories of good companionship and spectacular country.

As something of a footnote, when I saw the alternative exit route leading down to the Irenabyss, I made a mental note that I must, at some point in my life, do the descent of the Franklin River[74] and take the opportunity to stop and take in the grandeur of Irenabyss. I was not to know at the time that it would be fifty years before I honoured that promise.

---

74 Readers may wish to read my account of that eight- day white water descent.

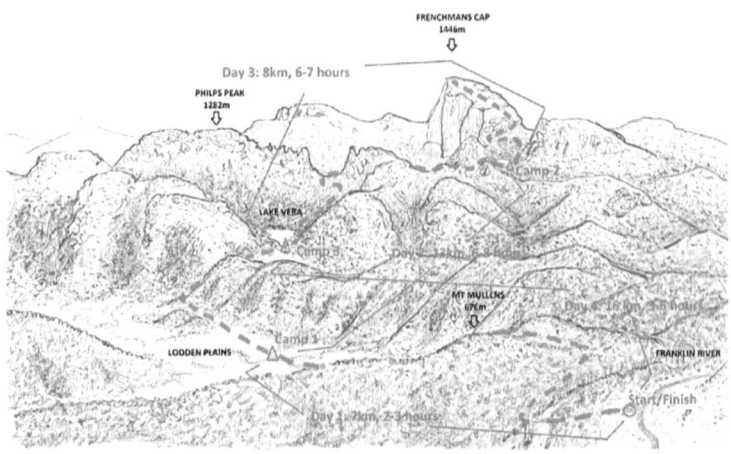

The route in to Frenchman's Cap

The Cap, seen from near baron Pass

The Cap, seen from the camp area at Lake Tahune

The summit route

Early Tasmanian Walks 3b

Mount Anne and the Mount Anne circuit 1972

Those who read my accounts of a visit to Lake Pedder and a subsequent traverse of the Frankland range may recall references to views of a faraway Mount Anne looking north from the peaks of the Frankland range. That was in the late 1960s. By the early 1970s I was working at the Rosebery mine on the west coast of Tasmania. That gave rise to lots of walking opportunities in the southwest and I began by completing a walk out to Frenchman's Cap.

A little later, possibly in 1972, I made more than one visit to parts of the Mount Anne circuit, starting with the track up to Mount Eliza from Condominium Creek. With the weather being what it is frequently in Tasmania, I was never able to complete the entire Mount Anne circuit and have no written diary of such a trip. However, I did venture up past Mount Eliza in both summer and winter and I do recall that the day hut just below Mount Eliza was being constructed about that time.

As was the case with the Frenchman's Cap record, I have chosen to quote extracts from John Chapman's *Southwest Tasmania*[75] as it brings readers up to date with the situation when that guide was published.

> Mount Anne is the highest peak in the southwest. With its sharp profile and huge cliffs it dominates the area. It is part of a small range of peaks that are composed of white quartzite capped by

---

75 Southwest Tasmania, published by John Chapman, 3rd edition, 1990 printed by Globe Press, page 174.

red dolerite. This is in sharp contrast to the surrounding white quartzite ranges of the southwest. The scenery and views in fine weather are superb. With Scots Peak Road passing along the foot of this range Mount Anne can be climbed in a long return day trip from the road. The recommended trip to attempt is the high level circuit. Although short, it is as good as any other trip in the southwest. Fuel stoves must be carried and used as the entire range has been declared a fuel stove only area. The Mount Anne circuit takes two long days for fit parties. However, three to four days is recommended to explore this area more thoroughly and to allow for poor weather.

On both the occasions I went to the foot of Mount Anne I was turned back by nasty weather. That is apparent from the limited black and white photographs that I took on those visits.

A far better idea of the quality of the Mount Anne circuit is provided by a seventeen minute video available on U-Tube. Titled the *Mount Anne Circuit Tasmania*, it was filmed by Cam Bostock and hopefully can be accessed using the abbreviated link[76] given below. It's an excellent coverage of the circuit, showing the campsites at Mount Eliza, the shelf camp as well as the Little Tarns. The views are superb and I could not help noticing the improvement in the quality of the track right round the circuit given that there were no tracks at all in the 1970s.

For those interested in the flooding of Lake Pedder and know what it looks like today, the old black and white prints looking down over Mount Solitary from Mount Eliza with the Frankland range in the background give an idea of how looked way back then. I did read somewhere that the pristine quartzite beach of the original Lake Pedder is still intact below the waterline according to divers who ventured to the bottom of the new lake equipped with camera gear.

---

76 https://www.google.com.au/search?q=mt+anne+tasmania

Early Tasmanian Walks 3c, Precipitous Bluff, 1974

An aborted trip and a cold walk in the snow

Location[77]

Set deep in the southwest wilderness, Precipitous Bluff (PB for short) is an impressive dolerite peak with a towering rampart of columnar cliffs facing out to the Southern Ocean. The problem is access as any prospecting climber faces at least four days' walk in, and out, and has to brave the frequent appalling weather.

History

Over the years climbers have braved the elements and explored a little of the enormous potential of the area. Details are scant but it seems the peak was first climbed by MacUrquhart in the 1930s. Dave Neilson from Melbourne is reputed to have visited and left a rope there in the mid-70s, but it isn't known what, if any, climbing was done. Phil Robinson, Tasmania's leading exploratory climber for many years, was there with Chris (Basil) Rathbone in 1986:

> We climbed a good long ridge to the summit, some short routes but the main face had blank corners (needed pegs which we didn't have) like the E. Face of Mt Anne. We had hexs and wires and two or three

---

77 Compiled from original material by Phil Robinson, Chris Rathbone, Steve Monks and Ross Taylor this content from http://www.thesarvo.com/confluence/display/thesarvo/Precipitous+Bluff

original Friends but we never used to aid anything in those days. If it didn't go free there was always another line to try.

In 1994 visiting Victorian climbers Steve Monks and Jane Wilkinson, undaunted by the out-there location and access problems, created a major multi-pitch wilderness climb, Precipitous Arête[23] committing themselves with the minimum of gear 'a single 30m rope and a handful of wires'.

The next new route recorded was in 2012 when Lachlan and Ross Taylor hiked along the coast from Melaleuca, up the lagoon and added The Paddy Line (380m, 18) – 'the easiest looking line up the main face'.

Access

These are not for the faint hearted!

Route 1 – from Cockle Creek follow the South Coast Track north for three days to New Lagoon, then wade up the river for another day to Damper Creek. From here, follow a taped 'track' for maybe four hours up to the cliff line. The track turns north here and follows the cliff base to a major gully. This has been climbed (difficult) as a way to the summit but the main route continues on for about another hour, then up and round another narrow gully before climbing more easily up the ascent gully, exiting when it ends and into the next gully which leads to the top. Descent is via this path. Camping is available at a rough campsite on the south bank of the Damper River (658850), or there is a small bivvy near a permanent pool about fifteen minutes after the track turns north at the base of the cliffs.

Route 2 – traverse the Southern Ranges for two to three days from Lune River via Moonlight Flats, Hills 1-4, Mount La Perouse and Pindar's Peak. This is quicker than the South Coast track although very exposed. Camp at a semi-sheltered hollow just below the summit.

The best weather is usually February and March although you can expect lousy conditions at any time. PB is in Tasmania's World Heritage Area and is a fuel stove only area. Full details on the South Coast track, access and transport are available in John Chapman's *Southwest Tasmania Guide, 2008*. See also TASMAP 1:25 000 Precipitous and/or 1:100 000 South Coast Walks, and http://www.parks.tas.gov.au/recreation/tracknotes/scoast.html for track information.

Diary of a trip that wasn't

Well, that was the plan. Precipitous Bluff. PB or Perwibbery Buff, as my then pre-school son John referred to it. I had talked about it so much around the home he had picked it up.

PB was a landmark overlooking New River Lagoon in the southwest Tasmania heritage area, close to the coast. Basically, it could be accessed three ways:

1. From Lune River via Moonlight Ridge, starting at Mystery Creek (and Mystery Cave); along the Moonlight Ridge Track to Pigsty Ponds (climb Mount Perouse); then on to Pindar's Peak; then to Pandani Knob, Leaning Tree Saddle leading to the foot of PB (east side) via the Kameruka lead. On one trip, I went as far as Pandani Knob but never as far as PB itself.

2. Via the South Coast Track, starting at Catamaran following the track past South Cape Bay, Shoemaker and Surprise bays, then all the way to Prion Beach where it crosses the New River. From there, wade up the lake shore to PB (west side) camp on Damper Creek. I never did this stretch as on the earlier trip to the East and West Arthur Ranges, we flew in to Cox Bight (30 km further to the west), landed on the ocean beach and set off north from there. PB was becoming somewhat elusive.

3. Fly in to New River Lagoon, landing by float plane at Damper Creek or near to it, follow the track from Damper Creek camp east, up to the base of the cliffs and follow the climbing topos from there. This was the plan and I arranged a float plane (weather permitting) with Jim England, who flew us to Cox Bight all those years ago.

In 1974 I started work as a lecturer in mining engineering at the University of Melbourne. In 1973, before I left Tasmania and my work at the Rosebery mine in the west coast, I was keen to tick off the elusive PB.

I was in Hobart, having organised some time off, when my father arrived, accompanied by Rajendra Singh Deswal, a friend of mine and the son of a surgical colleague of my dad back in Patiala[78], northern India. It was planned that we would fly in to New River Lagoon. But the weather was against us.

Each morning, we were ready to go, until the call came in from Jim cancelling the flight. Eventually we had to abandon the plan lest we ran out of time to allow dad or Raj to see anything of the Tassie backcountry I was so keen to show them.

What were we to do? We had all our gear and food and the easiest option was to drive to Derwent Bridge, the gateway to Lake St Clair, and take dad and Raj up to Pine Valley. The route was very familiar to me but it was winter and likely to be subject to heavy snow in places. Not deterred, we set off.

DAY 1: LAKE ST CLAIR

We left Derwent Bridge and left the vehicle at Cynthia Bay park headquarters at the southern end of the Cradle Mountain Park. Being off season, there was no boat taxi to the northern end of the lake and Narcissus hut. We thus had no option but to follow the track along the western shore of the lake, all the way to Echo Point and then on to the hut. But as we had arrived in the middle of the day, we did not reach the hut by nightfall and had to camp short, in a light A-frame tent with snow falling.

I had made up cold/wet weather gear for Raj and dad: parkas, balaclava and gloves, leaving it to them to bring warm clothing. We did not bring gaiters and walking poles did not exist. Dad wore his camouflage military trousers from our time in Vietnam. Raj also brought a warm scarf, seen in the old faded images.

I also had spare rucksacks: old H-frames with no waist or breast straps

---

78 Years before, Raj and I played cricket in his front yard as youngsters, that is until a cobra interrupted the game.

– very uncomfortable by today's standards. But it was all you could get back then. Raj's pack was even older – an early European design with a small A-frame, all in heavy canvas. All in all, we must have presented a rather disorganised outfit.

DAY 2: PINE VALLEY

It was a rather miserable night and we were up and off early, passing Echo Point and stopping later in the morning at Narcissus[79]. As we arrived, I cast my mind back to a previous visit with my brother and was reminded of the ghetto blaster he carried all the way to Pine Vally hut and back, playing haunting tunes like *Tamalpais High*[80] as we moved along.

What is now a three-hour walk to the hut was a different proposition back then. For starters there were no swing bridges across the two major watercourses, plus we had to confront winter conditions and snow. This meant that the forest route to the hut (not the exposed plains route) would be best.

By late afternoon we were still short of the hut and wading through heavy snow drifts in places. Dad was concerned as Raj was nearly done in – stopping to rest on his back pack and very disinclined to continue. But continue we must as another night in the cold tent was not part of my plan. We had to press on.

I did my best to reassure the others, but as evening approached with visibility down and light snow falling, they were visibly concerned. We were discussing our predicament as I looked about, looking for something familiar. And there it was: a crooked beech tree I had often photographed on previous trips. I knew exactly where we were. I said to the others, 'Wait! I know where we are. The hut is just up the rise from the creek. Follow me.'

And that was how we stumbled upon the old hut[81.] The snow was up half way to the roof and we had to dig out to open the door.

Dad and Raj were in a bad state – mild exposure and exhaustion – but

---

79   This hut now has radio contact with the Park office at Cynthia Bay.
80   On David Crosby's solo album.
81   It has since been replaced as described and shown later in this book.

they had made it! There was no fuel in the hut but I got a fire going and they soon cheered up and we cooked a warming meal. Dad said something about a 'close call' and 'you did well to get us here' or something along those lines. There was so much snow outside that we could not gather anything dry for the fire[82]. There was, however, some broken down, rickety, furniture which had to suffice. After all, the hut log indicated nobody had been here for several months and no one was likely to return until November. We were certainly on our own.

DAY 3: STAY OR LEAVE?

We ate well and slept the sleep of a tired party but awoke to poor weather and little opportunity to venture far from the security of the hut. Raj was still pretty buggered and dad was questioning the wisdom of us hanging around with time running out and the weather not looking good. He was right. We needed to get Raj back to civilisation while he was still up to the return journey. That meant retracing our steps to Narcissus, resting there and walking out to Cynthia Bay the following day.

It was a subdued party as we trudged rather glumly back through the dripping wet coming from above, the track very slippery and muddy and still under snow in places. Today, much of this route has been made safer with duckboards, which greatly reduce overall journey time – but for us, then, we simply had to press on.

Our packs were lighter and our spirits picked up as we crossed Cephissus Creek and then the Narcissus River (both on slimy logs) as the hut beckoned. Having left the greenery of Pine Vally, we emerged into more open eucalypt country which fringes the Narcissus River, heralding the proximity of the hut. My companions were understandably relieved to be able to call a halt, rest up, get dry and focus on the walk out tomorrow.

The hut is seen as the terminus for the Overland Track and sees tens of visitors every day in the summer walking season. There is jetty there now for the water taxi and a resident platypus which shows itself usually around dawn or dusk. The hut has been rebuilt compared to the hut we stopped in

---

82 In those days there was no stove, coal fuel or toilet.

on this trip. Still, it was roomy and comfortable and by evening, dad and Raj were in good spirits and pleased with their achievement – Pine Valley in winter – with no water taxi!

DAY 4: REDEMPTION

The homeward walk back down the lake was uneventful. We all walked strongly and made a familiar stiff, footsore return to the park office and camp area, where we rented an overnight cabin. Nobody wanted to drive to Hobart. It was afternoon and there were hot showers!

In retrospect, we were lucky not to get to New River Lagoon. The weather, plus the route from the lagoon up to the rocks of PB itself would have been too much for us. Even today, the route is very demanding – not so much the ascent of PB, but just getting there.

That's its allure. It's still there. I hope to get there some day, but the last time I checked, float plane access to Damper Creek on the shore of New River Lagoon was not allowed.

Precipitous Bluff climbing routes

PB from New River Lagoon
Courtesy: Phil Robinson, Chris Rathbone, Steve Monks and Ross Taylor

Wading New River Lagoon to PB campsite

Access ramp to the summit ridge, centre

The alternative trip to Pine Valley, with Dad and Raj

A very cold winter trip

How far to the hut?

Later Tasmania Walks 4, Cradle Mountain Lake St Clair, 1983

The Overland Track Revisited 1983-4

Day 1: Saturday 24 December 1983

The journey began on Christmas Eve 1983 with warm sunny weather in Melbourne as we took off from Tullamarine airport at 9.25 am on an Ansett F27 bound for Devonport. The flight was forgettable, save for the turkey sandwich with cranberry sauce. We touched down in Tasmania to be met by Maxwells Coaches in the form of a Land Rover which took us up to Waldheim, Weindorfer's 'home in the forest'[83] for $20 each.

After a gap of at least five years, two features of note sprang to mind. First, the road west to Tullah was in place, even if still four-wheel-drive only and, second, only ten kilometres of unsealed road remains on the Cradle Mountain road. The trip was thus very quick and we arrived at the ranger's house about 1:30 pm. The intentions book was signed and a $10 each fee paid for the right to walk the track. Lunch was taken in the day hut consisting of fresh green peppers, smoked ham, kabana, cheese, rye, Promite, nuts, sultanas, dates, chocolate and hot tea.

Light rain was falling as we strolled about the old chalet area, which still retains all its rustic charm, set as it is among the leafy glades of myrtle, pine and pandanus. How pleased we were to see the Bennett's wallabies and pademelons feeding freely about the picnic area which was deserted but for

---

83 A rough translation of 'Waldheim'.

about six cars. With the barometer steady and a temperature of 16° we set off for Crater peak at 2.45. Light rain continued to fall as we passed the summit in the mist, seeing nothing of the peaks but admiring and relishing the delicate alpine flora consisting of alpine boronia, scoparia ritchea, mountain rocket, pencil pine, cushion moss, sphagnum moss and much more.

Despite our heavy loads (Chantal[84] had 15 kg, I had 30) we made steady progress and reached Kitchen hut by 5 pm still much the same as it was back in the 1960s. We missed the right turn to Sutton's Tarn so ended up bashing and sliding our way down a shingly rock scree to reach the lake at six. Chantal was not amused by my short cut and adopted a typically feminine method of descent, characterised by many rests and bum slides. The tarn, set in a glacial depression, is shallow and ringed with graceful beech and pencil pine, sheltered from the wind, well wooded, and presents many cozy camping spots.

We found this magical setting deserted and quickly ran up a snug tent and soon had a blazing fire of pinewood. After we enjoyed a lazy dinner of soup, beef stew, fried bacon, Christmas pudding with butter, rum and sugar, the rain cleared to an azure sky. A red sunset blazed across the crags as the mist cleared off the summit of Cradle Mountain. As the light faded, the fire crackled, the birds called and the crickets chirped, all combining in Nature's chorus as a fine day came to an end.

DAY 2: SUNDAY 25 DECEMBER 1983

Overnight the barometer fell from 26.7 inches of mercury to 26.6. I woke variously at 5.30, 6.00, 6.30 only to see the cliffs surrounding the lake covered in mist. I rose at seven and lit a fire with the assistance of richia scoparia – the so-called kerosene bush to experienced walkers – and brewed coffee. There was a fairly heavy dew which dampened the tent fly and the firewood and the mist rendered visibility down to 100 metres.

Following porridge with sultanas, the mist began to lift and by 8.15 the temperature was steady at 11°. We decided to move with the prospects

---

84 Chantal my second wife, from France. My first wife, Heather, passed away from breast cancer.

of climbing Cradle Mountain or Barn Bluff fairly low. We made our way out past head of the Fury Gorge and on to the Cradle Cirque with the mist swirling around us and the wind cutting an icy bite. Climbs on either Cradle Mountain or Barn Bluff would have to wait for another day. So we went on past Benson Peak, then dropped off the Cradle Cirque and raced down to Waterfall Valley for lunch at the hut, which had changed but little since my last visit in the 1960s. While the native cats under the floorboards proved elusive to photograph, the old Bennett's wallaby complete with joey was more obliging.

During the afternoon the weather began to clear. As the peaks gradually appeared so did patches of blue sky as we trudged on to Lake Will. Though the track was fairly dry, a cold wind blew from the southwest all afternoon and made the going unpleasant. At the lake we camped on the first of the white shingly beaches looking out at Barn Bluff. It was the most sheltered of all the sites but still we needed to cook inside the tent (soup, stew, pudding again) and by 8 pm we were washed up and tucked in. The temperature had climbed to 13° and the mercury 26.75. The wind was dropping and as I zipped up the front of the tent mist was girding the Bluff. Chantal was already sound asleep.

DAY 3: MONDAY 26 DECEMBER 1983

Boxing Day 5 pm temperature 16° pressure 26.9. The evening sees us still camped by the shore of Lake Will[85] nestled on soft white sand that squeaks under your boots. The sky had clouded over again but the wind had dropped and nearly all the white caps on the lake had disappeared. A little bird chirps from a gnarled old pencil pine jutting out from the shore amid the clumps of red flowered scoparia.

I sit with my back against a rock, the billy warming on a little fire, feet up on an old log and above me through the woodsmoke towers the Bluff. We climbed it today in four hours return from the lake. The peak was clear, driven by cruel icy blast and conditions on the top were appallingly cold.

---

85 Little changed since my first visit some years previously.

Still, it was a grand thrill to steal the seldom travelled route in the brief clear weather around midday.

Innes Falls were visited in the morning around 9 o'clock. It was so cold that two layers of wool, parkas and gloves were required. By midday we were back and sheltering from the wind over lunch when the peak really became consistently clear.

Chantal is reclined on the log shaving her legs which will do nothing to help her left boot which has separated almost completely from its sole. As the flames of the fire flicker and I sit sipping coffee I wonder how we're going to get through the next seven days with any boots left at all on her feet. It is now 7:40 pm. Mist is circling the Bluff and the fly on the green Turka[86] tent has stopped flapping and tugging at the stone tent pegs. The setting is peaceful. Tomorrow swags were up for the Windermere and beyond.

DAY 4: TUESDAY 27 DECEMBER 1983

A long day, which eventually saw us camping at Old Pelion in the scrub at about 7 pm. We had an early start and braced ourselves against the cold wind on the open heath country that leads down to Windermere. Chantal was walking well despite one wired up boot and we didn't stop until we reached the lake. It was pleasant, sitting there on the grassy banks basking in the warm sun and eating chunks of chocolate.

Moving on, we passed through the button grass plains that lead to Pine Forest Moor. The going was good with fine weather and a generally dry track underfoot. About an hour on from Windermere and just past the moor, Chantal's other sole broke away from its upper. It too had to be wired up. Fortunately, this did not take long as I was carrying twitching wire in my mending kit and my knife had a saw blade suitable for cutting out slots in the flapping boot heels. The wire loops now on both boots held quite well for the rest of the day, only occasionally being torn off by twigs or rocks.

Chantal was in good spirits but obviously not satisfied with my food planning. She asked for lunch at 9.30 before Windermere and almost repeatedly after Pine Forest Moor until I gave in at Pelion Creek. The creek,

---

86   This two-man tent was an older A-shaped design and had no fly cover.

not marked on the map, is crossed just before the start of the Pelion West climb, and has a campsite, some wood and a nice set of falls twenty minutes upstream which we photographed. It was a pleasant lunch stop amid the babbling stream and the clumps of waratah and pandanus, sitting together on a warm rock sharing our small amounts of food with the exception of my super hot, year-old Calabrese sausage.

The track round to Frog Flats was negotiated non-stop in about an hour. The gentle downhill grade did little to please Chantal's slowly deteriorating demeanour. We crossed the Forth River at a log bridge at about 4 pm. I cannot remember seeing the flats so dry or devoid of leeches, even though I found one fat and happy one in my crotch next morning!

Up the Hill we trudged towards the Pelion Plains, the weather warm, the peaks standing out against the blue sky as the bush thinned out near the top. To avoid any unpleasant skirmish, I relieved Chantal of her load for a short while to enable her to adjust to the late afternoon fatigue that sets in so often after a long day. My head ached as I plotted upwards with thirty-five kilos on my back and fifteen kilos on my front.

Pelion Plains were reached in lengthening afternoon shadows and a stiffening wind. After roaming around the banks of the Douglas River which flows from Lake Ayr, we opted to camp just below the Old Pelion hut. Wood was scarce and as we were tired, we cooked up dinner on the kero stove and were thankful that the ground was soft enough to take green twigs as tent pegs. No sooner had we turned in for a well-earned sleep, than I heard a chomping noise going on outside at my pack. In the torchlight a Tasmanian brush possum with her young one on its back was well into an Alliance dehydrated sliced beef and beans. Despite me bringing both packs inside the tent, the persistent little fellow tried to force his way into the tightly zipped front flaps for more than an hour. This frustrating (for me as well as him) experience kept me awake as I repulsed each thrust of the nose through the hole with a prod with my torch. At last, it went away or I fell asleep, for by morning all that was left was the littered aluminium foil around the tent area.

DAY 5: WEDNESDAY 28 DECEMBER 1983

The day dawned clear and sunny with the wind still blowing gently from the southeast, which was a good sign. Already we had had five clear days in the park, which was unusual by any standard.

We got up around 8.30 and strolled up to the old copper mine workings about ten minutes down the Douglas River from the Old Pelion hut. We took some pictures and gathered firewood on the way back to see us through the remainder of our stay. A leisurely breakfast ensued, involving muesli followed by scrambled egg. Chantal knocked back some of her muesli but seemed to appreciate the egg powder creation which followed.

At exactly 12.00 we set off with a day pack for Mount Oakleigh. The weather was fine and we took our lunch and extra clothing. After an initial false alarm in which we followed the old Forth River track, we changed the plan: one person not two would visit Mount Oakleigh. Chantal decided time would be better spent doing anything but walking so with a little grace she retired. The climb took 3½ hours return and gave a good view of the entire central park area.

The best approach from Old Pelion is to skirt the button grass plains to the north of the Douglas River until the main summit track is reached. On the return a pleasant swim was had in the river – certainly a wash was overdue since my last which was before Christmas. As the sun set behind the ridge behind Old Pelion hut, we sat overlooking the river as we cooked our evening meal on a small fire. We made up for what the possum ate by adding mushrooms, peas and corn. Chantal approved of the stewed apple and pear which followed to such an extent that she refused coffee. Victory at last! As an end to the day, we built up the fire and shared rum and chocolate as we awaited the return of the possum.

DAY 6: THURSDAY 29 DECEMBER 1983

Despite the reappearance of the possum during the night, with each visit requiring attention, we both slept well and emerged from the tent at 7.30. It was shaping up already to be a fine clear day so we were away by 8.30, stripped down to our T-shirts with muesli and porridge in our bellies and heavy packs on our backs.

We passed the coolness of new Pelion hut where camp fire smoke drifted up through the trees and filtered the sunlight playing on the soft green grass. It would have been nice to stop for a while if we had had more time.

Chantal was sporting new look boots. The soles were wired at the front to the lace hooks and held at the rear with wire stirrups under the heels to stop them flapping. Additional laces were tied around the instep. This arrangement did not work very well and had to be adjusted every hour or less, much to my frustration and Chantal's discomfort. Nonetheless, she never complained even though her heels were extensively blistered at the end of the day by the upper rubbing on the sole's heel block.

I admired her determination as we climbed up the long haul to Pelion Gap. At the top, a marvellous view opened up. To the left Pelion East, to the right Mount Ossa. Ahead the Du Cane range and behind Oakleigh, Barn Bluff and so on. The warm sun and green grass invited us to lay down on our loads and take in the splendid setting. It is indeed rare in Tasmania to cross such high passes as these with fair weather enough to enable one to pause. After some dried fruit and chocolate, we took some photos and moved on down to Kia Ora hut, which we reached about midday. Down in the valley the bush was dry and hot, particularly through the button grass flats. At least the bogs that go with them were mainly passable.

A great thirst and sweat was upon us as we ground on to Du Cane, arriving at 1.00 pm for lunch. The old hut nestled under Castle Crag still commanded its legendary setting, looking out over Cathedral Mountain at the head of the Mersey Valley. It was somewhat sad to see the old stopping place barely habitable. The animals had nearly taken over and the flies and mosquitoes were most annoying. To sit on the grass and take in the view while resting the shoulders and feet was reward enough.

After Du Cane, the track follows the Mersey before rising to Du Cane Gap. Before leaving the Mersey access can be gained to several impressive falls on the river. We took in D'Alton, Boulder, Cathedral and Ferguson falls. Of all these, Ferguson falls were by far the most elusive but worthwhile. To see them was to remember Fergie, the honorary ranger at Cynthia Bay and his contribution to the southern part of the park. Fittingly, a memorial to him has been erected on a tree blaze at the turnoff to the falls that bear his name.

We pressed on in hot afternoon sun up and over Du Cane Gap. The scrub on the top obscured any real views and most of the descent to the new Windy Ridge[87] hut was completely devoid of any real campsite. Tired and a bit cranky we reached the hut and settled for a small flat spot at the rear of the hut[88]. At least the hut had a cold shower. Chantal was pretty knocked up and went to her pit straight after dinner, disappearing around eight.

As long as daylight lasted, I worked at stitching the makeshift mended boots together with wire. The exercise was slow and tedious as I had no pliers. By dark I had completed sufficient twitch loops to hold the whole show together. I turned in equally exhausted but pleased with our progress. It looked like we would easily reach Pine Valley for lunch the next day.

DAY 7: FRIDAY 30 DECEMBER 1983

Up at seven and away by 8.15. This is fairly good going by any standard if a tent is to be struck and stowed and a hot meal taken. It was with a sense of nostalgia that we reached the old pine at the entry to Pine Valley about 10.30.

I had passed this spot many times before and the valley has always been a special place for me. It was therefore significant that I climbed this way again with a special companion. We took the forest track and by midday our tent was up on the mossy banks of the Cephissus Creek with the water babbling along through the coolness of the lush setting. There was plenty of wood about, including some slabby pieces of pine, so with a well-placed sitting log, we enjoyed a very laid back lunch with an Englishman who we had met along the way and who agreed to come for an afternoon stroll and look at the Acropolis. I had skilfully proposed the climb to Chantal in terms of adjectives such as memorable, worthwhile et cetera – anything but words such as steep, hard and worse than anything to date, all of which were true. With her newly stretched boots functioning satisfactorily she readily accepted my suggestion

---

87   Now referred to as Bert Nichol's Hut

88   I don't recall but the hut must have been fully occupied.

to take a walk. Suspicion arose as I packed parkas, food, water and so on. Could these really be necessary for a short stroll?

Five-and-a-half hours later we returned with Chantal carrying fire logs and feeling tired and sore but agreeing the trip was worthwhile. The view from the top is the best in the park and takes in Ossa to the north, Frenchman's Cap to the west, Lake St Clair to the south with the dolerite columns of the arete dominating the eastern aspect.

Never has the summit been so mild and windless. At 5 o'clock the sun came out and the sky cleared. Gradually all the rock faces took on a richer and more detailed hue as we gazed at the Labyrinth, situated on the other side of the abyss. The peaks of Geryon were as awe inspiring as ever as we shared Mrs Robinson's lemon and barley water with chocolate and dates. The Tobler chocolate courtesy of Paris Croissant[89] in Melbourne and was a significant part of our menu over this trip. Regarding the actual climbing, we took two and a half hours up and one and a half down, allowing well over an hour on top such were the ideal conditions aloft.

Back at camp we benefited from the extended daylight until 9 o'clock and had a leisurely evening meal, wash and campfire chat. The pine log burnt vigorously as the light slowly faded, the blueness above giving way to a pink tinge showing over Mount Gould as we sat under a huge eucalypt. Coffee with rum ended the day as native cats, both fawn and dark, nervously flitted about in the shadows, surveying the scene. No doubt they had smelled the cabana fat from the sausage we grilled and added to our spaghetti and meat sauce.

By 9.30 it was dark and we found ourselves snug by the fire, Chantal holding a candle as we finished our track notes for the day. Above, amid the chunky branches of the large tree some stars appeared.

DAY 8: SATURDAY 31 DECEMBER 1983, NEW YEAR'S EVE

It is evening in the Labyrinth, with the sun sinking behind Walled Mountain, the last of its warmth and colour playing on the slabs of Geryon across the valley to the east. Our camp nestles among a small grove of

---

89 Where Chantal worked for a time selling fresh croissants and brioche.

pencil pines and rocks, sheltered from the gusting winds. Our tent looks cosy sitting on pineapple grass and heath with a clump of mountain rocket by the door.

Nearby lies Quiet Tarn, part of the tangled mass that makes up the Labyrinth, surrounded by the starkness of white dead pines. Here and there, clumps of waratah add splashes of red to the scene. A cozy fire burns by the rocky outcrop above the tent but among the wind gusts, the smoke cannot make up its mind which way to go. We have a casual heap of dry firewood over which I laid out a parka and a woollen pullover. It makes a good seat for two and gives a fine view of our surroundings.

The day started very lazily with the proclaimed lay in till 9.30. After eight days' toil on the trail and early starts, a short day warranted a late start. After emerging from the tent and stretching all was quiet and peaceful. The creek still babbled quietly and birds called. Lazily I took a wash and mooched off slowly upstream to photograph the Cephissus Falls while waiting for Chantal to rise. It was a pleasant stroll through the best forest the park has to offer, and I thought of my many previous trips which had brought me to this enchanted spot.

Back at the camp, Chantal had the breakfast fire going. The sun filtered through the trees as I walked and at the edge of the camp, the mossy banks shone in the dull light and blue of the campfire smoke curling slowly upwards towards the forest canopy. Hot porridge was coming off the fire which was crackling brightly. Scalding tea rounded off the somewhat limited breakfast. Sensing that the portion offered was somewhat lacking, I asked Chantal if she was satisfied. 'When is lunch was the reply?'

At midday we left for the Labyrinth, crossing Pine Valley below the hut and climbing steeply up the other side after negotiating an oozing swamp. The climb, through the heat of the day was very tiring and it was with a great sense of relief that we reached the top of the valley wall about 1.30. From this point we turned north and found a path to the first of many shallow tarns. It was after 2.00 pm so a small lunch was taken on some rocks by the water. But when we took a well-earned and refreshing swim we were invaded by ants from all directions. It was astonishing that so many could exist under every rock for many kilometres. It was virtually impossible to stop anywhere, even for a brief photograph or drink, so bad and persistent were they. Fortunately, they all went to ground at dusk and no longer presented a problem.

After dinner the sun was low in the west and the lighting sharpened, making for some marvellous photography. The sky took on a rich pastel hue, broken by cumulus and cirrus clouds of all colours. Down below, all the vegetation seemed to pick up enough light to lend the right amount of emphasis to each picture being shot. It was one of those moments when all becomes a blaze shortly before sunset. Back at camp, the rum and chocolate were on with the wind still gusting from all directions. By 8.45 the sun had dipped and it was time to don more wool and stoke the fire. It was New Year's Eve in the Labyrinth.

DAY 9: SUNDAY 1 JANUARY 1984, NEW YEAR'S DAY

I woke about 3 am to the sound of driving gusts of wind and a wild thrashing of our obviously detached tent fly, desperately trying to tear itself to pieces. Somewhat reluctantly, we emerged to re-peg it and were relieved to find that despite the wind it was not too cold.

After returning to our sacks we slept peacefully until about 8 am, although Chantal lay in her bag until tea, muesli and scrambled eggs had been delivered. The weather was on the decline and all the signs suggested we beat a retreat. The wind after being absent yesterday during a period of stable high pressure, was swinging from the north to the west and southerly quarters – a sign that the front was coming in. The barometer was falling from 27.6 to about 26.6 at 3800 feet over an eight hour period. And the clouds were massing, dark cumuli-nimbus and looking very ominous.

We thought it best to retreat, though two other parties nearby headed off for Hyperion and Geryon, leaving their tents thrashing in the wind. Ours turned out to be the better decision as by the time we had descended to Pine Valley and set up our camp again, the rain started in earnest. All afternoon parties dragged in from all over the place, wet and bedraggled. What began as a novelty ended up beyond a joke, with tents almost back to back all down the Cephissus Creek and people swimming and washing upstream from the campsites of others. Common consideration seemed to go out the window.

Our evening meal saw the last of our food mostly used up, with the rain still coming down steadily for the first time in nine days. Despite having a good fire well ablaze around a huge root, it was too wet to stand around. Turning in, it was comforting to reflect on having made the move at the right time, beating the hordes and staying dry.

DAY 10: MONDAY 3 JANUARY 1984

During the night it continued to rain quite heavily. The fly shed the water well but without any tent drains some of it ran back under the floor. The rubberised tent floor sealant had perished and I awoke to find my feet in a pool of water. Groping round in the dark it was soon obvious what had happened. My socks and shorts were soaked through, not to mention the bottom of my bag. I laid my parka down over the wet spot and covered it with my foam mat – that was enough to stem the flow and soon I was off to sleep again with my feet further up inside the bag.

By 7.30 we were both up, eager to leave 'tent city', particularly as it was clear and rain free. The fly was rolled up wet and the tent underneath it was dry save for the floor. We decided not eat and by 8.15 were away. Chantal's boots were still holding together which was some consolation for having to wear long johns – woollen ones – as my wet trousers were tied to the back of my pack to dry as we walked. The trip down to Narcissus was as uneventful as ever – it always seems to be a progressively developing anticlimax after Pine Valley. But you do notice the increasing appearance of hakea and bottlebrush as you get nearer to the lake and a noticeably greater and more diverse bird population.

Sitting around at Narcissus hut, we managed to get most of the gear dry and were enjoying the peace and quiet when, like yesterday, more and more people started to trickle in. After a while it became obvious that there would be many more than nine people, or more than one boatload, so by about 3 pm people started to get ready for the charge at 3.30 when the boat arrived.

Sitting on the edge of the clearing with a small fire to keep us warm we saw the MV *Tequila* rounding Echo point and we were away. Luck was in and we made it aboard. The seventeen-foot aluminium hull twin outboard engine powerboat had us in Cynthia Bay in thirty minutes. We took a bunk in Milligania cabin and settled in. Chantal bought bread, butter, chocolate and Coke (for the rum) and had a long hot and well-earned shower. I had an ear-splitting migraine type headache so took two Veganin and lay down for a spell. By about 6.30 I felt okay so we lit a fire and had a cup of tea before calling it a day. We were at journey's end.

Fauna Summary

The following is a complete list of animals reported as having been seen in the park. Those seen on this or previous trips are marked accordingly.

Monotremes
Platypus
Spiny anteater

Marsupials (Polyprotodonts)
marsupial mouse
native cat
tiger cat
Tasmanian devil
bandicoot
striped bandicoot

Diprotodonts
opossum mouse
flying opossum
ring tailed possum
bush opossum
wombat
bettong (Tasmanian rat kangaroo)
rat kangaroo (pademelon)

Bennett's wallaby

kangaroo

native rats

Park Birdlife

Birdlife is not as common in the park as might be expected. According to Sharland[90] these are the most common varieties:

Birds of prey

Wedge tailed eagle, white breasted sea eagle, goshawk

Water birds

Black duck, white faced heron, native hen, spur wing.

Parrots

Green rosella, eastern rosella, black cockatoo, white cockatoo, ground parrots.

Robins

Flame breasted robin, scarlet robin, dusky robin.

Honeyeaters

Yellow wattle bird, strong build honeyeater, black headed honeyeater, yellow throated honeyeater, crescent honeyeater.

Bell magpies

Currawong, black magpie, raven.

Smaller birds

Pipit, brown scrub wren, scrub tit, blue wren, ground thrush, cuckoos.

---

90 A Guide to the Birds of Tasmania, by Michael Sharland FRZS., published by Drinkwater Publishing

Equipment – Personal

Boots (with ankle support), shorts (one pair), long johns (one pair), woollen pullover, woollen shirt, socks (two changes), parka (Gore-Tex), over trousers zipped, mitts and gloves, balaclava, head torch, mess tin, spoon mug and milk shaker, toothbrush, snow glasses, pack, sleeping bag and foam mat, wool singlet, sun hat, fibre filled vest (Chantal only), cotton T-shirt, brush or comb.

Equipment – Party

Tent with poles and fly, 1 mm cord, billies (two) small in bags, water bottles to buy (1), stove and fuel (nine carried one litre kerosene), candles (about three), mending kit (with wire and rivets), first-aid kit (emphasising pain relief, cuts, blisters, muscle strain & diarrhoea), toilet paper, pot scouring pack, soap, toothpaste, maps and compass.

Guidebooks, notebook and pen, spare plastic bags, snow cream and lip seal, boot wax or dubbin, camera and film, mouth organ, water bag (canvas), gas cigarette lighter or dingbat[91].

Food List

The overall objective was to feed ten people for ten days and to end up with only a little egg powder, some soup cubes and a small amount of tea. If you plan on the basis of 1 kg of food a person a day, then the total weight of food for the trip would have amounted to about 20 kg.

However, some of our luxuries such as Christmas pudding would have added to this amount and we probably had closer to 25 kg all up, had we scheduled at this daily allowance. This means personal and party equipment needs to be kept to less than 20 to 25 kg, so that individual pack loads are not significantly more than 20 kg. Strong walkers can carry 30 kg which allows the weaker party members to carry as little as 10 to 15 kg.

Breakfasts

Ten serves of porridge, eight serves of muesli, milk powder equivalent to twelve pints twenty tea bags, forty spoonfuls of coffee or their equivalent,

---

91 Firelighter with flint.

powdered drink base for twenty litres, six tubes butter concentrate, half a kilogram sugar.

Lunches

One loaf rye bread or SAO biscuits, two tubes jam, two packets cheese, 1/2 kg dehydrated apple, 1/2 kg sultanas, 1/2 kg apricots, 1/2 kg dates, 1/2 kg nuts, 1/2 kg kabana sausage, 1/2 kg smoked ham, 250 g spicy hot sausage, six sesame seed/fruit bars, six blocks chocolate, one film can of Vegemite.

Dinners

Twenty cups of single serve soup, eight dehydrated dinners (Alliance), four packets dehydrated peas and corn, one packet dehydrated potato, two, one tin dehydrated egg.

The total weight of all the food was about 20lb which was very acceptable after being cut back to a daily allowance of one pound a person, about as low as you can tolerate. Chantal said she was always hungry but I felt okay for the most part.

Breakfasts were largely okay but could have used a little more porridge and some ground coconut.

Lunches were also okay on the whole. Rye bread should be replaced by two to three packets of dry biscuits. We needed more cheese, more meat and more fruit bars.

For dinners: the Alliance dehydrated meals give one and a half serves only and needed supplementation. We could have used more peas and corn. Also, one meal of spaghetti and one of rice would provide a welcome change. As a backup, we could have halved the dehydrated egg and taken some flour.

Also, some drinking chocolate would have been appreciated. As usual the lemon and barley water was great. A full tin was taken which is pretty heavy but it was nearly all used. The Twining's tea bags were indispensable as was the Tobler chocolate.

Summary

It is evening on 3 January 1984 and we have just returned from Tasmania. I have emptied out our packs, cleaned up and had some tea. Sitting at my desk in Moor Street, Fitzroy[92], I'm reminded as always of passages of the trip by bits and pieces that tumble out of my pack during the cleanup. It is a kind of bushman's debrief, like the notes of the song long forgotten but summoned up again by some strange twist of familiarity. So here I am living it all over again even though it has only recently ended.

The trip could be summarised simply as eight straight days of good weather and a bad case of boot failure – otherwise a great trip. Given the time of year, December to January, the weather should usually be good but experience has shown that very few walkers have that good a run so we were certainly very lucky. I carried a small barometer/thermometer which read in inches of mercury and degrees centigrade. The recorded readings are generally low due to the altitude, which averaged 2500 to 3500 feet.

Chantal's Lowa boots failed completely on the second day, the sole coming off both boots by day 3. How she completed a ten day walk without alternative footwear should be noted, as described in the track notes. The importance of a good mending kit cannot be underestimated if only one pair of footwear is to be taken. In the outcome she suffered little foot damage with the exception of some heel blistering caused before wiring the soles back on at Windy Ridge.

Chantal carried the Lutz Guide pack weighing about 15 kg which she managed well for her personal body weight of forty-two kilos (a ratio of .36). She needed help with her pack only twice on steep sections and then only when pretty tired. I carried a new Gregory Snow Creek – an excellent eighty litre adjustable sack which weighed thirty kilos with my body weight of eighty kilos and was also a ratio of .36). The sack was at all times excellent.

Transport costs are summarised as follows:

Melbourne to Devonport	$90 each
Devonport to Cradle Mountain	$20 each

---

92 Where we rented until I left for work in PNG at the Ok Tedi mine in Western Province.

Park fee	$10 each
Lake St Clair cottage	$11 each
Cynthia Bay to Derwent Bridge	$2 each
Derwent Bridge to Hobart	$13.90 each
Hobart to Hobart airport	$3 each
Hobart to Melbourne	$110 each

Transport to and from the park is now really quick and reliable. It is nonetheless a pity that many of the locals cannot hide their disdain for 'greenie conservationist bastards[93]' which appears to be their general impression of bushwalkers. A great deal more courtesy should be shown by these local as many of the visitors are from overseas and leave the park wondering how the place can effectively be safe in the hands of such dolts. Note that these same remarks cannot be directed at the park rangers, whose behaviour and efforts to interest the day trippers was exemplary.

The park fee of $10 is perhaps reasonable and is a quantum leap better than the $50 fee levied on a potential Franklin River rafting trip. The latter fee must surely be another slap in the face for the 'eco nuts who managed to stop our dam from going ahead'. This last return visit to Tasmania confirmed my view that the Hawke Labor government did the correct thing in intervening where the state government could not prevail in the national view[94].

During the first half of the walk, the number of people encountered was not too great. We would pass, say, half a dozen parties a day and the huts would have about the same number of parties stopping overnight at each location. We certainly appreciated our tent and aimed to camp away from huts where possible. This was not always the case as the country is sometimes very dense, rocky or exposed and the hut locations very timely. Windy Ridge and Pelion are good examples of potential saturation where it is difficult not to stay somewhere other than in the vicinity.

In the second half of the trip things did start to get a bit hectic. Pine

---

93 Probably less so today.

94 I was always opposed to the flooding of Lake Pedder and later still, the proposed dam on the lower Franklin river.

Valley became a joke, as described in the notes and would have been awful if we had to stay longer. The walk should perhaps be completed before new year or done in spring or autumn. Track conditions were very good for the most part largely due to the extended dry spell of weather. I came home with dry socks, which attests to the generally dry conditions and to some extent careful bog navigation.

The old red and white jam tins and tree blazes are now nearly all gone – they have been replaced by yellow PVC reflective triangular or square ones, generally nailed into place where appropriate and are quite satisfactory. Quite a few important signs were lost/destroyed/missing, which definitely caused some parties to miss some points of interest rather than lose their way. For example, there was no sign to Sutton's Tarn at Kitchen hut, no sign to Ferguson's Falls from D'Alton Falls, no sign to Ferguson's Falls, or any of the Waterfall Valley falls.

Many of the huts are in an advanced state of decay, at best rough and at worst no longer habitable. Example are Waterfall Valley, Old Pelion, Du Cane, Pine Valley[95]. It is certainly a relief that most of them have toilets and fuel (coal) but it does look as if these huts' days are numbered[96]. Waterfall Valley will likely be replaced by Cirque, Old Pelion by New Pelion old Windy Ridge by the new Bert Nichols. What happens to Du Cane and Pine Valley is not clear. My guess is that Du Cane will be replaced by Kia Ora, forty-five minutes' walk away, and that Pine Valley will be replaced by a large hotel type hut[97].

Not that the park needs more huts. Far from it as the idea should be to camp out. The problem that needs to be faced is that the point has been reached where too many people are using too few tracks and huts. Alternative routes are needed fairly urgently – and would be excellent projects for scout groups and so on if they could be given some incentive and encouragement. For example, the following would be of great assistance in reducing the pressure on the Overland Track:

---

[95] Many since rebuilt.
[96] The status of all huts referred to here can be looked up on Google.
[97] A new Pine Valley hut was completed and was in use by about 2010 at the latest.

- A route from Frog Flats to Mount Thetis – Mount Ossa – Pelion Gap;
- A route from Kia Ora hut to Big Gun Pass, Lake Helios and the Labyrinth; and
- A route from the Labyrinth to Mount Gould and Gould Plateau.

Finally, for photography, I took and used the following: Minolta 303 35mm SLR; Makinon 25 to 80 mm zoom with macro and a 1A skylight filter; three rolls Ektachrome 200 ASA slide film, colour and a utility camera clamp

Setting off from Waldheim

Leaving the Pelion Plains

Snowed in at Waterfall Valley

Our friend at Waterfall Valley

The wired up boots

On Barn Bluff cirque

Camped in the Labyrinth

Later Tasmania Walks 4, Cradle Mountain Lake St Clair, 1983

Resting before Mt Olympus, with brother Zeke

He carried a ghetto blaster, too...

Boiling the billy

With Heather and kids, 1970s

On the Overland Track with Heather

Later Tasmania Walks 5

Cradle Mountain Lake St Clair National Park and the Overland Track revisited 1987

This was the second trip that I did with my then wife Chantal to the Cradle Mountain Lake St Clair National Park in November 1987. As far as I can recall, I had finished work with BHP as a mine manager in the Pilbara iron ore country and was about to start a new job in Perth as a regional general manager, with the task of opening up some new underground mines. The diary opens with a title Two Weeks at Waldheim or Waist Deep at Waterfall, the subtitle referring to getting snowed in at Waterfall Valley as mentioned in the following diary notes.

As usual, the notes were written on a day-by-day basis and I have not attempted to edit them. The photographs also taken at the time and the heritage notes included by the national park staff were again current at that time. The accommodation arrangements at Waldheim will have since changed and different arrangements[98] may well apply today.

Introduction

Sitting here in Binya hut at Waldheim on a crisp but clear November evening and staring out the window at the soft cushion moss tussocks and sphagnum being grazed by the Bennett's wallabies it is hard to believe it is four years since Chantal and I last visited this place and completed the Overland track.

---

98 Google Waldheim Tasmania Accommodation to see today's options

Watching the wood smoke curling up from the pot belly stove through the King Billy pines and hearing the shrieks of happy children gambolling around the cabins[99,] reminds me of many previous visits over almost 20 years. Very little has changed – apart from the old Beltana cabins which have been replaced. The rustic charm still remains: power from 4.30 pm to midnight, no power points or refrigerators; just a shower block of toilets and wood sheds. Adults pay $7.50 a night, children 6 to 16 years $3.75. The Waldheim Chalet still stands, though it has seen better days and the wildlife still abounds. More than half the wallabies are carrying joeys, which is a good sign.

There are a number of day walks around Waldheim now – many of them well benched and graded. Boardwalks extend out over the button grass areas and the rougher quartzite sections are well drained. Signposting is also of a good standard.

Having walked through the park more than once and visited Pine Valley many times, we decided this year to come in November and base ourselves at Waldheim for a two week stint. November was the only time available as far as work was concerned and it offered the chance to beat the December invasion of tourists. We drove in from Devonport on Friday the 13th with about twenty pounds of food, augmented by fresh steaks, bread, eggs and beer. Spirits were high and the weather was fine.

DAY 1: FRIDAY 13 NOVEMBER 1987

We arrived after lunch and settled in at Binya hut, the weather fine with a cold wind blowing. Unloaded all the gear and food while Chantal fed wallabies and black currawongs. We decided on a short walk which Chantal suggested should take about one hour. Soon we were off in the car to the Dove Lake car park with a daypack of parkas, camera, gloves and balaclavas.

Enthusiasm was lowered a few notches when we alighted at the car park in an icy wind. Spirits un-daunted, and with the peaks clear, we set off for Lake Lilla with whitecaps running on the lake. Lilla offered a little more shelter so after a short stop we pushed on to Wombat Tarn, a somewhat

---

99   I brought my own children here as toddlers in 1974.

less used path than the 'tourist highway'[100]. The tarn was small but very attractive set among the pines with a backdrop of Little Horn. We sat on an old pine log and took it all in. Stillness in the water, fresh air and a light pack. The wind was still blowing up on the Marion lookout so no time could be lost running up there for a view. We stopped at the junction of the track from Crater Lake as we had been gone an hour and the temperature was falling fast. Cloud was scudding in over Cradle Mountain and the weather looked threatening. From our lookout we could see down to the car park – Chantal tugged my sleeve so off we went, reversing the route in about forty-five minutes.

Back safely in the hut, we soon got the evening meal under way: noodle soup, steak, mashed potato with peas and corn. This with beer and Jamaican rum, helped down with raisin buns. The extreme cold kept Chantal in the hut, but I could not resist those famous Waldheim showers! Happily, they still lived up to their reputation, just the thing after a walk in the hills. Back in the hut, Chantal could not be raised. Boots were oiled and lights were out by 9 pm. By 10 we were both too hot in our Everest bags – the stove was still well light – so clothes were shed and I slept soundly till the alarm went off at 6 am the following day.

DAY 2: SATURDAY 14 NOVEMBER 1987

I rolled over after the alarm sounded and slept on until 7 am when I jumped up, dressed and put the porridge on. The sky was clear and there had been frost – the sign of a good day. By the time the porridge was served with some milk and coconut, Chantal was calling for tea and toast – the tea courtesy Twining's Darjeeling teabags and the fruit bars as before. Despite the six eggs on hand, neither of us had room for any.

By nine, Chantal had showered and we felt ashamed at not having yet set off somewhere. With our daypack from the previous day, plus a lunch, we departed up the 'horse track' about 9.30 in perfect weather. The going was very easy and we reached the Crater Lake boat shed by 10.30, finding it bathed in sunlight and tranquillity, with clear, tea brown water over

---

100 The main Overland Track south.

quartzite sand and the familiar old shingles making it the iconic shelter I remembered so well. Up above, the crags were clear and inviting, all was still with the absence of yesterday's cold blast.

The track led on to Marion's Lookout, viewed in perfect conditions about 10.45. On over the plateau we walked, after holding hands in the open sections, until we reached Kitchen hut about 11.30, track conditions being mostly dry. So perfect was the day, we agreed to climb Cradle Mountain, setting off a few minutes later. The summit was reached at 1 o'clock (after some coaxing near the top) affording a clear 360 degree view which included Frenchman's Cap and St Valentine's Peak. Lunch was taken just below the summit on a grassy tuft, in warm sunshine and in full view of the winter snowdrifts. Shirts came off as did gaiters and we settled back and enjoyed the tinned fish, smoked meats, cheeses and dried fruits.

Leaving at 1.15 we were soon rock hopping downwards with great speed, Chantal with sore heels and I with sore toes. Passing many other parties, some with quite young climbers, we were soon down on the plateau where we took the westerly leading face track to Little Horn. At the base of the horn, after passing through much fagus and King Billy, we could look down on lakes Wilkes and Dove, a splendid sight!

I changed the Kodak 200 ASA 24-shot print film and loaded a 24-shot Ektachrome slide film (also 200 ASA) while Chantal ate some Cadbury dark chocolate and drank freely from her water bottle: time.. Various routes on Little Horn were considered but left for another day as we headed steeply down the trail to Lake Wilks which was reached at 3 o'clock. Though we were both footsore by this stage we could not help but marvel at the beauty of the setting. On the far side of the lake a waterfall danced noisily; on this side a creek babbled. Pines reached up for the crags, mingling with the eucalypts swaying gently in the breeze. A perfect day campsite was found near the water's edge, tempting us to return late and enjoy the enchantment of an overnight stop, especially with such a plentiful wood supply. On we went down to the Ballroom Forest. Once reached, it offered cool shelter from the afternoon sun and that tranquillity all Tasmanian trampers will recognise. It comes from the quiet majesty of the tall pines and myrtles shadowing the pandani and other lower-level trees and sheltering the velvet-like forest floor. The lake's quartzite beach was occupied so we pressed on, pausing only for a photo t about 4 o'clock. It was now a tiring slog back to camp, reached at 5 pm soon followed by a visit to the showers.

A first-class day walk! Splendid views, mostly moderate going, good climbing and plenty of interest.

DAY 3: SUNDAY 15 NOVEMBER 1987

We woke and arose late – not surprisingly after the long previous day, and took a leisurely breakfast while stretching tired legs and gazing out at the weather. The peaks were clear, the temperature was mild and a gusty wind was blowing.

By 11.30 we had packed four days' food and were off up the horse track once again with light packs. We stopped at the scout lodge near Crater Lake as Chantal was feeling unwell with hay fever and a head cold and needed some pack straps shortened. We were greeted by the lodge occupants and offered hot tea by the scout leaders, the enjoyment of which was marred only by the incessant ramblings of one of the leaders who was a hopeless gear freak[101]. The lodge site is impressive, located high in Crater Valley with views of Waldheim and Crater Lake. Probably the site of Ronnie Smith's original hut.

On we went up to Crater peak stopping for lunch behind a large sheltered rock, just short of Crater peak lookout. After munching on some biscuits with cheese and meat Chantal felt improved. The wind had eased and the visibility was good. We made good time over the open plateau, passing Kathleen's Pool on the left and dropped down to Suttons Tarn on the track running southwest from Kitchen hut. Arriving about 3.30 pm we made ourselves comfortable among the pencil pines at the eastern end of the lake, finding plenty of firewood for our needs (no stove was used on the entire trip).

The twilight was cold and required two layers of wool so by about 7 pm, after the usual dehydrated meals for dinner, we were inside the tent. With

---

101 A term used to describe people who are obsessed with the latest outdoor or climbing gear.

our new Everest bags we will able to sleep unclothed with the bags zipped up, such was the warmth of the Fairydown Sting' two-man mountain tent[102].

DAY 4: MONDAY 16 NOVEMBER 1987

I climbed out of my bag for a leak and weather check about 6 am. Mist was down all around the camp so I turned in again until about 8. Got up and made tea and porridge for Chantal who then came to life feeling better than the previous day but with feet sore from heel blisters. The weather suited a lazy start and fitted in well with our plans for a short walk around the cirque and down to Flynn's Tarn via Lake Rodway.

By 11 am the peaks were clearing so we set off, Chantal going non-stop up to Kitchen hut and on to Fury Gorge camp, where we enjoyed lunch with billy tea overlooking that grand and cavernous gorge flanked by the awesome remoteness of Barn Bluff. Patches of blue sky and sunshine appeared fleetingly but on the whole, cold wind and bleakness, were the overriding memories. The camp is exposed with room for one or two tents, with ample firewood and water. After lunch we trotted down around the cirque where, at the head of the track down to Lake Rodway, Chantal required extra plaster on one heel. That done and moving well we headed down to Scott Kilvert hut, by the lake, arriving about 4.30 pm to find it empty and dark. The large A-frame structure with a sleeping loft seemed rather bigger than necessary though a fitting memorial to the schoolboy Kilvert and his teacher Scott who perished in the area in 1965.

We took a photograph and moved on to Flynn's Tarn, not far away, where we camped on an idyllic promontory with a dramatic panorama of the west face of Cradle Mountain. The site appeared to have received little previous use, had plenty of wood and was quite sheltered. After pitching the Sting we ran back down the track along the creek which flows into Lake Rodway. At one point the creek flowed over open rocky ledges to provide an ideal bathing location. We took full advantage.

The views of Mount Emmett were great; the weather chilly. We used my blue-black bush shirt as a towel and returned to camp with a full canvas

---

102 Much later, I used this tent on the North Ridge of Mountt Everest.

water bag. For something different we tried the Alliance dried fish and parsley sauce and found it quite good. There were few complaints either about the plum pudding with rum and sugar (heated using the double billy steaming technique). Light rain started to dance on the lake, birds called and a waterfall cascaded into the lake after murmuring and splashing its way through the fagus and over the rocks. It was awe-inspiring and magical. Seated on a log we wrote postcards and boiled the billy before turning in.

DAY 5: TUESDAY 17 NOVEMBER

We enjoyed the beauty of the campsite and the prospect of a short day to Lake Wilks so did not leave until late. We sauntered along, stopping to photograph Artists Pool and the smaller pool before it in cloudy but clear conditions of high overcast haze. Chantal changed into shorts as a helicopter flew back and forth with building materials for the new commercial hut near Cirque Hut.

I was feeling poorly and we wondered if the tent allowed enough air in, overnight. We both had the same head cold. Whatever the reason, we took Panadol tablets and moved on up to the emergency shelter underneath Little Horn, where we took lunch amid the foraging forays of two black jays, anxious to share our lunch to any extent possible. We guarded the last of our Sao biscuits, some of which we lost to the jays at Fury Gorge.

After lunch we took the face track and climbed up steeply, dropping packs at the foot of the Little Horn summit track. From there, the track took about half an hour only, affording a much better view than that of Cradle Mountain main summit, taking in Lake Rodway, Flynn's Tarn, Mount Emmett, Hanson's Peak, Twisted Lakes, Lake Dove, Marion's lookout, Lake Wilks and Weindorfer's Tower. The latter was named after Gustaf Weindorfer by two Australian climbers who did the first Cradle Mountain traverse.

The large black jay joined us on the summit, clearly still requiring sustenance. As we had nought to offer, we climbed back down to regain our packs at the turnoff, passing through boulders and pineapple grass, then open heath and arriving back after a one-hour excursion.

Shouldering our packs we were soon descending from the face track to

Lake Wilks where the tent was up by 4 o'clock. Down came the mist and with it the rain, detracting considerably from the immense charm of the site's location directly under Weindorfer's Tower with two cascading creeks feeding it over crags closed in pandanus, fagus and King Billy pine. To the east, on the other side of the track, there was good firewood to be found.

We were unanimous in our assessment of the evening meal – disgusting – and vowed never again to try Alliance's savoury mince and spaghetti. Two other walkers passed through while we sat in the tent so we did not see them, thus completing two days without contact with others – surprising, for November and the mild weather usually combine to make the place usually popular. It was a fitful night: Chantal thirsty and me still with a headache though we both rose next day pretty well refreshed and ready to run home to Waldheim.

DAY 6: WEDNESDAY 18 NOVEMBER 1987

The minor discomforts of the previous night behind us, we were up early for tea and porridge amid failing weather. Mist was down, the peaks were blanketed and the crags around the lake barely visible through driving mist and rain. We lost no time breaking camp and were off by 8.30 with very little other than our basic gear. Most of the food was gone, having been carefully apportioned back in Waldheim before we set off.

Going well, we reached the beach on Dove Lake in forty-five minutes and walked through to Waldheim in just under two hours, non-stop. All afternoon the weather deteriorated so we drove down to Sheffield and restocked our food. Chantal tried to shower before going to Sheffield but the water was cold (ladies' taps left on). On return, however, the legendary wash house was back to its usual standard. I washed, shaved and cleaned my teeth. It was good to be back for a spell in our little cabin.

We checked in to Amarina a four-bunk cabin not far from the Binya cabin that we occupied before. We lit the stove and cooked up quite a meal: steak and onions with cabbage and chips, and tinned fruit with a Seaview 1984 cabernet, topped off with currant buns. By 8.30 Chantal was sound asleep for the night on the lower bunk, with her bag unzipped and opened out so warm was the cabin interior. I read a book on the life of Gustav Weindorfer[103] till the lights went out at 10.50 and then slept soundly.

DAY 7: THURSDAY 19 NOVEMBER 1987

Rained in at Waldheim. What follows are some reflections on Weindorfer's home in the forest, some fifty-five years after the founder's death.

After Weindorfer's passing in 1932, Lyle Connell took over at Waldheim with his wife Margaret and ran the chalet until they sold it to the government in 1945. Lyle Avenue was established and some logs were taken from the forest by Ronnie Smith and G Stubbs for the timber minesweepers. Connell was the first Cradle Mountain park ranger who with Bert Nichols, was responsible for much of the Overland Track as we now know it. Connell built the Weindorfer monument and also Hellyer's at Cradle Mountain.

In 1967, on my first visit to Waldheim, the original chalet still stood. However, in 1976 the National Parks and Wildlife Service (NPWS) removed it, causing a public outcry which resulted in the current replica being constructed. Only the original bathhouse still remains, currently used as a storage shed.

The future of the park seems to be in a state of evolutionary change – what with commercial huts going in and the controversy surrounding the camping ground (see newspaper clipping). One gets the impression that even the rangers' disagree with some of the things which are going on. As always, the place cries out for more money and manpower. Walking around Waldheim in the rain and mist, the place is rather sad and dishevelled in appearance. Weindorfer's dream was realised with the formation of the national park in 1947 and World Heritage listing in 1982 but strolling about the chalet today, one wonders at the tangibility of progress since Connell left in 1945.

The overnight cabins and shower blocks, the toilets and woodsheds are major additions, but the sad neglect to Waldheim's replacement chalet seems something of a pity. The tracks around the chalet are boggy from being trampled by innocent weekend visitors and in need of work . The museum

---
103 A Man and a Mountain, by Margaret Giordano, Regal Publications (reprint) 1989.

and day hut are dank and dilapidated – no doubt waiting, like the rest of Waldheim, to assimilate with some future changed identity carved out for it by bureaucrats.

The spirit of Gustav is still here but one wonders if 'Dorfor's' dream will live on into the future, half a century after his passing. Viewed from the window at Binya hut, the rain continues to fall, the setting is bleak and sad are the expressions on the drenched and wretched wallabies. Weindorfer's Forest continues to flourish now that the scars of 1945 are mostly gone. The birdlife has changed little, but the native cats seem scarcer and more timid than ever.

A senior ranger, John Walters, was living in Amaroo while working on the camping area down near Black Bog Creek. He too was somewhat reticent about new-wave parks but spoke in glowing terms of the C Multrum organic dunny, capable of handling 80,000 craps a year and all sorts of other gear. Another gear freak and the first Tasmanian I've met who insisted on drinking Swan Special Export beer. Also the first hut I've seen with a TV and dishwasher too. Looking in the trip book, we noted about five parties had set off on trips during the day despite the weather. Later one pair (a housewife and her Scottish sister) came in very wet after an episode in the Ballroom Forest when they lost the track. All smiles after that, visiting the shower block and a hot cup of tea.

We really set to over dinner trying to do something creative with the rissoles. After the noodle soup we fried them with some onion and tomatoes, added spices and beer, then served them with mashed potato and peas. The result was edible, topped off with a fruit bun and some coffee. We finished the washing up at 9.30 and read for two hours until lights out.

DAY 8: FRIDAY 20 NOVEMBER 1987

Got up around 7.30 to see some patches of blue sky. Feeling confident that the day might prove more active than the last, I made breakfast for Chantal and got her up. Alas, all was not well. She had not slept well and I still had a bad dose of hut diarrhoea. Unperturbed, we decided on a day walk to Lake Hansen, Twisted Lakes and return via Truganini Point or Dove Lake.

We took a lunch, parkas, gloves and balaclavas and set off, somewhat surprised at the amount of rain that had fallen overnight. The camping area down by Weindorfer's 'dump' had been washed away and there was quite a deal of flood damage. We stopped at the ranger's station to check the forecast (none) and to sign the trip book.

Then we were off! Leaving the Dove Lake car park at 10.30 in freezing wind, we climbed up to the saddle before Hansen's Peak to find the wind raking the top with great ferocity. We kept the hoods of our parkas up over our faces and scooted off down to Hansen's Lake where there was some shelter under the pencil pines where we paused and ate some salted peanuts.

It was 11.30 and we were going slowly. In addition to our own problems, the track was everywhere a raging torrent and all the bush was dripping with water between showers. Passing the Twisted Lakes we battled a full-on southerly, heads down, hands gloved. Down at the ranger's emergency shelter we got out of the wind and ate some lunch feeling pretty disconsolate. Outside, the mist and rain swirled around Little Horn and creeks cascaded in bounding, spontaneous waterfalls down from the crags into lakes Wilkes and Dove. Quite a display, but cold.

As a climb on Hansen's Peak was not on, we set off about 12.30 for the Lake Track and were soon descending from the plateau, sloshing our way down the slippery tea tree roots through dripping rocky erosion gullies, over irregular button grass mounds, through tangled undergrowth and making the usual diversions around oozing bog holes.

The lake had risen about a metre overnight, causing the beach at Truganini Point to all but disappear. All was windswept, boggy and waterlogged. Overhead, the sun tried to poke through the clouds but inevitably the holes closed and the heavens opened up. We got back to the car at two o'clock and shook out all the wet gear. Back at Waldheim, all was quiet. I loaded some 400 ASA film and got some good shots of Bennett's wallabies, plus some forest scenes. The leeches, meanwhile, had had a shot at me!

With a fire on back at the hut, the clothes were soon dried out and I opened a bottle of Boag's beer, and laid out some of the plant specimens gathered during the day — native laurel, banksia, sassafras, melaleuca, myrtle and some lichens. The barometer read 26.8 inches and steady and the helicopter was back in the air.

DAY 9: SATURDAY 21 NOVEMBER 1987

Weather foul. Went to Devonport, got some money out of the hole in the wall and did a little food restocking. We had lunch by the Mersey River, in the car, with a hot barbecue chicken and a bottle of Boag's beer. We watched the ferry *Able Tasman* set off, racing a steam train and some relay runners heading for Burnie.

Back at Waldheim the weather was still foul, hailing in fact. Frustrated, we drove back to the Middlesex plains and up Weaning Paddock Creek to the Quaile's Falls track. The falls, named after Roy Quaile, who established the track in 1912, were well worth a look, being about seventy-five metres in height over three big cascades. Back from the falls about 7 o'clock we slept in the back of the car after scoffing breadstick with cheese and meat, fruit loaf, beer and an excellent Mildara Coonawarra Cabernet Merlot 1982.

DAY 10: SUNDAY 22 NOVEMBER 1987

A freezing clear night heralded clearing weather. The wind dropped during the night, so did the temperature; not surprisingly, getting started was painful. Up at Waldheim the peaks were out, so after a quick hot shower we set off for Waterfall Valley with three days' worth of food. An icy wind was blowing in our faces as we walked up to Crater Lake, so much so that we checked the lake shore for a campsite in case we had to retreat.

We were making good time, though, since our 9.20 am start we pressed on up to Marion's where we took in the view eating muesli bars as we sheltered behind a beech tree. Then it was on over the plateau to Kitchen Hut which we walked through at 11.30. A fresh dusting of snow adorned the summit rocks on Cradle Mountain and Barn Bluff.

We reached Fury Gorge campsite at midday and called a halt for lunch, again admiring the wonderful view of Barn Bluff and the gorge while waiting for the billy to boil. With hot black coffee steaming from a large enamel mug, it didn't seem nearly as cold, so after a forty-five minute break we were off again, still wearing two layers of wool against the elements.

Little by little the afternoon warmed up. By 2 o'clock we were at the edge of Cradle Cirque where we photographed the old signpost standing starkly against the gaunt and awesome solitude of the high desolate plain and the dramatic backdrop of the Bluff. If the top was windswept and bleak, then the boggy descent took us to a warm and inviting camp – the ever-appealing Waterfall Valley, set on the edge of a small plain, nestled by some gnarled old myrtles with a beautiful old hut sitting peacefully on a velvet-like grassy setting. This was to be our home for a while, complete with its resident Bennett's wallabies, both with joeys in their pouches. Lowering our packs gently on to the turf at 3 o'clock it was evident the rest of the day would be balmy. All around the rim of the valley waterfalls could be heard – all no doubt working vigorously after the heavy rains of the last three days.

Flowing over the valley rim in a generally westerly direction are numerous creeks all feeding the Hartnett Rivulet, thence to the Forth River. All cascade over the conglomerate cliffs and most are easy to find. Between 3 and 4 pm we visited three before turning in for the day, leaving two more for exploration next day. Though essentially small, all the falls enjoy a beautiful setting among the pencil pines, and against the blue afternoon sky the light for photography was excellent. Weary of feet and legs, we trudged back to the hut which we were glad to find fully rebuilt since our last visit four years previously. Despite needing a good sweep out, it was most cozy with four double sized beds and a coal-fired pot belly stove. What with two skylights and two large windows, the whole interior was really pleasant and bright.

By the time we had settled, more wallabies had arrived to greet us, taking the total to four – all with joeys. How we regretted leaving our cabbage at Waldheim! Basking in the sun outside the hut we witnessed something of a furry maternity session at dusk as they gradually settled down in the bushes by the camp, just in time for the wombat parade. Wispy pink cloud hovered over the purple peaks and there was the sound of running water as we stared lazily out of the window at nature's twilight pageant. Joeys darted about, never far from their mothers, wombats grazed and moved cumbersomely onward, and birds returned to their nests as darkness filled the hut and we waited for the native cats after first making fast our food supplies.

DAY 11: MONDAY 23 NOVEMBER 1987, WATERFALL VALLEY

Hut-bound in atrocious weather. Driving wind pounded the hut until it shuddered, letting icy blasts in through every crack to chill the body. Full to the top, the pot belly stove fought to take the edge off the cold hut interior. Outside all is bleak. Driving mist runs along the ridge tops where the peaks disappear in the void; the plain vegetation lashed by the wind, bending against the onslaught; pools of water everywhere on the sedgeland and lone, disconsolate wallaby stoically accepting all the elements, shaking now and then to lighten her coat of its sodden load.

Incessant rain rattled on the corrugated tin roof, falling at a crazy angle as it runs off the eaves; a contraption to collect droplets from a hole by the stove flue; cold metal billies and an assortment of food bags on the old plank bench where I write.

Barometer 26.1, down seven points overnight, temperature 7 deg inside the hut. All day long the deluge continued unabated. By late afternoon the stream behind the hut broke its banks and flooded the plain while the sheets of rain turned intermittently into hail. The water ran down to the edge of the button grass where the Overland trail signs stood in a lonely vigil in the face of the wind in all its full fury. At 7:55 pm: the rain eased, the sky showed patches of blue and clouds rushed wildly by Barometer up slightly at 26.2, wind easing, floodwaters subsiding. The great storm was passing.

DAY 12: TUESDAY 14 NOVEMBER 1987

It had been a clear cold night. Stars were visible and the wind had vanished. The Southern Cross blazed. But as we snoozed away under the smoky pencil pine beams of the hut Nature was preparing another surprise.

The barometer fell to 25.8 inches and the sky closed. Back came the wind and with it 200 mm of snow. This was in November!

The scene outside at seven o'clock was extraordinary to say the least. Visibility was down to 500 m, a dense blanket of snow covered the entire plain and there was most atrocious wind imaginable. A full blizzard was raging!

Each blast of the wind shook the hut and snow came in through the roof's ridge flashing as we struggled to rekindle the stove. The inside temperature had dropped to 2°C. Down to our last dry twigs and paper, we struggled desperately to light the fire, finally winning out with the help of some offcuts of Masonite. Soon all was aglow and we felt more able to assess the situation.

We were due back at Waldheim on the 24th — well no chance of that. We would have to sit out at least another day. Food was re-rationed. Cold muesli for breakfast followed by a wood gathering mission out in the full force of the gale — a miserable job — but the wet pile of snow-covered fuel soon dried behind the stove. It was muddy work with all the bog holes covered with a concealing layer of snow.

About midday I visited the waterfalls, again under appalling conditions, and attempted to photograph them in the full spate of the storm. About an hour of this and it was back to the refuge with wet feet. All else was dry under Gore-Tex overpants and Typhoon japara parka.

Chantal had hot tea awaiting my return after which the usual lunch followed. The afternoon the storm showed some sign of easing: patches of blue sky, weak, fleeting rays of sun, then more snow. We waited, recognising the need to move next day. Barometer 26.1, temperature 10° inside the hut. By 6.30 pm there had been no change and we recognised that tomorrow we would have to make a dash for Waldheim.

Day 13: Wednesday 25 November 1987

I got up three or four times during the night to stoke the fire and check the weather. It was calm and generally free of snowfall, with clear patches appearing around 4 am. Outside, the water bag had started to freeze, sitting on an old shingle with hard snow. It was nearly time to go.

Anticipating the big push, neither of us had slept very well, as is usual in such circumstances. Despite this, Chantal was up before tea was made and was busy packing, without the usual coercion being required. The old mother wallaby arrived for her morning feed, almost completely fearless of us, as if she had accepted us as members of the wild folk, as did the animals except the Purun Bhagat[104] in Kipling's story. After a quick breakfast of tea and porridge, we were soon packed and ready to go. The log was signed; the stove was stoked (lest we had to return), a full stack of dry wood was left. The benches were cleaned and the floor swept. We donned two layers of wool with parka, gloves and balaclava as well as trousers and overpants, gaiters and boots. Lunch was carried in our pockets and all gear was given last minute checks

At 8.30 packs were up and we closed the hut door, saying goodbye to our good friend and her joey. She seemed to understand that we were passing on and thanked us for our kindness to her during our stay. Immediately we were fighting the elements, knee deep in snow as we crossed the plain to rejoin the main track. For the first section, up to the Cradle circuit rim, we were blessed with sunshine and stillness. The firm crust of snow carried us over the tea tree bogs and it was a joy to be under way at last, our snow glasses shielding our eyes from the intense snow glare. Chantal shed a layer of wool, I shed a parka as we motored on upwards.

The sun disappeared when we reached the rim and the wind stepped up its tempo as a dirty black cloud approached. Undaunted we pressed on, munching a muesli bar for courage. By the time we reached the turnoff for Scott Kilvert hut and Lake Rodway, all layers were back on as the full fury of the storm hit. It was already too cold to stop. We pressed on, pleased with our progress and the fact that the wind was side on, from the northwest. We were about one hour out from the hut – reasonable given the knee deep snow and the need to plug fresh steps all the way.

The next hour took us across the high country at the foot of Cradle Mountain to Fury Gorge camp, under very heavy drifts in places. The wind

---

104 From The Miricle of Purun Bhagat, Kipling's second jungle book written in 1894. Purun Dass is a high caste Brahmin, highly educated, and a powerful figure as Prime Minister of one of the semi-independent Native States. At the peak of his career, he casts aside all possessions, takes a staff and begging bowl, and becomes a wandering holy man, 'Purun Bhagat', depending on charity to live. At last, he comes to the high Himalayas, where his people had come from, and finds a deserted shrine high above a mountain village, where he makes his home. For many years he lives there, fed by the devoted villagers, making friends with the wild creatures round about, monkeys and deer and bear, and pondering on the meaning of existence.

really handed out a belting, making us glad of hooded parkas and gloves. We maintained a steady, slow but deliberate rhythm until we reached the dead eucalypts and finally the pencil pines and babbling stream. It was one more hour to Kitchen hut and still snowing.

We each took a leak, ate some peanuts and took a photograph before moving on. The track was lost under the deep snowdrifts, so only the snow poles gave any indication of the route. In places we sank to the waist, in others we sank knee deep into bogs or streams lurking under the soft surface. It was tiring work, but very encouraging to see our progress. Our feet were still dry and almost warm, helped by oiling the boots before departure and the dry snow conditions. The proofed gaiters and overpants kept our legs dry as we sledged on. Visibility was quite good, though the peaks appeared for no more than brief instants, like the fleeting glimpses of blue sky above the mirk. The mixture of rocky dolerite and peat bogs along this section made many slips and fall throughs inevitable. Despite this, we reached the rise, turned north and slid down into the hollow that houses Kitchen hut right on 11.30 where we had a twenty-minute lunch outside the hut sitting on the snow talking to an animated and optimistic Swede waiting for a climb on Cradle Mountain. Our talk was cut short by another fierce snowstorm and we up and left taking the Marion's Lookout track as it ran east from the hut and had the wind on our backs.

Some very deep drifts were encountered before we were safely on the cordwood paths. These had little snow on them and took us safely to the lookout where footprints from the summit led down the other side. Appreciating the easier going we dropped down to the saddle below the lookout in a driving snow storm then continued down the track to Wombat Tarn, again affording good shelter. Soon we were below the worst of the weather and stripped off, sloshing our way down the track, which had become a raging torrent of snowmelt. Dry feet became a thing of the past as we crossed the button grass, walked the boards and motored in to Waldheim at 1.30. Once again, the showers lived up to their reputation and we reestablished in Binya hut to dry things out. It had been a significant alpine traverse considering the conditions.

All our gear was turned out in the little hut, sorted and dried. Chantal headed by instinct and inclination for the showers while I split some firewood, ran up some washing lines and started an evening meal. It was to be our last night in Waldheim so a farewell dinner was planned but Chantal jumped the gun, drank all the wine while the soup was being prepared and announced, 'I'm beat – time for bed'. Despite this veiled threat she stayed up for a great meal of leftovers washed down with the Boags draught. I had some more of this after dinner and banter with senior ranger John Walters and turned in about 10.30.

DAY 14: THURSDAY 26 NOVEMBER 1987, LAST DAY AT WALDHEIM

Up early I was off before breakfast, still in drizzly rain. Although wearing shorts, gaiters, woollen shirt and parka, it was cold when I reached the Knyvet Falls track at 7 am. My feet were soon wet from the soaking my boots got the day before and the wet undergrowth, but the short stroll down to the falls was rewarded with a couple of good photographs. I also photographed some waratahs in the Waratah track at Pencil Pine Lodge (now Cradle Mountain Lodge).

Back at the hut, Chantal had made a very pleasing cheese and spice omelette which I enjoyed while she fed the local wildlife all our leftovers. It was sad to be packing up and leaving despite our poor run with the weather. We had become very adjusted, very assimilated with the place. It had been the ideal location to unwind after working the last year in the tropical heat.

Of our fourteen days we had managed six out on the track of which three were in bad weather; three good days out of fourteen was not as good as last time. The heavy snowfall had been most unseasonal but presented the unexpected bonus of excitement that also tested our gear to the full and gave the chance for some winter photography. Even being hut bound at Waterfall Valley was a bonus as the experience was special in many ways. And the forced walkout to Waldheim was good experience for Chantal.

The accommodation cost $20 a night at Waldheim only and nothing when on the track. The showers were great and, as always, the Waldheim locals and houseguests friendly and courteous.

As we drove down the white crusted quartzite past Weindorfer's dump and turned our backs on the mist-enshrouded Little Horn, we felt the pangs of leaving. Although the weather down on the Middlesex plain was clearer, it made little difference to the fact that we were once again leaving our 'home in the forest', Weindorfer's Waldheim. Fifty-five years on from his death, his vision of a people's wilderness park lives on into posterity.

Equipment (For Two)

- Boots (Asolo Scarpa),
- Shorts,
- Breeches and pullover
- (Chantal),
- Wool shirt (80/20 wool blend),
- Bush shirt (John, 100 per cent wool),
- Socks (two pairs on, one spare),
- Parka (1 x Typhoon japara, 1 x Gore-Tex cagoule),
- Overpants (Gore-Tex with zipped legs),
- Gaiters (Cordura, with zips),
- Gloves (80/20 fingered and fingerless),
- Balaclava (silk for lightness),
- Torches (preferably headtorches, spare batteries),
- Mugs (two enamel, large),
- Spoons (two x large, one teaspoon),
- Toothbrushes and paste,
- Snow glasses (carry a spare pair),
- Packs (one 80 litre, one 50 litre),
- Sleeping bags (two Fairydown Everest high loft, two Thermarests),
- Wool singlets,
- Long Johns (for sleeping),
- Hat (walking sticks optional),
- Duvet (Chantal, sleeveless),
- Boot wax (Sno Seal or dubbin),
- Tent (Fairydown Sting),

- Cord (three 5 mm and one 4 m each),
- Billies one small, one medium, bagged),
- Water bottles (two of one litre),
- Water bag (canvas, five litre),
- Stove (Camping Gaz and gas cannisters),
- Gas lighter (two plus matches),
- Candle (four hours burning),
- Mending kit (rivets, wire, tape, pliers, needle and dental floss),
- First aid kit (plaster and analgesics, diarrhoea),
- Toilet paper (plastic trowel useful),
- Pot scourer,
- Soap (one cake or powder),
- Maps,
- Compass (barometer and thermometer optional),
- Notebook (pen and larger felt pen),
- Plastic bags (spare Ziplock type),
- Lip salve,
- Camera,
- Knife (two Swiss army type),
- Firelighters (just a few),
- Mouthorgan (optional).

Clothing

- Daytime: one layer wool – upper body,
- Evening: two layers wool upper body, possibly one layer wool bottom,
- Sleeping: one layer wool top and bottom,
- One wool layer only for bottom half in the form of long johns,
- One cotton singlet for hot days,
- One pair of shorts for hot days,
- One pair dry socks for sleeping.

Most people on the Overland track wear short pants with boots and gaiters. When it starts to rain it is important that the parka covers the bottom of the walker's shorts.

It is also important that overpants have zipped legs so that they can be slipped on over boots, thus saving time when it is raining.

I have always found it a good idea to carry lip salve, a Swiss army knife and a cigarette lighter in my pocket and some would say toilet paper as well.

FOOD NOTES

Breakfasts:

Tea, (tea bags to taste), coffee (instant or coffee bags), sugar (brown, bagged), milk powder (1/2 litre a day, plus a milk shaker), porridge (single serve sachets), coconut (desiccated, bagged), sultanas (bagged), muesli (alternate with porridge), cooking oil (in a tube). Extras (for emergencies) – egg (powdered, bagged), flour (bagged).

Lunches:

Sao biscuits (pack carefully in takeaway food boxes), smoked meat (salami, kabana etc), cheese, dried fruit (apricots, dates, sultanas), nuts (salted and honey, roasted), sardines (or tinned pate), drink base (powder, bagged), high energy snacks, chocolate (one block every three days), muesli bars (two a day, one each),lifesavers (or optional equivalent).

Other: jam (small container), honey (ditto), Vegemite (ditto), chilli (flakes), onion (or garlic, powdered), curry (powder, optional).

Dinners:

Freeze dry – (one packet a day, shared), peas and corn (1/2 packet a meal), potato (powdered, say 500g), tomato paste (in tube), soup (sachets, single serve), plum pudding (small, 500g).

Extras – rum (small flask), pancake mix (instead of flour), fruit buns (or heavy raisin bread), dried apple   (for stewing).

At Dove Lake

The Weindorfer memorial

One of the many tarns

The refurbished Waldheim 1980s

The boathouse at Lake Dove

The Barn Bluff cirque

On the summit Cradle Mt

Cradle Mt and Little Horn

The Waldheim bathouse

DEPARTMENT OF LANDS,
PARKS AND WILDLIFE

Receipt No 3634

Cradle Mtn   Date 26 / 11 / 87

RECEIVED from Mr Dunlop

....by Cash/~~Cheque~~

the sum of Fifty

............................dollars and ———— cents

being for Accommodation for 6 nights
in several cabins
less $70 deposit R/N 4351.

$ 50.00   *J Adams*
            Receiving Officer

Lake Will, Little Horn and Cradle Mt.

Barn Bluff from the summit of Cradle Mt.

Later Tasmania Walks 6

The Walls of Jerusalem and Cradle Mountain, 1991

An account of a four-day solo trip to both parks in 1991, told through pictures, music, prose and verse.

> So come with me you say
> To where the Southern Cross sits high upon your shoulder,
> Come with me you say
> Each day you turn the clock you're one day older,
> While the blood runs colder.
> But that anchor chain's a fetter,
> And with it you are tethered to the foam,
> And I would not trade your life for one hour of home.
>
> From the words of the song by Eric Bogle

DAY 1: 25 APRIL 1991, UP INTO THE WALLS

Leaving my hire car at the Fish River car park I was quickly up into the eucalypt forest, following a clearly marked track leading up the hill from the small toilet block. The tall gums waved gracefully in the breeze as I steadily ascended. Steep in places, the track crossed a couple of small creeks before breaking out into more open country after about forty-five minutes. By a creek, nestled by some pencil pines and gums, I came upon Trappers' Hut and signed the logbook. A rather downmarket shelter, it offered only a bunk and no fireplace, so my thought of calling a halt was cancelled. It was only about 3 pm so I pushed on.

The track rose for another few hundred feet and then flattened out, travelling easily over dolerite boulders and through low eucalypt (not unlike the Labyrinth in the Cradle Mountain Park) until the lakes of Solomon's Jewels were reached. the track passed close by attractive, shallow tarns, ringed with pencil pines,. I motored on, keen to get 'somewhere' before nightfall, as the wind was getting up. The forecast was good, but large dark clouds looked ominous.

Late afternoon brought me to Wild Dog Creek at the foot of Herod's Gate. I knew there was no hut until well past Lake Salome so, in a strong wind, I elected to bivouac the on the soft grass near the stream well sheltered by bushes. I was soon brewing up, quite snug with a bag and Gore-Tex bivvy sack. The noodles and stew went down well with a bread roll, but in the dark it was hard to see what they looked like. It was getting colder so I snuggled down deep into the bag and wired up for sound, munching on chocolate and finishing the last of the black tea. With the hood pulled over my face I slept like a log. Only twice only did I wake, once to the eerie moonlight and the thump of a wombat and the erratic scurry of native cats, the other to the joy of a starry clear sky. This and the crimson sunset of the previous evening heralded a fine day to pass through Herod's Gate.

Warm in my sack, cold outside, clouds scudding overhead, the wind running through the snow grass. Cold gear discarded in the snowdrifts awaiting morning and the uncertainty of the coming day.

> Daylight again
> following me again
> I think I hear a hundred years ago
> How my fathers bled...
>
>   Words and music by Crosby, Stills and Nash

Like the Anzacs, this being Anzac Day[105], the song continues...

---

105 This was, I guess, a lone Anzac Day remembrance for me. I recalled my time in Vietnam in 1965 as the song played.

All the brave soldiers who cannot get older,
They are calling after you.
Do you find the cost of freedom buried in the sand,
Mother Earth will swallow you and lay your body down.

Up at first light about 6 o'clock I forgot yesterday's hangover and moved out quickly after a cup of tea and a biscuit. The bivvy sack was covered with hoar frost but the bag was quite dry – surprising considering the soggy ooze I had been lying on. It was cold, requiring fur hat, fingerless woollen gloves and sleeves down. I trudged up and passed into Herod's Gate. Behind me, pink with the early morning light, Barn Bluff punctuated the horizon.

I fumbled in the cold with my camera refusing to fire up until changing the batteries. Then I was away. Mist drifting across Lake Salome, catching the sunlight on the sundew and pineapple grass. Spongy, wet cushion moss and prickly scoparia were gentle underfoot as the sun crested the dolerite blocks behind the lake, bursting upon me and warming my numbed extremities. A diamond hard morning.

Steam rose off the bushes and drifted across the open sedge and heath leading to the Pool of Bethesda. Leaves sparkled in its light and all was still. Pencil pines run down to the shore of Lake Salome and fringe the Pool of Bethesda which offers some perfect sites for camping nearby. Though not a deep pool and boggy around its edge, it rivals Artist's Pool and Flynn's Tarn (in the Cradle Mountain Park) as the most picturesque glacial tarns I have seen. Sunlight low in the sky and filtering through the pines offered some excellent photographic opportunities before I ambled on across the foot of the Temple to the Pool of Siloam near Ephraim's Gate. This pool, larger than the Pool of Bethesda, was also one of great beauty with its fringe of snowdrifts and rust red sphagnum moss among the pines.

I returned to Lake Salome and on to Herod's Gate arriving about 10 am and feeling warm. Near the head of the lake were snow grass flats, ideal for a casual rest. Having had not much for breakfast I settled for an early lunch using the warm sun and gentle breeze to dry out my bivvy sack and bag over a large scoparia shrub. Wild Dog Creek gurgled by, fish swam by unafraid and red mountain rocket blazed away in small clumps edging the stream. It was a truly peaceful spot, lending itself well to some snaps of the Gate and Barn Bluff, much further away. The good weather was in possibly for one or two days. If I ran, I could be back at the car by 12.30 and at Waldheim by 2.30 and Waterfall Valley by six. Could I do it? Why not try?

> Of war and peace the truth just sets,
> It's curfew goal it glides,
> Upon four-legged forest clouds,
> The cowboy angel rides,
> With his candlelit into the sun
> Heading for the gates of Eden.
>
> from *The Gates of Eden* by Bob Dylan

Only a day was spent in at the Walls[106] because the weather demanded that I move across to Cradle Mountain without delay to take full advantage. Although the Walls offered some excellent glacial tarns and grand stands of thousand-year-old pencil pine, I could see no deciduous beech (Nothofagus *gunii*) which I had come here to photograph.

The decision was an easy one. Wired for sound, I descended Herod's Gate to the thumping sounds of Chuck Berry, followed by the more compelling notes of Bob Dylan's *Gates of Eden*. Back at the bivvy site I pressed on past Solomon's Jewels down to Trappers' Hut and then into the tall eucalypts running down to the car park. By 2.30 I was at Waldheim after stopping at the corner store at the Cethana turnoff for fifteen dollars of ULP (seventy-two cents a litre) and a hot pie with sauce.

DAY 2: 26 APRIL 1991, WALDHEIM AGAIN

The old place looked much the same, the Weindorfer replica still standing and looking well, as did the bathhouse. I was pleased to photograph them in good weather as most of my previous visits had not enjoyed blue sky, and I had lost most of my Waldheim slides.

---

106 Later on, I made quite a few return trips.

It was a relief to see that the huts and shower block had been retained after the scare referred to in my previous accounts. Several families were in residence though the ranger's HQ had been shifted down to the park boundary at Pencil Pine Creek, quite near to Pencil Pine Lodge. The airstrip was also revitalised with tourist joy flights, which made the next two days a little bit like Mount Cook in midsummer (when the joy flights buzz about overhead like blowflies above the glacier). I lost no time in parking the car at Weindorfer's monument and taking off across the boardwalk for the horse track at 2.30.

> Eight miles high[107] and when you touched down,
> You will find that it's stranger than old...
> Nowhere is there warmth to be found,
> Among those afraid of losing their ground...
> Down below they are huddled in stores,
> Some laughing, some shapeless forms
> Sidewalk scenes and black limousines
> Some living, some standing alone...'.
> Words and music by The Byrds, but sung here by Leo Kotke

Bumping along across the boardwalk, I appreciated the smooth surface provided by the pine boards cut from the tree with a billet knife and therefore not as smooth as milled timber. But my limbs were weary and feet sore from the run out from the Walls. On the other hand, my pack was light, the sun warmed my shoulders and a fresh breeze cooled me as I passed by the button grass plain near the foot of the Horse track. The quartzite gravel crunched under my boots as I swung up towards the scout hut, working up a puff and a sweat on the brow.

The hut was reached in half an hour from Waldheim. I downed my pack and ran down to Crater Lake to see the boat shed, surrounded by golden beeches. All was a blaze of colour with the water lapping at the quartzite beach near the shed. After a short pause to take it all in I returned up the

---

107 Song originally banned in the USA when released.

hill to my pack. Above the hut, the track angled up gently out of the beech thickets on to the open heath, driven usually by snow and wind. On a lesser day others would perish here – today I was to pass on untouched to Crater Peak with a bottle of Boag's beer sloshing around in my belly, as I straddled the drifts of dazzling snow. Creeks babbled, stones clinked, currawongs called. But Crater Peak was cold and I stayed only for a moment, following a fast walker up ahead with yellow pants.

I reached Kitchen Hut about 3.30 so the pack was dropped, music turned on and the descent to Sutton's Tarn began without delay. The waters below beckoned and tired legs drove me on with only dried dates and apricots to chew on,.

Well I'm running down the road
trying to loosen my load I've got seven women on my mind
four who want to own me two who want to stone me
one says she's a friend of mine.
   Words and music by the Eagles, sung here by Jackson Browne

The lake waters were placid, the sun filtering through the pines and beech as it westered low in the western sky over Fury Gorge. I walked the quiet shores on tired feet with only a camera in hand, a fur hat and shorts, rather taken by the serenity of the spot and the haunting tune of *Mr Tambourine Man* by Bob Dylan. I recalled the earlier camp at this spot with Chantal as I padded over the flat vacant tent site we used. I wished she was here with me to enjoy the perfect afternoon as I reluctantly headed back to my pack.

Thanks to Buddy Holly 'raving on' as of old the climb back did not take too long nor did it tax me too much. How could I complain? 'Yellow legs' was coming down off Cradle Mountain after an astonishingly short ascent. I waited to congratulate him at the turnoff to the climb. After a couple of minutes he, or more correctly, she was with me. Heidi (I made up her name) was German and in good form. 'You,' she said, 'are a real Australian that is Aussie climbing person; therefore I will photograph you now.' That was more or less how it went. 'Zese Australian walkers climb very slowly,' I think she went on. Evidently so, I thought, as she took her pictures. 'See you in Barcelona, yellow legs,' I said.

'Pardon me?' was the expected response as I wired up for sound and bid farewell to Heidi and left for Fury Gorge with the sun low to the west over Rigg's Pass.

'We may never pass this way again,' went the plaintiff lines of Seals and Crofts as I pulled into Fury campsite on a perfect evening. With the afternoon beams of light thrusting down into the gorge and a perfect view of the Bluff, I was tempted to stay but thoughts of the stove at Waterfall Valley beckoning me with its warmth. Out of the dead stick country, across the heath and down into Cradle Cirque I raced, stopping only at the Waterfall Valley turnoff to photograph the Bluff in the westering sun. The snow grass glistened under the weak sun's rays as a wombat raced by, startled by my sudden arrival. Then it was down the hill and across the boards to the hut. I had completed the afternoon traverse from the Walls of Jerusalem right across to Waterfall Valley hut at Cradle Valley.

Notes on Waterfall Valley revisited

It had been a pretty ordinary night in the hut as I surveyed the scene on a fine clear frosty morning. There were four wide bunks at Waterfall Valley – wide and hard. While it proved okay to leave the sleeping mat at home (anticipating sleeping on the ground), those bunks were a different proposition. But after a long day's walk from the Walls, weariness overcame discomfort. I was just sore from yesterday.

The hut, with its waterfall cascading gently by the door, was just as I'd left it on our last visit. Those in residence, as usual, had difficulty with the pot belly stove but before 7.15 am all had departed on the track south, about the same time as I left to photograph the waterfalls. I mentioned earlier that I caught the falls basking in the early morning light and ended up quite excited, firing off a roll of Ektachrome 200 ASA[108], ripping my duvet in the scrub bash and ditching another pair of Bolle sunglasses. It was good to come

---

108 Unfortunately, I have found since that slides do not keep well in the tropics where I live.

back to an empty hut, to sit back over some cheese and biscuits and reflect on past happy times here wile jotting down those thoughts, spurred on by the inspirational view across the 'wallaby plain' as I called it, to the valley rim.

The sun was well up, all the frost had gone and what wind there was barely ruffled the trees around the hut. I decided on a leisurely stroll back up the boards to the rim, then round to the drop off and down to Lake Rodway. It was a repeat of the Cradle circuit that Chantal and I completed together some years ago. I had enjoyed Flynn's Tarn and Artist's Pool so much that I was keen to return. So swags were up and I was off back up the hill. In no time I was on top of the rim, cresting it easily in about twenty minutes as a result of a greatly improved track. It was windless and balmy, with walkers everywhere on the main track, which I backtracked to the Lake Rodway turnoff. From the drop off signpost the view back to Barn Bluff was a mass of golden beech filling the yawning cirque in the midday sun. I took it in, lingered a little, savoured it and then turned my back and plunged downward at the start of the back circuit. The heath gave way to beech, the beech to eucalypt and finally the eucalypt to paperbark, which thrived in the swamps that fed the lake. Run-off from above is very intense as the Permian conglomerate has little permeability. Notwithstanding this, the swamps were not too bad, easily negotiated by a combination of root stepping and stone hopping.

Down at the lake the waters were tranquil and the hut[109] was empty. Outside an inviting ground log beckoned and I took up residence, partaking in some more of my flexible menu, washed down with the surprisingly warm lake water. Soon my little book came out and I caught up on some reminisces of the Walls. It was important to capture these fleeting thoughts before they vanished from any hope of recall.

The thoughts poured out on to the paper in a continuous flow. I scribbled on, oblivious to the passing of time, pausing only to drink or munch on a biscuit, dried apricots date, or chocolate. Before too long the sun dipped behind Cradle Mountain – about 3.00 pm – and it got too cool to continue. A little stiff, I got up from the log and hobbled about. I could hardly move! I put

---

109 Scott Kilvert memorial hut.

the hut logbook back in the large A-frame hut, (how do they ever warm it up?) shook my head at the vastness of the great empty space and closed the door. It confused me that Scott Kilvert should be so large and yet Waterfall Valley so small —on that very evening Waterfall Valley had thirteen occupants to Scott Kilvert's nil.

No more hard bunks for me — I saddled up and trudged off stiffly up the short rise that leads away from the hut and the button grass flat towards Flynn's Tarn. I paused where the creek flowed over the conglomerate beds below the tarn. It was here that Chantal and I took our baths when last we passed by. I warmed to the memory but also because I knew our campsite was not far from this spot. The late afternoon lacked the sun of the other side but was compensated for by the shelter from the westerly breeze. As a result, the place was peaceful, somehow calmer than the rat race of the usually crowded Overland track. Not that you'd know from the galaxy of sounds and music that propelled my every step. As I pulled into my favourite spot on the point by Flynn's Tarn, Roy Orbison was on and he opened the section that follows with its reference to my mystery camp.

DAY 3: SATURDAY 27 APRIL 1991, EVENING CAMP AT FLYNN'S TARN

Darkness falls and she will take me by the hand
Take me to some twilight land
Where all the love is grey where I can't find my way
Without her as my guide .
Night comes I'm caught beneath her spell daylight comes my heavens turned to hell .
Am I left to burn and burn eternally '
She's a mystery to me,
She's a mystery girl.

Mystery Girl, words and music by Roy Orbison

Here I am back at mystery camp at Flynn's Tarn, just off the track, out on a point jutting out into the quiet waters, set under the dolerite crags of Cradle Mountain, all clothed in golden beech. A warm fire at my back as I sit on a rock listening to the Big O with the smoke drifting over my head as it wisps on down the creek to Lake Rodway. A quiet windless night, though clouds were gathering overhead billowing across from Little Horn away towards Mount Emmett. The old campsite was still as I left it – the banksia firewood still under the bush where I left it (no fires they say at park headquarters – well tonight I will have a small one as there is ample wood and I'm sleeping out on the cold earth). The flat rock is where Chantal and I sat, the vacant tent spot awaiting our return. A light breeze rustles the leaves of the gnarled eucalypt by the fire but the birdcalls of our last visit are absent. Only frogs croak now and then. I regret being alone.

A makeshift groundsheet was down, long johns donned with down vest and the billy was on for soup which, with a tin of herrings and some biscuits, was about all I had left in the tucker-bag, plus some tea, dried dates and hot chilli scroggin[110]. Unfortunately, the Rycroft shiraz and the Boag's beer were in the car waiting my arrival tomorrow so it would be a meagre evening meal. It was 4.30 with plenty of light left for cooking.

High up on Little Horn the sun played on the dolerite columns. Lower down the prominent Permian conglomerate overhanging was strikingly in view. In the foreground the lake shimmered, dead stick behind ghostly white, blending with the grey conglomerate, golden beech and green pines. Some of the older pines, long dead, reached out over the lake shore, older than we know. Up on Cradle Mountain, a rockfall and scree chute ran down through the thickest, richest patch of beech yet seen on this trip. The colour was breathtaking as an aircraft flew overhead, passing to the right of the Horn.

Soup's on! A lamentable instant sachet affair called 'Mushroom Cuppa Soup'. Ordinary flavour which hangs on to your tea if you don't wash your mug out properly. I was, however, surprised, amazed and eternally grateful for the squashed Anzac Day bun from Deloraine which, when toasted over the fire, went down tremendously well after the herrings in tomato paste. (Thwack went the springy tin lid, covering all and sundry with orange coloured oil!) The billy was still boiling so after a hot cuppa, I cleared the fire which could be stoked up and enlarged slightly. A pity the banksia breakfast

---

110 A trail mix of nuts and fruit, usually.

wood burns so quickly. The plane I noticed earlier flew back over, passing Mount Emmett as the last rays of the sun caught the tumbledown summit.

Later, at 5.30, under Cradle Mountain, there are pink clouds overhead, crimson swirls around the crags, snowdrifts in dark gullies and a cold wind that suggest I turn up my collar. With duvet zipped up and fingerless gloves on, Dan Fogelberg is back on the air, doing *Sutter's Mill* while evening falls and I draw another cup of tea and chomp into the last of my block of Nestle club dark chocolate.

Well they came from New York city and they came from Alabam'
with their dreams of finding fortune in this wild unsettled land.
Some fell prey to hostile arrows as they tried to cross the plains'
and some men died in the Rocky Mountains with their hands froze
to the reins.
Some would fail and some would prosper,
Some would die and some would kill,
Some would thank the Lord for their deliverance,
Some would curse John Sutter's Mill.'

           Words and music by Dan Fogelberg

It is evening as I turn in. Dusk surrounds me and a full moon has appeared above a conglomerate rise to the east. All is quiet but for the rushing stream tumbling into the lake from the crags above. The sky has a purple hue and the waters are still on the lake. Above Little Horn the first stars appear, punctuating an almost cloudless night. Soon I will be stretched out gazing up at them.

Stretched out on the soft ground, I was much more comfortable than on the hard bunk at Waterfall Valley. And warmer too in my bag and bivvy sack. Even small huts can be very cold at times. Right above Mount Emmett, the Southern Cross hangs, suspended over the Cradle. Just left of Weindorfer's Tower I see Orion's belt, part of the Big Dipper. *Holy shit!*, I called out loudly as a satellite shot across the sky. The vastness of the firmament on that peaceful night was certain to stay with me. The tape gave way to *Duelling*

Banjos and I recalled similar wilderness scenes from the film *Deliverance* and its soundtrack. As I dozed off in my fur hat and gloves the lilting strains of *The Tambourine Man* came back to me as they had earlier in the day.

And take me on a trip upon your magic swirling ship
my senses have been stripped
my hands can't feel to grip
my toes to numb to step, wait only for my boot heels to go wandering...

Take me disappearing through the smoke rings of my mind
down the foggy ruins of time, far past the frozen leaves
the haunted frightened trees out to the windy beach,
far from the twisted reach of crazy sorrow.

Yes, to dance beneath the diamond sky with one hand waving free,
silhouetted by the sea, circled by the circus sand
with all memory and fate driven deep beneath the waves,
let me forget about today until tomorrow.'

Music and words by Bob Dylan

As I closed my eyes and pulled the hood of the sack tightly over my head, I had that sinking feeling that the weather was on the way out.

DAY 4: SUNDAY 28 APRIL 1991 THE JOURNEY ENDS

Slept well. Did not have to complain about hard bunks and the biv was warmer than the hut. Don't believe me? Well, I rose late, – about 6.45 and well after daybreak, though the sun was still behind the range to the right of Little Horn. The fire took hold first try and raced away, but the wind had changed from last night. Mist and cloud raced overhead, the main peaks were 'under', the wind was intensifying and the temperature was down. It was crapping out[111]

---

111 I picked up this term from NZ mountain guides in the Southern Alps.

Hardly enlivened by this observation, I completed an even more meagre breakfast than usual, a cup of black tea and a SAO biscuit, and called it quits. What a time to strip one's long johns and duvet! As a luxury, I spoiled myself with clean socks and retained my gloves and wool hat, spreading the fire as a last ceremonial gesture to this special place, putting the burning pieces in the nearby pool. With my pack on my back and the site checked, the place was dead again. A sad look over my shoulder and that was all. Strange how this moment can often be like leaving a friend…

Feeling slightly jaded I moved on, past the little pool and on to Artist's Pool, quite close to the saddle below the Horn. I attempted one or two shots but suspected that the light was a bit 'off'. There was not much choice as the blue sky was fast disappearing. Having shot the second 200 ASA Ekta I decided it was time for the faster 400 ASA. I could not find it so loaded 400 print film instead. (Luckily I had tossed it in at the last minute, even if I did forget the Rycroft red wine).

On the other side of the saddle, Cradle Valley was heavily clouded in. I reckoned I had about half an hour left for any landscape shots so headed up the face track. The sign carved in rock at the base of the Tower read, 'Summit thirty minutes.' In that time, I climbed the thing, took some pictures, crapped in a deep chasm and scrambled back down to my pack and was on my way. The wind on top was fierce as I fumbled with the time delay on the Minolta.

Across the face track, the climbing possibilities of Weindorfer's Tower suggested it perhaps be visited another day. I paused near Smithies to wait for a break in the mist over the Horn but was denied. I fired off a shot in anguish and bagged the camera in despair then headed off into the wind and mist, sleeves rolled down and hat with ear flaps down.

I had no reason to be disgruntled at the thought of being homeward bound. After all, the track was downhill, it had not rained in four days and the falls on the creek below Crater Lake were very pretty. The boardwalk leading up to them had been constructed very artistically, leading up to the falls through sassafras, myrtle and tall pines. A currawong danced along the handrails as I went, eager for a morsel no doubt.

I had that 'trip's over' feeling again as I climbed the final steps to Waldheim, only to be confronted by a grotesque fire engine red hose reel. Sidestepping the thing, I gently lowered my pack on the porch and fetched a cold bottle of Boag's. I sat on a pine bench gnarled by the years, and set to drinking it. It went down well though I was slightly chilled by the lower temperature from the wind.

Shaking off my lethargy, I shot off almost the last of the film in the forest leaving one or two for 'this was me'[112] shots at the end. Then it was off to the new look shower block and a hot shower. Emerging a new man, I left quickly, stopping only briefly at the ranger's headquarters and visitor centre to check out. It was a dash to Wynyard, dropping the hire car and catching the plane with a minute to spare. A quick change in Melbourne and I was back in Perth that afternoon. Flynn's Tarn to Perth in a day!

Safe In The Harbour

> Have you stood by the ocean on a diamond hard morning
> and felt the horizon stir deep in your soul
> watch the wake of the steamer as it cut through the blue water
> been gripped by a fever you just can't control?
> Ah, to throw off the shackles and fly with the seagulls to where
> green waves tumble before driving sea wind,
> Or to lie on the decking on a warm summer's evening
> To watch the red sun burning beneath the Earth's rim.
> But to every sailor comes time to drop anchor,
> Haul in the sails and make the lines fast.
> You deepwater dreamer your journey is over
> You're safe in the harbour at last.
>
> Words and music by Eric Bogle

In an earlier trip account, I made an oblique reference to the realisation that very few poets, writers, artists or songwriters have spent much time

---

112 Yes, the word 'selfie' was not in use back then.

portraying the hillman's love for his hills. Certainly not to the extent that the low country and the sea figure in our everyday lives. Rudyard Kipling, in his verse *The Sea and the Hills*, almost paradoxically asks us, 'Hast thou desired the sea, the smell of saltwater unbounded, the heave and the roll, the curl and the crash of the breakers wind hounded...so and even so do the hillmen desire their hills.'

His analogy relating to the seafarer's love for the sea and the hillman's attraction to the high country, draws the reader to a rather abrupt somewhat unexpected statement. Understand the hillman by your more readily understandable typical seafarer – this would seem to be the message.

I have always found this perhaps the most compelling answer to the often asked question, 'Why do you people do this'? As nearly everyone knows, during the golden years of British mountaineering, the legendary Mallory, who was lost on Mount Everest in an epic above 8000 metre climb, answered, 'Because it is there!' Doubtless it was there but my guess is that as a hillman, he desired his hills not only as the seafarers loved the sea but because his exploits into the high country extended his level of consciousness, broadened his horizon and satisfied to some extent h vision. The Eric Bogle song continues:

> Some men are sailors but most are just dreamers
> held fast by the anchor they forge in their mind
> who in their hearts know they'll never sail over deepwater
> to search for a treasure they're afraid they won't find.
> So in sheltered harbour is they cling to their anchors
> bank down their boilers and shutdown their steam
> and wait for the sailors to return with the treasures
> that will fan the dull embers and fire up their dreams.

One can't escape the similarities in the convictions of both men. Mallory on the one hand was obviously not a writer at all! When people asked him the question it was born of fascination, an enquiry into the perception and motivation of the seasoned adventurer. I suspect that they would have been much more satisfied with a reply in the form of *Safe in the Harbour* as it says much more but would the reply Mallory gave been any less enduring? Remember that when Hillary came down off Mount Everest in 1953 his prosaic response when asked how the climb went' was something like, 'We knocked the bastard off!'

Perhaps many would counter that it is the sailors who are the dreamers and that so-called dreamers are the real, sensible, 'normal' people back in the towns with their feet firmly rooted in the real world of making a steady living. These people would contend that normal people keep their minds on the job, dismiss flights of inner fantasies as the feckless shortcomings of immaturity, even though their search for job satisfaction and 'quality-of-life' may be as empty as their understanding of why the sailors sail and the hill men climb. So lost, can they accept that daily work can be typified by a working environment soured by the negative energies of those safe in the harbour, but harbouring a latent wish to do something else, because it is there. I have always been profoundly saddened by this and sorry for all those concerned. The Eric Bogle song continues:

> And some men are schemers who laugh at the dreamers
> take the gold from the sailors and turn it to dross
> they are men in a prison they are men without vision
> whose only horizon is profit and loss.
> So when storm clouds come sailing across your blue ocean
> hold fast to your dreaming for all that you're worth
> for as long as there are dreamers there will always be sailors
> bringing back their bright treasures from the corners of earth.

Then there is that Mo Anthoine's phrase which, on the Richter scale of literary abominations rates about 6.5 of 'feeding the rat[113]'. Mo reckoned there was a rat living inside every true mountaineer which, if not fed, gnawed away at the insides of his host. Graphic, imaginative. But some would say rather disgusting.

---

113   Feeding the Rat, by Al Alvarez, first published 1988

According to Mo, the rat could only be fed on a regular diet of frequent trips to the hills. Should the owner be foolish enough not to feed it, then the familiar frustrations of a land-locked sailor would surely result. Whether graphic, imaginative or disgusting, the phrase has taken on cult status since Mo has largely left the scene after his notable exploits in the 1960s and 70s with Joe Brown and others.

Back at home, the rat can be partially fed by 'playing' with one's equipment, whether in the back yard shed, in the study or on the living room floor. As an alternative, sorting out all the trip photos can assuage for a time that thirst that comes from within. But before too long, unless old age catches up or you get 'banned from the bush'[114], you feel the need to head off once more. Armchair mountaineering, immersed in the epic deeds of others as each page of another glossy mountain saga unfolds, will no longer suffice. Just as the sailor can no longer linger safe in the harbour, so must the hillman depart for the hills, a rat to be fed, to knock the bastard off, because it is there.

Mountaineers in captivity are easily recognised. Without their clothing and equipment, away from the crags and the misty high places, seemingly stripped of their stage on which to play out their calling to the high hills, you can pick them out. Their unmistakable signature betrays them. Kipling, in his work *Kim,* recognised it even if disguised like the handshake of a Freemason when he wrote,: 'Who goes to the hills goes to his mother.'.

The music score which accompanied this walk

Crosby, Stills, Nash and Young
    Judy Blue Eyes
    Cowgirl in the Sand
Crosby, Stills and Nash
    Daylight again
    Find the Cost of Freedom
    Southern Cross

---

[114] A domestic related family travel restriction.

Barbara Streisand
- Evergreen

Seals and Crofts
- We may never pass this way again

Harry Chapin
- Taxi
- Greyhound Bus

Simon and Garfunkel
- I am a Rock
- Sounds of Silence

Emmylou Harris
- Spanish Johnny
- Here, There and Everywhere

The Fureys
- When you were Sixteen

Bob Dylan
- Mr Tambourine Man
- Gates of Eden
- Knockin' on Heaven's Door
- Tangled Up in Blue

Jackson Browne
- Running on Empty
- The loadout/stay
- Take it Easy

Deliverance soundtrack
- Duelling Banjos

Buddy Holly
- That'll Be the Day
- Rave On

Easy Rider soundtrack
- Born to be Wild
- Wasn't Born to Follow
- The Weight

Dan Fogelberg
> Leader of the Band
> Sutter's Mill

Fleetwood Mac
> Rumours
> Go Your Own Way

The Who
> Pinball Wizard

Chuck Berry
> Sweet Sixteen
> Johnny B Goode

Leo Kottke
> Eight Miles High
> Pamela Brown
> Medley (with Joy of Man's Desiring)

Roy Orbison
> Mystery Girl

Travelling Wilburys
> Album, volume 1

Eric Bogle
> Lock Keeper
> Safe in the Harbour

Food List

- Absolute minimalist approach for this short walk.
- Breakfast: Black tea
- Lunch: SAO biscuits, tinned fish (3), cheese, pepperoni, dried fruit, nuts.
- Dinner: soup or noodles, dehydrated meals, chocolate.
- Backup: muesli bars (4), lifesavers, fruit buns (3), drink base.

Equipment

- Absolute minimalist lightweight approach.

- Pack (50 litre), sleeping bag (fairy down), bevy sack, Gore-Tex, (foam mat optional).
- Stove and fuel, billy, spoon, scouring pads,
- parka (Gore-Tex) long johns, wool singlet, spare socks, overpants (Gore-Tex).
- Head torch, penlight, candle, camera and film, lens filters, camera clamp, mending kit, Swiss army knife, first aid kit, gaiters.
- Mug, canvas water bag, gloves,, hat, balaclava, boot wax or snow seal, sunglasses, toothbrush and comb, map and compass, pen and paper, lip sealer, toilet paper, cigarette lighter and matches, Walkman, tapes and batteries, down vest

Camps by the Pool of Bethesda

The Pool of Siloam

The Pool of Siloam

Unamed pool nearby (SE) of the Pool of Siloam

Pool of Bethesda

And in 2003

Dixon's Kingdom hut in 1991

Pool of Bethesda

Jaffa Vale and Solomon's Throne

Jaffa Vale in 1991

Jaffa Vale in 1991

Looking down to the Pool of Bethesda

The route up Solomon's Throne

A perfect camp

Later Tasmanian Walks – 7

Return to the Walls of Jerusalem, December 1995

DAY 1: THURSDAY 28 DECEMBER 1995

Above all else, it felt good to be back on the track into the Walls. It was four years since my last visit – four years too many and my heart lifted as I pushed up the familiar track from the car park, soon leaving the large eucalypts and approaching Trappers' Hut. I had left it late, leaving the car park at 3 pm, but there was plenty of time with daylight saving and the southerly latitude on my side. The weather looked very promising with a large high on the Great Australian Bight, so after some deliberation, I left the tent behind and pushed off.

Trappers' Hut was reached in an hour, and I found the climb a little tough in the hot afternoon sun. But once past that, the going past Solomons Jewels and on to Wild Dog Creek was easier. Since my last visit much of the boggy area has been duckboarded which makes the walking even more pleasant. I got to Wild Dog Creek about 5 pm, the site of my bivvy last time on the way in. This time, however, it was still warm and there was little wind – plenty of time to push on to Herod's Gate, where I remembered there was a good place to stop for the night.

Lake Salome shimmered in the late afternoon sunlight as I entered Herod's Gate. I crossed to the north side where there was still an hour's sunlight and found the campsite on the edge of the first clump of pencil pines. It was a pleasant spot, with soft snow grass and a high rocky backdrop. The pines offered shelter from the wind and there was plenty of firewood, though I used a stove as required by the park rules. Every now and then the wind blew gently enough to cool my brow and discourage the mozzies, but not so strong as to blow out the stove. There was enough light to cook by so I made some Maggi two-minute noodles followed by a fiery hot Asian pasta dish. I left some for breakfast and cooled off with a fruit biscuit and tea. It was a warm night. I laid out a foam mat and tried to sleep in my bag, dressed in woollens. But it was too hot and the mozzies buzzed around my head in swarms. Eventually I stripped off, put the bag inside the bivvy sack, which has a mozzie net and slept like a log under the stars till 7 o'clock the following day.

The morning was chilly out of the sun and I needed a wool shirt as I fired up the stove to cook the leftovers and some tea. By 8 o'clock I was away back to Herod's Gate and on to the Pool of Bethesda via the south side of Lake Salome. It was pleasant, thumping along the boards, wired for sound, listening to Pete Seeger and some reggae. A clear morning sun glistened on Hall's Buttress and also on the tufts of velvety snow grass. By eight thirty I was at the pool.

DAY 2: FRIDAY 29 DECEMBER 1995

The Pool of Bethesda is one of the best spots in the Walls area. Along with Jaffa Vale, it ranks as the favourite spot to camp, ringed as it is with ancient gnarled pencil pines and blessed with spongy soft snow grass and superb views of the valley and surrounding crags. There A number of people were camped there but not conspicuously, and there was room for plenty more tents. A fantastic place. I strolled around the pool taking photographs then headed up to Damascus Gate sucking a peppermint lifesaver and pounding out the reggae. It was starting to warm up as I reached the gate, but I still wore my wool shirt and had applied a layer of lip sealer against the wind.

Damascus Gate gives an excellent view of the vale of the same name and the pine forest that leads down to Dixon's Kingdom Hut at Jaffa Vale. It is one of the most impressive stands of pencil pines I have seen. And the setting at Dixon's Kingdom Hut is breathtaking. The hut is located on the edge of a pencil pine grove, high in Jaffa Vale, not far from the Jaffa Gate, which is the gap between the Temple and Mount Jerusalem. There are plenty of mossy soft spots for camping above the hut and with sweeping views down the valley to Lake Ball.

Not far from the hut entrance there is a fine gnarled old log which provided an excellent spot for a mid-morning break. I sat there quietly with the sun warm on my shoulders and ate an orange I brought from the Melbourne Hilton where I had checked out after work. It was very pleasant. The wool shirt was off for the rest of the day and the stream babbled away next to the log. Above there were fine views of the Temple and Hall's Buttress, perfectly framed through the pencil pines fleetingly reflected in the pool's limpid water.

After a long photo stop, I moved on to the saddle above Jaffa Gate. A staked route led to the top then off to the right up to the flanks of Mount Jerusalem itself. The climb to the top of Jerusalem was not difficult with a faint track all the way and passing two or three small tarns. The summit gave a good view of all the Cradle Mountain peaks as far south as Acropolis in Pine Valley. Allow about two hours from the Pool of Bethesda.

I didn't stop at the summit but pushed on down the northeast scree slope to join up with a small creek running down to Zion Gate. There was lovely photography on offer at several appealing pools but it was hot and I wanted to press on to Lake Tyre for a drink and some lunch. About ten minutes later, after some light scrub, I saw the lake shore of the lake appear through the trees . There was no track after the Jerusalem summit. Lunchtime was a peaceful Lake Tyre stop with cool water to dip into and a flat block of dolerite to sit on and bask in the summer sun.

After coming down off Mount Jerusalem I stopped at midday by a flat rock near the creek that drains into the lake from Zion Gate. A delightful spot with a gentle breeze ruffling the lake's glass-like surface and moving the tops of the brave little pencil pines pushing up between the mossy rocks. Across the water I saw two groups of tents — one by itself and four others. It looked as if they were here to fish for mountain trout. Behind the tents the pines thinned out and the ridge ran up to a blocky outcrop. Overhead the sky was blue with a wispy cirrus cloud here and there. Flies and mosquitoes buzzed about but lunch was all finished and packed away. The herrings in tomato sauce were tasty on flat bread, with some pepperoni sausage, nuts and dates. I couldn't find the SAOs so assumed I had left them in the car. What I had was plenty, washed down with plenty of cool water from the lake. I decided to complete a circuit back to Lake Salome by traversing from Lake Tyre to Lake Sidon, then climbing Ephraim's Gate to exit at the Pool of Salome – this would enable me to camp at the Pool of Bethesda, which was assured of late afternoon sun.

Leaving Lake Tyre after a pleasant stroll around the southern shore, following a faint wombat pad, I struck out through the bush for Lake Sidon. The going was rough but not too bad. After a while I could see the lake which made route choosing easier and speeded my progress. The pack wasn't too heavy but by the time I reached a small tarn not far from Lake Tyre my feet were feeling sore. They take a while to warm up after lunch or an overnight stop. I named the pool unofficially the Pool of Isabelle and took some pictures and trudged on wearily, reaching Lake Sidon, with its two islands, at 3 pm, about an hour after leaving Lake Tyre. I was starting to tire (no pun intended) but picked a good route up to Ephraim's Gate, and made steady progress.

The bush was very thick but I was soon through it and snapping pictures at the top. A panoramic view of the West Wall again framed by pines. Just below the top is the Pool of Siloam, closed to camping because of its very fragile shoreline and peaty bogs. No matter, Bethesda was my aim, reached about 4.15 pm. It was good to put down the load and unwind down by the shores of the pool. Warm enough to swim (some people were) but I preferred not to foul the water supply any further. I found a spot to camp at the northern end of the pool with some soft grass and a log to sit on. It was a peaceful evening with a pink sunset over the crags and lengthening shadows among the pines throwing a magic light. The stove purred, the tired body unwound, birds called and wallabies grazed quietly by the pool, seemingly wary and man shy.

Sitting on a wood block, padded with a pair of canvas Karrimor gaiters and a foam mat, I cooked noodles and pondered upon the richness of the setting. Still the wispy cloud, a silver moon rising through the pencil pines and, later still, the Southern Cross blazing in the lower sky. Nearby, a soft patch beckoned. Throwing down the mat I stretched out in the bivvy sack and zipped up the mozzie net. Lying back comfortably, it was a dress circle view of the peaks and pines seen with the majesty of moon and stars. There was, or seemed to be, peace in the firmament as I drifted off into cloudland.

DAY 3: SATURDAY 30 SEPTEMBER 1995

I slept until about 7.30. It had been a somewhat hot and sweaty night in the sack but I felt refreshed after getting up, stretching and having a look about. It had been warm enough to open up the sack but there were too many mosquitoes for that — so I had to sweat it out. Despite that, I got a reasonably good sleep, waking once or twice to roll over or have a drink of water. Clouds had gathered overnight and blanketed the sky shrouding the peaks early in the morning. But they made way as the morning passed for to leafy, puffy cumulus here and there, with higher windblown streaks of cirrus. Day three of the big high. Little wind and warm.

Taking a daypack with lunch and a camera I set off at about 9.00 am back up over Damascus Gate. The shirt came off before too long as the camera worked away in the early morning light. It was a beautiful stroll down to Dixon's Kingdom through the majestic stand of pine forest. The Dixon's Kingdom hut was built in the early 1950s by Reg Dixon and his son Bobby. It was renovated and extended in 1979-80 by Roger Scholes who featured the hut in a film about the high country.

Dixon was a local bushman from the Meander, Deloraine, Mole creek area who had a pastoral lease on the Walls from 1946 to 1972. He grazed the high country by summer and trapped there in the winter. Today the pine log and shingle hut is under conservation — not for residents — but would give good shelter in winter.

Walking through the forest, with sphagnum moss, cushion moss and pineapple grass underfoot, the sensation is like walking on thick carpet under the coolness of the canopy overhead. Out on the grassy meadows, alas, the biting mosquitoes and March flies came in dense clouds, attacking at will. Not so bad at other times of the year, but right now it meant moving on. Back up towards Jaffa Gate, route stakes offered a rest for my camera clamp so grabbed some self-portrait shots with a pleasant backdrop. Below the hut, you can see Lake Ball, but well before that there is a green shelf about twenty minutes' walk towards the lake. Excellent shots of Hall's Buttress (King Solomon's Throne) can be taken from there with reflective pools to complete the scene perfectly.

After passing through Jaffa Gate, I continued into the grassy valley below the east wall on Mount Jerusalem. Stopping at midday by a grassy tuft and a shallow stream, I took some lunch and drank deeply of the scene. Overhead, broken cloud was gathering, the hot sun burning me only when it came out from the cover. One more rain-free night?

It was a relief to have a gentle breeze across the grass, flicking the daisies back and forth and caressing my burnt shoulders. The idea for the afternoon was to pick up an open lead up on the Temple then to sidle north to the Gate of the Chain, thence on the flat through to the Pool of Bethesda. An open lead to the left presented itself and after a last drink I was up and at it.

Following the lead up a boggy wombat pad with scratches and holes, I reached a large fallen pine log. From there it was into the scrub along random animal trails until I had enough height to sidle round and down a little on to the wide saddle – the Gate of the Chain. A good view of Solomon and Barn Bluff was photographed before sidling at the same height left to the larger rock I'd recce'd the night before as a waypoint for the track home. This led directly down to the Pool of Bethesda – perfect navigation!

It was 1 pm and I had been going strongly. Sunburnt, yes, but feet and legs strong. The camp was deserted, so I moved my gear down to the water – a perfect spot, under two twin pines with a flat rock to sit on. I settled in and got some water in the water bag. Lunch was the usual flat bread, sardines, biscuits and dates. Not bad, with a gentle breeze and a little music. March flies and mozzies came in for the kill, but were repulsed occasionally by the breeze. At least I could write! Not like at Dixon's Kingdom.

Drip, drip, drip went the water from the bag (hooked up in the pine to keep cool) down into the billy. Without the music turned on, it and the buzz of the flies was all you could hear. Ants scurried among the pine needles, picking up scraps. They made a great fuss over the sardine oil on the rocks. I oiled my boots with Sno Seal[115], adjusted some of my gear then put my feet up for a while and relaxed. It had been a short but pleasing day.

At 3 o'clock, rested and fed, I decided to run up Solomon's Throne (which used to be called Hall's Buttress) to check the weather to the west and get some aerial shots of the area. The climb from Damascus Gate was easy and quick — I was on top by 3.30 snapping views of Frenchman's Cap to the south, and much of the Cradle Mountain area.

It was cool and windless on top as I sat on the warm rocks in just a singlet. The weather to the west looked still clear, though grey cloud was building up around the mountains. Down below, I could see my camp at the pool was getting overcrowded so I located a nice looking alternative from my lofty perch and headed down. Got back to the pool by four o'clock. A few last shots of the pool with 400 ASA Ekta and I trudged out. They were swimming in the pool again!

My new camp about 400 metres back towards Herod's Gate was off the track to the left up on a little hill I called the Hill of Grace. It offered a clump of pines, a babbling brook and soft ground, set against a mighty backdrop of rock. Wallabies grazed tamely nearby on the snow grass as I sat on a log making tomato soup and cheese and bacon mashed potato. I had hoped the aerial attack would be lessened away from the pool but no such luck. The March flies were gone but the mozzies and sandflies were a real pest. They gave no relief, even when the evening breeze from the north had me in a woollen shirt with gloved hands. It was now 6.00 pm, calm and cool, with crickets calling and the mozzies buzzing about. Occasionally a blow fly called in and then buzzed off. There were three wallabies grouped about 100 metres from my camp. Nibbling quietly, they were unconcerned by my presence.

Either it was cooler night or I was feeling the cold more. On went the long johns and wool singlet and shirt. It will be interesting to see how the sack and bag perform tonight. I'll still need the net — the mozzies are into me right through the long johns and socks. Couldn't write any more — the

---

115 The warmth of the sun softens the wax.

clouds of them were carrying me away! It was 6:20 pm and calm. Hopefully no rain tonight. Cloudy sky.

DAY 4: SUNDAY 31 DECEMBER 1995

It took a while for the stars to come out. And then only briefly. The evening mist came down after 8.30, hanging over everything like a shroud. The wind was gentle, though chilly, and did little to discourage the insects. Bagged and netted, I was hot, steadily shedding clothes until I was in a singlet and jocks, listening to music as I drifted off to sleep on the soft ground. Above the clouds, the Stars of Warburton[116] were looking out for me.

I woke with a start. What was that sound? In a flash I knew what to expect. Unzipping the fly top I bounded out with my torch which I'd left close at hand, expecting nocturnal visitors. A large Tasmanian possum was up the pine tree where I'd hung the food[117] and scrap bags[118]. I put both in my pack and placed the pack under my feet at the foot of my bed so to speak. She was persistent. After several attacks and a brief encounter with the billy of evening 'mash' she gave up and mooched off into the darkness. I didn't wake again until shortly before dawn when I was roused by the sound of rain on my bivvy sack. But it was a heavy dew, driven by the wind. Rather bleak in fact. But warm as toast in the bag. You've heard the saying, 'It's nice to be in bed when it's raining.' Well the feeling was the same in that snug bivvy bag. Why move? Why panic? All was secure, warm and dry. My equipment was made for this... I rolled over and slumbered on until getting up at 7.10 am.

It was a bleak, windswept vista. Reminiscent of *Wuthering Heights*, I could imagine that woman calling out 'Heathcliff, Heathcliff' her cry being lost in the wind-driven mists. The tops were clouded in and, unlike yesterday, were unlikely to emerge by 9.30, if at all.

---

116 Words and music by Midnight Oil.
117 The chuck wagon is the name I use for the food bag. I usually carry so little food that it all fits into a small string topped bag. At this stage it contained a little cheese, dates, nuts and some muesli bars – plus some coffee.
118 The scrap bag is a plastic shopping bag used to collect waste packaging which is returned to civilisation. It contained teabags, orange peel, sardine cans and soup packets – possum heaven!

Not much point in hanging around. After four rain-free days it was time to head out. After considering a stockman's breakfast[119] I opted for a cup of tea and some reheated mash from last night. Both were forgettable – eminently – and the Optimus 00 kero stove was hard to light in the wind, notwithstanding the fact that I had perfected an outdoor 'rough and fiery' method of starting it.

A marvellous advantage that comes with travelling ultralight is that packing is a breeze. It all fits into a fifty-litre pack with oceans of spare room – and there's less to get wet if it rains. Despite the heavy dew, the bag was dry though the inside of the Gore-Tex Early Winter bivvy sack would need drying out back in Perth. It worked very well just the same. The rest would have all fitted easily into a shoebox – parka, down jacket (J and H 'dumper') woollens, stove, gaiters, mat and camera.

Taking a shot of 'bleak house' for the record, I shouldered arms and eight o'clock danced around the campsite to an Irish jig by Tommy Makem and Liam Clancy[120], waved to my furry friends in the mist and marched down from the Hill of Grace to the duckboards.

Come fill up your glasses and let us be merry,
for to rob and to plunder it is our intent,
as we roam through the valleys through the hills and the roses,
and the beauty of Kashmir lay drooping its head.
English traditional folk song performed by Steeleye Span

My boots clumped over the duckboards once more as I trudged down to Herod's Gate in the driving mist. It occurred to me that my feet were hardened but it was cool enough for gloves even though I still wore short pants (my only longs were long johns and fully zipped Gore-Tex North Face overpants – both not needed as it turned out).

It would be the last trip for the shorts – they were completely thrashed to bits; legs torn away, pockets holed through and the arse out completely on

---

119   Aussie expression meaning a piss and a look about.
120   All God's children have a place in the choir.

one side. I must have cut quite a sight in my Coonskin hat and moustache; a bit like a Tassie version of Davy Crockett.

At nine thirty I stopped by one of the Solomon's Jewels tarns — a really nice small one, just off the track, with a perfect rock to sit on looking out over the water towards Lake Loane and Trappers' Hut. There were wild water lilies on the surface of the tarn, like the more familiar domestic version, but smaller. First time I'd seen them. Very peaceful. Cheese (cheddar with peppercorns), flatbread (last of), smoked oysters (last tin) and poor man's wine from the streams of the mountains.

I stashed the Swiss army knife back in its leather pouch on my belt (a plaited RM Williams version) and calmly watched the water — drops of rain and mist broke the surface here and there. Birds called. Solitude.

Two other 'escapees' passed by on the main track. Did they see me? In a moment they were gone. Even the mozzies were not too bad.

It was now ten o'clock and there was a plane to catch. Shouldered the load — very light even on sunburnt shoulders, and set off down to Trappers' Hut where a young couple were still preparing to leave after an overnight stay. The original trappers were Dick and Ray (Boy) Miles and their uncle Ray Walters (possibly Reg) who built the hut in 1946 from timber slabs and shingles. In those days there was good money to be made from wallaby and possum skins, though it's not so today.

The animals were caught in snares which had to be tended. From accounts, Miles and Walters had several thousand in the area. They dried the skins on the wall of the hut inside. Not sure what they did with the carcasses. In 1969 the hut was demolished and rebuilt in the same design by the Hut Preservation Board. It had become so rundown that a complete rebuild was needed.

The replacement is true to form, with split shingles on the roof and slab boards and bunk area. It would easily overnight a group of four to six but its location is a slightly odd in that it is five or ten minutes' walk below the edge of the central plateau in the last of the larger stands of eucalypt at the top of the 'grunter' up from the car park, about an hour's climb. Downhill, it takes about half an hour and it's hard not to break into a jog. In places the track is quite steep, but wide and offering a good footing.

I put on the Jimi Hendrix and some reggae and raced down to the logbook station near the car park in quick time. Signing out, it was hard to find my 'in' entry; it was three pages back! Amazing to see so many entries. Car park was not quite full. Also, two commercial, mountain guide vehicles.

Changed into my street clothes. My street shoes felt soft and light – luxurious in fact. The pack went into the boot, dirty clothes and boots into the sail bag. What's that at the rear of the boot? It was the missing Sao biscuits! I slid behind the wheel of the hire car, looking but not feeling clean. It felt good to be heading home after another mountain odyssey.

> I've strayed on the side of twelve misty mountains,
> I've walked and I've crawled on six crooked highways,
> I've stepped on the side of seven side forests,
> I've been out in front of a dozen dead oceans,
> I've been ten miles in the mouth of a graveyard
> it's a hard, it's a hard, it's a hard and it's a hard
> it's a hard rain's gonna fall.
>
> Words and music by Bob Dylan

As I turned the ignition key, the first spots of rain began to fall. It rained for the 156 km back to Wynyard, and flight 6326 with Kendall Airlines from Burnie was nearly fog bound. The weather had completely closed in. I said 'Happy New Year' at the desk as I dropped off the car keys at the Avis counter and flew out at 5:15 pm.

Ultralight Food List

In keeping with management's aim neither to fill nor satisfy

Mornings:
- black tea,` evening leftovers

Midday:
- flat bread and tinned fish, cheese, dates, nuts, pepperoni sausage.

Evening:
- soup and noodles.
- Extras: biscuits (forgot them), muesli bars (4), peppermint lifesavers (1 pack), fresh fruit (2 pieces).
- Binge out on return? No.
- Target weight. four x 600 g, say 2.4 kg
- Would have liked some orange Tang

Equipment

Pack, 50 litre:	Clothing (worn)
foam mat	singlet
sleeping bag	shorts and belt
bivvy sack	wool shirt
water bag	socks two pairs
stove and fuel	boots
billies, two	hat
bowl	
mug	
spoon	**Clothing (carried)**
mending kit	long johns
torch, two	wool singlet
medical kit	down jacket
Walkman and tapes	parka
Candles	over pants

Snow seal
map and compass
camera gear
Swiss army knife
Cord
Sunglasses
guidebook or map
note paper and pen
toothbrush and paste
Would have liked? insect repellent and suncream

gaiters
gloves
balaclava, silk

Epilogue

I am a truthful man from the land of the palm trees,
and before I die I want to share these thoughts of my soul.
My poems are a soft green
my poems are also flaming and crimson
my poems are like a wounded fallen seeking shelter in the forest.
With the poor people of the earth I wish to share my fate.
The streams of the mountains please me more than the sea...
        – Jose Marti 1852 – 1894, Words adapted to the tune
                                          Guantanamera

The connection in Melbourne was close, very close. I had to run from gate 14 round to gate 6 and only just made it. Mr Newman from 7 A had to be 'moved'. As soon as I boarded, the door closed, we pushed back and were on our way to Perth, taxiing off in pouring rain. After what Qantas refers to as dinner, munching on an Eskimo Pie, I gazed out the window at the cotton wool cloud blanket below me and felt pleased with myself.

    It had been a great trip. The weather was perfect, the gear worked well, nothing of significance was missed or forgotten. Others might have been looking forward to their New Year's eve festivities – not that I was not – but the high was still very strong. As Rudyard Kipling wrote in Kim, 'He goes to the hills goes to his mother'. And as it was for Kim with the mountains stirring a feeling in him which the lowlands could not offer, so it was that I felt heightened as always by the effort, and grateful for the break from the daily grind of minerals related work.

I felt pleased with the time for more creative thinking, allowing 'glimpses of notes like the catch of a song' to float in and out of my head as 'echoes of boyhood shall bear them along[121]'. Catches of phrases, sometimes whole verses, songs, past memories and the grandeur and oneness of the hills surpassed, as usual, my more normal instincts for food and to a lesser extent, sleep.

Bowling along the stony path, thumping on the boards, lightly treading in the sedge and cushion moss or forging progress through the 'wait-a-while', I had mental glimpses of other great adventures and a feeling of getting older. The college anthem of my boyhood drifted back to me:

Forty years on growing older and older,
shorter in wind as in memory long,
what would you now, were that once you were younger,
twenty and thirty and forty years on.

Struggling to remember the words, I keep coming back to, '... visions of boyhood shall float them before you, echoes of dreamland shall bear them along'. Like in the song, nostalgic trips seem to float so many things back to me[122]. Returning to the hills is not just 'feeding the rat' as it was once described. It's as if one needs to pause, look backwards in a mood of contemplative reflection, then to look forward, hopefully with a clearer view as to one's future direction. With more inner peace and a feeling of greater confidence.

In these days of politically correct doublespeak, I guess they call this self-empowerment! It used to be called self-actualisation! But in any event, it 'took me disappearing in the smoke rings of my mind, down the foggy ruins of time, the haunted frightened tree, far from the twisted reach crazy sorrow'. Yes, I drank deep of it and felt satisfied.

---

121 From Forty Years On, the song of Harrow, the UK public school.
122 At this point, I still had three Himalayan expeditions ahead of me.

Yes, to dance beneath the diamond sky with one arm waving free,
silhouetted by the breeze,
far from the circus sands
with all memory and fate buried deep below the waves... '

I allowed myself for a while at least to 'forget about today until tomorrow.[123]' But I came back to reality. The sun was lower now on the western horizon. The movie (something about killer whales and a Willie), which I didn't watch, has finished and the 'cattle are lowing'. I tore back the Velcro tab on my Heuer[124] diver's watchband and set the time back by three hours – it is 7.00 pm and forty-five minutes to Perth.

Time to let go. Join hands again with the living. Daylight again... the end of 1995... Australia remembers.

Perhaps I should unpack quickly, wash all the clothes and put everything away. That way the reminders of the trip may recede quicker. No sights or scents to distract the senses; only the gashes on my hands (from a fall), the scratches on my legs (from the unyielding horizontal scrub), the bandage on my toe (toenail in-cut), flaking skin (face, hands and shoulders got the worst of it) or the greasy hair need be reminders, which will pass.

After all, it's New Year's Eve. Out with 1995 and in with the new year. We are five years from the end of the twentieth century. The new year is unsullied and still pure – like the 'hammer of justice – the bell of freedom[125]'.

---

123 A few lines from Bob Dylan's Mr Tambourine Man

124 Later called TAG watchpieces.

125 From If I had a hammer, sung by Peter, Paul and Mary in the 60s.

Later Tasmania Walks – 8

Solo trip back to the Walls of Jerusalem, 2003

I did not do any walks in Tasmania between the mid-nineties and the new millennium. After I returned from Khan Tengri in 1999 and Mount Everest late in 2001[126,] I don't recall doing very much away from work in 2002. The following year however, I did a solo trip back to the Walls of Jerusalem in December of that year, some eight years after the 1995 trip. This is a description of the Temple circuit, Walls of Jerusalem National Park in Tasmania.

Foreword

It is late afternoon at my camp by the Pool of Bethesda, at the Walls of Jerusalem Park in Tasmania. The shadows are lengthening as I sit on a large rock by the tent waiting for the stove to boil the billy. On the edge of the grove of gnarled old pencil pines, two Bennett's wallabies are grazing nonchalantly, unconcerned by my presence as I moved quietly to the stove and prepared chicken and corn soup in an aluminium bowl.

It is peaceful, even more so when the wind drops, allowing you to feel the warming last rays of the sun. Behind me, the nearside of Solomon's Throne is nearly all in shadow, but the Temple still is adorned with golden light, its brown dolerite boulders falling almost to the shore of the Pool of Bethesda. The wind rustles in the pencil pines; currawongs call from afar; the wallabies twitch their ears. All must know the evening is approaching.

I took the chance to fly down to Tassie following a board meeting in

---

126 These expeditions are described in The Wandering Pilgrim, Volume 1, my first book.

Melbourne and spend four days here, hoping for reasonable weather. It is mid-December, a nice time to come, but time is short as I must leave for France soon for a northern hemisphere Christmas with Chantal and Isabelle[127].

These notes describe a pleasant walking circuit which can be done in a couple of days, three if you take in some of the peaks on offer as well. Places worth seeing, good campsites and so on are described together with a general description of the route.

The Walls of Jerusalem Park is among the best mountain parks in Australia, offering superb outdoor experience for all ages. A walk map and notes available[128] on the net are recommended. This was my third trip into the Walls.

DAY 1: SATURDAY 13 DECEMBER 2003 ...AND THERE'S CRICKET ON THE RADIO'

I landed in Devonport about 9.30 am, watching the waves of Bass Strait lap the northern shores of Tasmania as we came in low along the coast and touched down. I had no after-effects from Christmas dinner the night before at the Naval and Military Club with my sons John and Andrew, but was suffering the closing stages of an attack of 'jungle fever[129]' with the usual days of headache and fever gradually passing.

It had been good seeing the young men again. We had a pleasant dinner together and parted in good company. After collecting the Avis hire car , I stopped in town to gather some last minutes supplies before heading out through Spreyton and Sheffield. The second cricket test was on in Adelaide and Ponting was approaching two hundred runs against the Indians. The radio reception dropped in and out so I stopped at Gowrie Park (the former HEC construction camp) to change clothes and pack my rucksack for the walk in later in the afternoon.

---

127 Chantal had taken our daughter to complete some French schooling and further violin tuition.

128 The reference I used then was Cradle Mountain Lake St Claire and Walls of Jerusalem National Parks, by John Chapman and John Siseman, published by Pindari publishers, 1990.

129 I have been positive for Ross River fever and dengue for many years, picked up who knows where or when. around 2025 I started taking medicinal cannabis oil which has caused the symptoms to all but disappear.

By the time I reached Lake Rowallan and the Walls of Jerusalem car park it was 1.20 in the afternoon. There were six cars parked there. Ponting was on 205 and the Aussies seven wickets down for 520 or something. I locked the car and set off. The weather was fine, with showers occasionally requiring windscreen wipers when driving in, but now it was clear and warm enough to climb in only a shirt. I had a fair sweat up as I laboured up the path, but my legs felt strong and I reached the hut without stopping.

For this trip I had opted for the 80-litre Gregory sack – more comfortable than the 50-litre Camp Trails which I carried last time, despite its unusable extra space. As soon as I was under way carrying about 26 kg it felt much better. Good decision. The track led up fairly steeply to the Trappers' hut located on the edge of the Great Tiers, at the top of the eucalypt forest which fringe the slopes below the Tiers themselves. It has water but the hut itself is only much use as a lunch stop as it has no bunks. Allow an hour from the car park to the hut. There are two streams along the way so no need to carry water.

Leaving the shingle slabs of the old hut behind I continued without stopping. Not far past the hut, the track splits. To the right is the route to Lake Loane and Lake Adelaide. This track continues down to the Junction Lake and crosses over to the Cradle Mountain Park where it joins the main Overland track.

To the left, the track to the Walls of Jerusalem continues. Up here on the Tiers the wind had sprung up and sheets of rain, hail, sleet and snowflakes were driven in the strong southerly. I kept moving to keep warm and passed the tarns named Solomon's Jewels after about a further twenty minutes. The ruffled water of the lake also showed the strength of the breeze. The eucalypts bent and swayed, the stony track clinked as stones were overturned by my Raichle mountain boots as I rushed on towards Wild Dog Creek, where I bivvied on a previous trip[130] and woke buried in snow.

Imagine my surprise when I arrived this time to find a toilet and planked pine camping platforms, all nestled neatly below Herod's Gate. It seemed so incongruous as I passed by, not stopping, and climbed up to the gate – the entrance to the Walls themselves.

---

130 Refer to the earlier chapter on the 1996 trip.

Entering Herod's Gate under the towering King David's Peak I turned to look back. The weather had closed in and it was cold and blowing hard but rather than stop to don wet weather gear, I ran along the duckboarded path and reached the Pool of Bethesda after a three-hour journey from the car park. Time and the weather allowed little time to admire the Pool of Siloam, a short walk to the north of the track, – it could wait until the weather improved.

Right now I was cold and wet. Up with tent by a grove of pencil pines. Cold fingers fumbling, I crawled in, taped up some sore toes and put on an extra singlet and long johns. Down came the weather, so dinner was cooked inside the tent vestibule, snug with feet inside my warm sleeping bag. Sixties music from the Walkman soothed me as I cooked soup, stew and coffee. There was enough water to cook with as I had brought a five-litre canvas water bag. This means you can cook and wash up in bed without exiting the tent at all. The weather had closed in and even though it remained light till about 9.30, it was clear it would be a wet night. The wind buffeted the tent fly against the tent wall, but it was warm and dry. I drifted off to sleep listening to more music, waking only for pee about midnight. Surprise! The sky was clear and my lodestar, the Southern Cross, was visible.

> Got out of town on a boat for the southern island, sailing a reach before following sea
> I was making for the trades on the outside
> on the downhill run to Papeete.
> On this heading to the South lie the Marquesas,
> we have 80 feet of water line, nicely making way
> in a noisy bar in Avalon I tried to call you,
> but on the midnight watch I realised why twice you ran away.
> Think about how many times I have fallen, spirits are using me,
> larger voices calling,
> what heaven brought you and me cannot be forgotten.
> I have been around the world…

When you see the Southern Cross for the first time you understand
why now you came this way,
but the truth you might be running from is so small,
but it's as big as a promise the promise of a coming day...
    From *The Southern Cross*, words and music by Crosby, Stills and
Nash.

DAY 2: SUNDAY 14 DECEMBER 2003, THE TEMPLE CIRCUIT

After the three-hour walk in to the Pool of Bethesda in poor weather I slept well — cozy and warm in my Everest bag. So much so that I did not wake until 8.30. Gone were the fever and headaches. I felt well. Outside, however, the weather had closed in with mist engulfing the camp and rain squalls moving in. There was nothing for it but to roll over, put the billy on and enjoy a leisurely breakfast in bed. With Big Bill Broonzy singing the blues and pounding out on his twelve string guitar, I sipped coffee and watched the mist outside the tent flap swirl about among the pines. 'Polyanne drove steel like a man[131]'.

The morning passed pleasantly with breaks of sun and clearing cloud, despite getting wet while attempting to photograph the Pool after breakfast. It was boggy and soft around the edge but clear and showing little sign of environmental damage. I trod carefully and chatted to a Swiss couple on a day trip. Returned to camp to find the break in the bad weather on the move. It was fining up. Time to move.

The plan was to do what I call the Temple Circuit, starting from the Pool of Bethesda. It climbs up to the Gate of Damascus between the Temple and Solomon's throne. From there both peaks may be climbed. Then the route descends to Dixon's Kingdom hut among the pines of Jaffa Vale — a beautiful spot and a great place to take lunch sheltered by the pines.

From there, climb up to Jaffa Gate and follow the track on to the summit of Mount Jerusalem, returning to Jaffa Gate for a rest. Then follow the grassy slopes and creek down to the unknown named valley on the eastern side of

---

131 A line drawn from John Henry. Broonzy performed this at the Melbourne Town Hall without amplification!

the Temple, passing nice little tarns and assorted loan pine stands. There is a larger tarn below the east wall surrounded by conifers which also can easily be visited. From here, grassy slopes lead up around the north side of the Temple to a grove of dead pine, which is passed through on the west side to the Gate of the Chain from where it is a straightforward descent back to the Pool of Bethesda.

The words of the *Gates of Eden* came to mind...

Of war and peace the truth just twists its curfew'ed gull it glides,
  upon four-legged forest clouds the cowboy Angel rides,
  with his candle lit into the sun though its glow is waxed in black,
all except when 'neath the trees of Eden.

The savage soldier sticks his head in sand and then complains
unto the shoeless hunter who's gone death but still remains
onto the beach where hound dogs bray at ships with tattooed sails,
heading for the Gates of Eden.

With time honoured compass blade Aladdin and his lamp
sits with a group of utopian monks side-saddle on the golden calf,
and all the promises of paradise you will not hear a laugh,
all except inside the gates of Eden.

The motorcycle black Madonna two wheeled Gypsy Queen,
and her silver started phantom cause the grey flannel dwarf to scream,
and two wicked birds of prey who pick up on his breadcrumb sins
and there are no sins inside the gates of Eden.

At dawn my lover comes to me and tells me of her dream
with no attempt to shovel a glimpse into the ditch on what each one means,
at times I think there are no words but these to tell what's true,

and there are no truths outside the gates of Eden.'

— Taken from Bob Dylan's epic song of the same name.

I left at 11.30 am and returned about 5 pm, including the climb of Jerusalem and plenty of rests and camera stops. The valley between Temple and Jerusalem is pristine and deserted. Wallabies are everywhere and it is sheltered from the wind. The going is easy though there is no track and it is boggy in places. A good idea is to plan the route from Jerusalem before descending as the views of the route from above are very useful. Allow about five and a half hours for the circuit. This includes the climb of Jerusalem. Add extra if climbing Solomon's Throne and/or the Temple.

My description of the circuit follows:.

I set off from the pool with lunch and camera gear in my pack. As always, it was pleasant work, swinging along the duckboards in clearing weather. The climb up to Damascus Gate was short and the track beautifully stoned. On top, it was not yet clear enough to climb Temple or Solomon's Throne, so I pressed on down through the verdant upper reaches of Damascus Vale, then descended into the pines of Jaffa Vale. All the way to Dixon's Hut the track was stoned and boarded – ideal for rumbling along with the Walkman plugged in.

By the time I pulled in at the hut, sun was breaking out and filtering the light through the pines on to the lush mossy areas around the old shingled hut. The hut was smaller than I remembered it. Evidently the older, larger part had fallen down and been removed. This was a pity, as my earlier pictures record a far larger and more fitting structure than what is left. Below the hut is Jaffa Vale, where patches of scoparia have taken over from the open grass. Down there, however, are some nice views of Solomon's Throne. I got some shots in clearing weather with three cameras: the old Minolta X 700; the Canon elf with Advantix film; and the Canon elf digital camera. Back at the hut I loaded a role of 400 ASA in the Minolta and pressed on up to Jaffa Gate, snapping the Temple along the way, looking upwards and away to the left as I climbed. It was lovely walking with excellent views.

From Jaffa Gate the track veers off to the right and winds up through dolerite at the start of a 1500-metre Ridge climb to Jerusalem's summit. Attractive tarns are passed before the route opens out and gets windy with height. I needed a pile jacket. The summit is gained after about half an hour from the gate offering 360 degree views. On the top, sheltering from the wind among the rocks on the eastern side, I enjoyed SAO biscuits with green peppercorn pate, smoked cheese, hot salami and dates. I was also a little dry by this stage so on the descent I drank freely from my Camelbak[132] as I trotted along and listened to the music.

The descent was unkind to my sore toes, which needed to be taped up some more on my return, and after a dip in a small tarn on the way back. Back down at Jaffa Gate, there were some delightful grassy spots just off the track to the north where one could sit peacefully and take it all in. Mossy grass, babbling stream, graceful pines, smooth rocks, all seemingly in harmony with a clear sky overhead. I stopped for a while simply to take advantage of such a pleasant wayside resting spot.

The descent down the north side of the gate was gentle and pleasant, opening out eventually on to a broad open valley ringed with peaks. Strange that it has no name, like the nameless tarn at the base of the East wall. Wallabies were grazing as I sidled round the flanks of the Temple, keeping to the open country and following the best route as seen from higher up on Mount Jerusalem. Gradually, the route turned to the left and started to climb up to the Gate of the Chain. Open grasses after crossing the mossy brook led up through scattered scoparia to a grove of ghostly white pines – burnt some aeons ago. Underfoot it was spongy and soft, with sphagnum moss and water oozing up around my boots. The grazing wallabies ran ahead as I broke out into more open country, just below the Gate of the Chain. Large brain moss was scattered among flat dolerite blocks.

Plodding upwards to the music, I was jerked back to reality as I stepped forward and nearly stepped on a young tiger snake. At the last moment I lengthened my step and hopped over it. It remained still and spat at me before moving on. Moments later I was standing at the Gate – nearing the

---

132 Commonplace now, the water bottle-in-pack has a tube and mouthpiece, allowing a drink on the go.

completion of the Temple circuit. From here it was a gentle descent to the Pool of Bethesda. I followed an open stream gully down to the mossy plain, hopping over the firmer pineapple grass where needed. Just below the pool, a grove of pines is reached through which one rejoins the camp.

Two wallabies were back in residence grazing peacefully. So quiet was it without the breeze that I could hear one of them chew as I prepared the evening meal before nightfall. The end of a pleasant day.

I sat on a nice flat rock by the tent and took in the scene. In the distance above the Pool of Siloam rose the rocky mass of Zion Hill. In the near ground were old pines, gnarled and white of limb but with soft green celery tops. A grassy flat with some low scrub and rock surrounded the tent. Occasionally one of the Wallabies would put its head up, look at me, scratch its furry coat and resume grazing. Overhead the sky was clearing. Tomorrow would be a fine day.

By nightfall I was in bed snoozing and listening to music with a candle burning by my head. At midnight I awoke to noises at my feet. Torchlight revealed mother possum and her baby full on into my food supplies. Once shooed off, they scurried away – only to return for the bacon bits spice bag. The mother loved those and chomped on them eagerly, her wide eyes staring at me. At last, she left, her baby clinging to her furry back. Large Tasmanian possums can be a problem as they will quickly eat a hole in a tent or fly or tent wall if unattended. After I brought in all the food from the vestibule and zipped up the inner door they stayed away. No doubt foraging with their fellow nocturnal dwellers, the native cats, wombats and Tasmanian devils. After all that midnight commotion I slept undisturbed until waking 7.30 to find the sun already well up. I blinked, stretched, scratched my head and wriggled out of the bag. Off to do the peaks!

DAY 3: MONDAY 15 DECEMBER 2003

Ten minutes from the camp, I was up at Damascus Gate, entering the Gates of Eden as it were – a gentle alpine meadow taking its name either from the song or from paradise itself. Eagles soared above my head. Wallabies bobbed. The moon hung, crescent shaped, just to the right of Solomon's Throne, which I climbed on the way through the gate at its foot.

On to the Vale of Damascus. Here I was treated to some amazing mountain photography in the soft early morning light and clear still conditions. At the Vale of Damascus, I found some of the most pleasant campsites I have seen anywhere. Just superb[133]. I marvelled at the place and lingered on a flat rock while snacking on crackers, smoked cheese and salami. After changing films, I wandered back up to the gate and climbed the Temple itself – an easy, marked track leaving the main track at Damascus Gate. The views were expansive, similar to those of Solomon's Throne and Jerusalem. Of the three, Solomon's Throne and the Temple were the most memorable. It took no time to return to camp for lunch and a wash in the pool. Then it was back to the flat rock to meditate and write these notes.

The plan for the afternoon was a visit to the Pool of Siloam and Ephraim's Gate. Travelling light, I set off at 1.30, wending my way down on to the plain, angling down along animal pads from the pine grove surrounding Bethesda. Once down, there was a striking view of Barn Bluff seen in the middle of Herod's Gate away to the west. A cooling breeze was coming through the gate and up across Lake Salome when I reached it, then further northeast out on the cushion moss below the Pool of Siloam. Working my way through the pines and keeping an eye out for snakes (there were several) I soon reached the cool waters of Siloam, three or four times the size of the Pool of Bethesda.

At the far end there is a rock you can dive off (and deepwater) so I opted to have a swim rather than venture on through Ephraim's Gate. I did a short recce on the far side, which showed a scrubby descent to Lake Sidon. Back by the swimming rock by 2.45, I warmed my back in the sun to dry and wrote down these notes, with a cool breeze at my back. The only sounds were the birds chirping and the crickets creaking. Occasionally a blowfly buzzed by and the water lapped the flat rock below my feet. Those sounds and the breeze in the pines completed the setting.

It was getting hot in the sun. I slapped on some cream and slowly

---

133 Ideal spot to photograph the Wailing Wall, the ridge separating Solomon's Throne and Mt Moriah to the south.

dressed. I couldn't help noticing that my shirt and shorts were falling apart completely. To finish the day, I planned to locate the small auxiliary pool below Ephraim and inspect the pine grove on the northwest shore of Lake Siloam. The auxiliary pool was immediately southeast of the main pool, with their shores about 150 metres apart. This pool is very shallow and resembles the Artist's Pool at Cradle Mountain,. Its shore commands a panoramic view of the entire West Wall, from Solomon's Throne to King David's peak. Well worth a visit but both pools are boggy along their shores and not really suited (or open) to camping.

I returned to camp about 4.30 in warm sun to find all as I had left it. The inside of the tent was furnace hot so I opened up the front and rear flaps to allow the breeze to flow through. The food was all hot – and the chocolate melted but leaving it out was not an option. I unpacked my camera gear and filled the water bags in the pool. It was pleasant being able to drink deep – not like in the high alps where water is so scarce. I mixed up a litre bottle with Raro lemon crystals and drank it all down. At 5.30 I started getting the evening meal started: put the pasta in the pan to soak, added coriander and chives; chopped up the half onion the possum left (pity about the hot chilli), added the flavour sachet and finally chopped up the pepperoni sausage. By 6.00 pm, the stove was purring as my alfresco kitchen took shape by the large 'cooking rock'. The meat and pasta went down very well with an English muffin – which I had found to be too dry for breakfast (without margarine or butter). While there was hot water on the stove, I finished off by washing the pan and making coffee.

By this time the sun was low over the West Wall. I cleared the site of every piece of kit, making sure all was safely in the tent. Then I headed down to the lower pool for a last wash and change of underwear for tomorrow's walk out. The shadows lengthened and some photos around dusk had beautiful texture of shadow and light.

By 7.15 I was back on the 'writing rock' completing these notes. In retrospect today was perfect. Probably one of only twenty or so every year for this location so I counted my blessings – particularly when you consider the last trip in here, when I also had some fine clear days. Even the evening has been perfect – no mozzies – only a few blowflies, but nothing that bites.

Mozzie net tonight as a precaution (fitted with zippers to the front and rear tent entries). Also needed to bag up the food and sleep on it to discourage a return visit from Mrs P.

All peaceful around the pool as I write, reading glasses pushed over my sunglasses doggy style. The native fly life sparkles in the dwindling sunlight, the currawongs have gone to roost and the wallabies are grazing down by the pool. The dead pines cut a stark relief against the skyline, etched by a golden sun and clouds of flies. Crickets are creaking. Grasshoppers leap on to my boots, moving on to my felt hat. Cobwebs in the bushes shimmer in the breeze. Low light made the grass stems shine like dew.

Fed and washed. Time for some music. Strolled down below the camp, along the boards towards Damascus Gate. In the twilight there were at least thirty Bennett's wallabies grazing lazily, some even lying down. It was possible to pass within a few metres of them. Back at camp the flies had gone and it was wonderfully still. Crosby and Nash were singing *Requiem to the Whales* which seemed appropriate as the last rays of the sun left the tops behind me and even my Walkman batteries ran flat.

For the first time since I awoke that morning, it began to feel cold. One last check of the site and then into the tent I crawled, leaving the fly door open at the front I zipped up the mozzie screens and lay on my Thermarest looking for any in insect life.

The gear was all sorted and laid out: torch, candles, music, balaclava, fingerless gloves, clean socks, cigarette lighter, glasses, pen, notebook, map, water bottle et cetera. Then feet were checked and taped up for tomorrow — a walkout with full pack will impact toes descending from Trappers' Hut. Sorted film into exposed cans and fresh ones for tomorrow. Toilet paper for my shorts pocket. Lip seal. Swiss army knife. Camelback suspended from tent roof, boots oiled up. Food stowed. Okay, all set. Relax.

 Fairport Convention
  Si tu doit partir?
 Joni Mitchell
  Both Sides Now

Bob Dylan
> Pat Garrett and Billy the Kid

Crosby, Stills and Nash
> Wasted on the Way
> Southern Cross

Creedence
> My Back Door

Bob Dylan
> Mr Tambourine Man
> Gates of Eden

Cat Stevens
> Miles from Nowhere

Paul Kelly
> Bradman
> Special Treatment

Emmylou Harris
> Ponco and Lefty
> Spanish Johnny

Bette Midler
> Wind Beneath My Wings
> From a Distance

Mary Chapin Carpenter
> The Hard Way

A peaceful night. Got off to sleep about ten and woke about 12.30 to check for possums and went outside to 'check the weather'. Fine and clear. Quite warm. Slept in only a singlet and got through about a litre of cold drink from the Camelbak hanging from the roof. The sun crested the Temple in the east and played on the tent fly about 7.15, warming it and causing me to stir. Opening my eyes, the first thought that came to me was 'where am I?'. Straightaway I knew. Miles from nowhere.

Miles from nowhere guess I'll take my time, oh yeah to reach there.
Look up at the mountain I have to climb, oh yeah to reach there.
Lord my body, it's been a good friend, but I won't need it when I reach the end.
Miles from nowhere not a soul in sight, oh yeah but it's all right.
I have my own freedom, I can make my own rules, yeah the ones that I choose.
Lord my body etc
Miles from nowhere, guess I'll take my time, oh yeah to reach there
Miles from Nowhere, words and music by Cat Stevens

DAY 4: TUESDAY 16 DECEMBER 2003

I crawled out of the Fairydown Sting mountain tent, scratched my head and took a look about. Nobody in sight, it was as if the park was empty and I had it all to myself. Miles from nowhere.

After emptying out all the kit and throwing the sleeping bag over the tent fly to air out, I soon had the stove roaring. The last of my food was a cooked breakfast which, according to the label, consisted of 'eggs, bacon and beans'. In went the hot water. Not too bad. Followed this with 'lemon and honey hot drink' left over from my Everest trip. Also quite good. That completed the formalities of breakfast, something more than the 'stockman's breakfast[134]' admittedly but still put together with a minimum of fuss in about five minutes.

I turned off the stove, let it cool, then drained the fuel into the Sigg[135] bottle and dismantled it and stowed it in its bag. It was time to strike the tent. There was a small tear in the fly by the door – and I made a mental note to get it sewn up. I laid out the tent – packed the fly on top and stowed it along with the pegs and aluminium shock tubes. With not much else to pack, I was on the way by about 8.45.

Jackson Browne was on as I listened to 'running on empty' and skipped along, my feet warming up, boots reverberating as they hit the boards. I was

---

134 Aussie slang for a piss and a look about.
135 Bombproof aluminium bottles in 1.0 and 2.0 litre capacity.

at Herod's Gate in about twenty minutes, saying goodbye for another year to the Walls of Jerusalem.

Epilogue

The notes stopped rather abruptly at Herod's Gate, didn't they? The truth is, from there back to the car park it's just a two and a half hour downhill run back to the car park and the madness of civilisation. With each step of my sore feet, I was sad to be heading down. It had been a great trip.

There was the walk in, in wind and rain on the Saturday, a cold arrival and evening meal in the tent, with feet in the bag for warmth. Then the joy of the clearing weather on the Sunday. Misty at first with showers till mid-morning, then a clear afternoon that allowed me to climb Jerusalem and complete the Temple Circuit.

On the Monday, following the circuit the previous day, I was gifted with perfect weather and ascents of the Temple and Solomon's Throne, plus the delightful visits to Damascus Vale and the pool of Siloam and the Gate of Ephraim. Hard to top that, which accounts for the down beat tone of the last day, Tuesday, the walk out.

People-wise, the park was fairly quiet. On the walk in there were six cars at the car park and eight to ten parties in the intentions book near the start of the walk. On the way out, the situation was similar. In the Walls proper, I met about six of these parties. One went on through to Cradle Mountain, meeting the main trail down near Narcissus Hut on Lake St Clair. There was plenty of clean water and certainly no need to carry any, though I opted for the one litre Camelback as a personal preference as one can drink on the move. I have again included a food list. The equipment list was similar to that in my last account, apart from the larger Gregory 80 lite rucksack.

This was my third trip into the Walls. My last visit was some eight years ago and there were signs of improvement to the tracks since then, with duckboards in the boggy areas much appreciated and stepping stones in many other areas. This has saved the track from degradation remarkably well.

There is scope for additional trails to be put in – the Temple Circuit and also a route out to the Wailing Wall, returning via Damascus Vale. Later still, a route out to Lake Thor and Lake Sidon, returning via the gate of Ephraim would be a worthwhile addition.

Without these additions it is still a grand walking area —one of the best anywhere. Not too strenuous, yet challenging. Not too remote, yet not overcrowded. Not too 'improved', yet having good tracks to walk on. Also offering country open enough to allow reasonably safe navigation.

Later still...

It's new year now as I write my last reflections – which often is the case after I have stuck in the photos in my diary and captioned them following sorting and rearrangement.

I am en route to Toulouse via Paris, following another trip to the Sahara hot on the heels of the Walls of Jerusalem trip. The solitude and peace of the place made a marked contrast to the busy pace of large French cities and already I feel, in myself, a yearning to return before too long[136]. My feet are almost fully mended after receiving some treatment from the old Raichle walking boots which will now be retired. Now I have only two black toenails as a reminder of my third trip into the Walls.

This year, 2004, promises to be a busy one with quite a few business trips (Algeria, Egypt, New Zealand at a minimum) already in the frame, plus the big expedition to Broad Peak[137] in June and July.

All going to plan I will be back unscathed from my fourth Himalayan trip by August and might be able to see Chantal and Isabelle for the last of their northern summer holidays.

That will leave Christmas 2005 for a planned Christmas dinner at the Walls once again. Isabelle has yet to choose which of the three camp sites she'd like. She has until year's end to decide.

---

136 To feed the rat?
137 8000m in altitude in Pakistan, adjacent to the notorious K2.

Food List

Mornings
- Breakfast cereal or muesli, milk, coffee, powdered egg, dried meat.

Midday
- Fresh fruit, SAO biscuits, smoked cheese, pate with peppercorns, tinned tuna, salami, dates, salted peanuts.

Evenings
- Dehydrated meals: lamb, beef, macaroni,
- instant soup: chicken and corn, curry laksa, tom yum, bread, English muffins, coffee, chocolate.

Drinks
- Coffee and tea bags, lemon and barley hot drink, RARO drink crystals: orange and lemon.

Later Tasmanian Walks, 9

The Walls of Jerusalem with Chantal and Isabelle, December 2004

Introduction

This was a summer holiday trip for my wife Chantal and daughter Isabelle, which was agreed following my previous trip to the Walls of Jerusalem in December 2003. Chantal and Isabelle were briefly back from France from December 13 2003 to January 8 2004, allowing time for me to show them the best features of this Tasmanian National Park.

The girls arrived in Melbourne from Hong Kong early on Monday 13 December and recovered for the rest of the day at my son John's home in Northcote. We ventured out briefly to get some outdoor clothing and food supplies for the trip. Isabelle had bought a video camera in Hong Kong with the intention of making a video of the trip. By the time they had arrived in Melbourne, she had mastered the technicalities and was busy filming everything. Consequently, we decided that this written account should take the form of 'notes to be read in conjunction with the official video'. The video[138] includes footage shot at John's home, our visit to my uncle Jamie in Torquay plus John's holiday home in Anglesea, where we packed up for the trip and fed the birds on John's veranda while enjoying a sumptuous meal of meats and wines.

---

138 The video went back to France with Isabelle and I never actually saw the final version.

On Wednesday 15 December we drove from Anglesea to Melbourne airport and flew to Devonport, arriving about 2 pm. By the time we'd picked up the hire car and bought the last of our food and driven to the Walls of Jerusalem car park, it was sometime between 4 and 5 pm. There was daylight until after 8 pm so we kitted up (having previously stopped to change into our walking clothes at O'Neill's Creek picnic site at Gowrie Park) and set off up the track. The plan was to camp for our first night up on the Tiers somewhere past Trappers' Hut at Solomon's Jewels.

This plan allowed for two full days (Friday and Saturday) in the Walls of Jerusalem with Sunday for the walk out and the flight to Melbourne and Perth. Weatherwise this was sensible as there was a strong chance that we might lose one day to poor weather. But as it turned out both days were fine, despite it raining on all three nights we were 'under canvas'.

On the Sunday morning, we struck camp with heavy rain easing and walked most of the way back to Trappers' Hut in mist and showers. Herod's Gate was blowy and cold, swathed in mist and chilling rain. By Solomon's Jewels, it was clearing, showing patches of blue sky. After a cup of tea at Trappers' Hut, we could repack the parkas for the run downhill to the car park, arriving at 10.15 after starting at 7.45. Actual walking time was about two hours.

We quickly drove back to Gowrie Park, changed our clothes, dropped off the rubbish in Sheffield, where we stopped at the Highlander tearooms for tea and sandwiches (Chantal and I) and a pie[139] (Isabelle). We fuelled the hire car in Devonport and checked in at the airport just before 3 pm. The flight to connected in Melbourne with the flight to Perth, so we planned to meet my son John in Melbourne and collect the extra luggage and Isabelle's violin. I called John from Devonport airport and arranged to meet him at arrivals in Melbourne with the gear. He was just finishing work (with Customs and Immigration at Melbourne airport) and would have all in readiness.

All went well. We checked three more bags and headed for the Qantas lounge showers, lugging two more handbags plus the precious boxed

---

[139] A homecoming Aussie experience for Isabelle, no doubt.

Panting[140] violin. After a short wait we were off to Perth on the final leg home. We settled in, wound back our watches three hours, pulled the peanuts out of the 'mini chuck wagon' and ordered a beer. We had earned it.

A rough summary of the trip is:

Day 1:   Getting there
Day 2:   Into the Walls: Solomon's Jewels, Herod's Gate, Lake Salome
Day 3:   Roaming inside the Walls: Damascus Gate, Jaffa Vale, Dixon's Kingdom
Day 4:   Visiting the pools: Bethesda, Siloam
Day 5:   Walking out

With Isabelle on the video camera throughout, I elected not to keep a written trip diary as I was guiding the other two and needed to give them my full attention. In addition, a detailed description of the various appears in the notes associated with the trip the year before.

As we were a walking party of three, the lists for equipment, food and first aid from the previous trip descriptions can be used as a guide.

---

140   A violin by the maker of the same name in Perth. Now quite valuable to collectors.

Recent Tasmanian Walks, 10

A short fishing trip to the Walls of Jerusalem National Park, January 2016

Note the different access to Dixon's Kingdom and Jaffa Vale via Lake Loane, then Lake Ball, from the south.

DAY 1: SATURDAY 9 JANUARY 2016

The Dash 8 touched down on the tarmac at Devonport and taxied to a halt about 2.45 on a warm afternoon. I was back in the Apple Isle. It seemed an age since I lived and worked here in the 1970s though, on the face of it, little had changed.

I collected a hire car and stopped in the IGA at Spreyton for some last minute supplies and was soon off again through Sheffield, under the lee of Mount Roland, and on through Gowrie Park to the start of the walking track towards the end of the Mersey Forrest road. The road was pretty rough towards the end and I reached the car park about 5pm, with plenty of daylight to spare.

By about 5.30 I had togged up with gaiters and boots, loaded up the pack with food and fishing gear, and was ready to set off with a prodigious load. Up the track to the Trappers' Hut I laboured, surprised to find that I could still manage the ascent to the Western Tiers in an hour, despite the load and the warm afternoon sun. Breaking out of the denser eucalypt, I didn't stop as I was keen to press on to a better campsite at Lake Adelaide.

The track continued to ascend for another hundred metres or so before the fork was reached and I set off south for Lake Loane, across mixed heath, richea and cushion moss, snaking through stony patches and dry bogs before circling the western side of the small lake at 7.00 pm.

Hoping to reach Lake Adelaide before stopping, I pressed on with Hardy fly rod[141] in hand and my load starting to make its presence felt. The sun was quite low in the west now and I needed my hat to shade my eyes as I wearily crossed an open button grass plain studded with the odd dolerite boulder, then up over a gentle rise, down the other side until the pencil pine grove at the north end of the lake at last came into view. I hauled in at 7.45 as dusk approached.

The camp site, sited on mossy ground among the pines, is a short walk from the water's edge and is idyllic and solitary. I was alone under the open sky as I set up my tent and set up a nice fire[142]. Sitting on a log, I enjoyed fried bacon with onions and some spicy soup and coffee. That night, even though the wind was up a bit from the south, I left the fly off and so could see the stars through the flimsy tent fabric. I dragged all my gear inside as a precaution against pilfering by the prevalent native cats, possums and wombats. Comfy on my Thermarest[143], I eventually drifted off to sleep after much rehydration with Gatorade. It had been a long afternoon.

DAY 2: SUNDAY 10 JANUARY 2016

The day dawned fine, though a low mist over the water drifted among the eucalypts on the western edge of the lake. I was up at 6.30 but packed up in a leisurely manner and left at 8.30 after a cup of tea and not much else. Shouldering the pack, I was reminded that it was not much lighter than yesterday.

The unmarked fork led uphill from the lakeside track, more or less in line with the northernmost point of the lake. I could easily have missed it had I not been looking for it in just about the right spot. It climbed steeply

---

141 A Hardy No. 6 bought for me by my mother in Scotland in the 1970s.

142 Fires are not permitted in the park, but a safe fireplace was available, the area around it was clear and there was abundant firewood.

143 Inflatable sleeping mat.

before easing off on a higher plateau where Lake Ball nestles at the foot of the Temple and Jaffa Vale. As the track eventually neared the lake, it skirted the northern edge in rough tea tree country with boulders and tree roots that made for slow progress. About half way along the lake was the Lake Ball Hut – a pencil pine slab and shingle structure with a sleeping bench and a fireplace that nestled in a thick grove of twisted, ageing pines. It was 9.30. I stopped for a drink and took photos of the historic hut before moving on with slightly better going as the lake shore opened out at the base of Jaffa Vale.

It started to get quite warm. The sky was clear and the heat was amplified by being radiated back off the open button grass plain near the lake. The track gradually climbed upwards. In the distance, the upper reaches of Jaffa Vale revealed Jaffa Gate, the saddle at the top of the valley, under wispy, high cloud. Towards the top, the valley opened out into a meadow of cushion moss and pineapple grass, with myriad streams gurgling under foot. The ground was spongy to walk on as I hopped across the many mossy, underground stream courses. Dixon's Kingdom Hut drew closer and I eventually dropped my pack outside the door at 11.30, glad to finally be back there again.

After the three-hour pull up from Lake Adelaide, I was feeling the strain of the morning march. I stood up, stiff as a board, and staggered about for a while until I gradually came good. It was a wonderful, warm day with quite a few walking groups lunching around the grassy surrounds of the hut. I had decided to pitch my camp here and do a recce in the afternoon of the lake country to the east of Mount Jerusalem. After a chat I moved away from the hut area and set up camp in the pines further up the hill. It was a lovely, inviting spot: soft, mossy grass, plenty of shade and protection from the weather and a superb setting. I sat on an old pencil pine log and enjoyed a long lunch before setting off on the recce.

I felt free in sandals and an open shirt, racing up the track to Mount Jerusalem, first along the sun bleached duckboards, through the scoparia[144] around the Jaffa Gate, then up the stony way to the upper reaches of the mountain approaches where low heath bent against the stiff wind. Peering down the eastern flanks, I saw a route down to the lakes, though it would

---

144 The kerosene bush – a great firelighter...

be a bit of a bush bash at the bottom. Buoyed by the fact that the way was open for tomorrow, I turned on the music and reversed the route, stopping at a tarn for a swim out to a smooth 'sitting rock', out of the wind. Dried off and dressed, I was back at the camp in a matter of minutes. It was 3.00 pm.

Afternoon tea consisted of SAO biscuits with cheese, fruit, salted peanuts and a couple of chocolate biscuits with plenty of Gatorade. By 4.30, the flies were bad so I climbed into the tent, zipped up the nets and snoozed until 5.30 with the breeze blowing in one end and out the other. Once the plague had subsided, I was back out on the log, getting the fishing gear together and a light pack ready for the following day.

After a spicy 'freeze dry' for dinner, I was tucked in by about 8.00 pm.

DAY 3: MONDAY 11 JANUARY 2016

I was awake by 6.15. It was another fine day in the making, this time with no morning mist up this high. I wasn't particularly hungry — I guess a bit excited to get off to the lakes — so after not much to eat at all I was away in earnest[145] a little after 8.30.

By 9 am I was back at yesterday's high point where I left the marked trail to the summit and sidled off to the west, gradually angling towards the lakes far below. At first the going was easy, across open heath. Lower down it became more rocky, before hitting the eucalypt and tea tree and descending into nasty thick scrub. Near the lake shore there was a grove of pencil pine and very thick sphagnum moss, before I broke free and found myself on the cushion moss surrounding an unnamed tarn. I circled around the shore and crossed over to a larger lake which looked promising, but a bit wind exposed. The northern shore appeared to offer the most shelter so I worked my round to it, through tenacious, low scoparia bush.

I finally arrived at a mossy shore about 9.45, though the wind was still blowing across the water and the conditions not settled for fly fishing. Nonetheless, I was here and it was not going to get any better. So, with mixed anticipation, I pulled out my reel and fly box from the pack and opened the

---

145 The camp site has ample fresh water and a new addition since my last visit — toilets, complete with advice not to put used toilet paper down the hole (?)

cloth end of the two piece fly rod cover. I drew out the two delicate pieces and went to join them at the ferrule located at each end…only to realise that one end had broken off! When? Where? Here I was, after three days on the track, arriving at the lake with a broken rod which looked pretty much unfixable.

I tried fashioning a dummy ferrule by whittling some pencil pine with my Swiss army knife. It came away and broke immediately. In some ways, it was more of a joke than a disaster as I had an idea there were no fish about anyway. so I took off my Keen[146] sandals and replaced them with walking boots and gaiters and simply packed up for the return journey.

It was 10.45 as I set off, confident I could reverse the route easily. I got through the worst of the bush-bashing through the scrubby lower reaches quicker than I expected and was soon bounding up over the rocks with the summit in clear view above me, having identified a few rock cairns I had left when marking the descent route earlier that morning. I saw bushwalker people assembled on the summit and joined them about 11.45 am. They were a happy, older group, and were pleased to see me again after we had chatted the previous evening back at the Dixon's Kingdom campsite. I took some photos for them before heading back down ahead of them. I reached my camp at 12.45 and had a simple lunch of biscuits, cheese, nuts and fruit, ahead of breaking camp and heading off.

The idea was, that in the event that fishing was off, I might as well fly home a day earlier. To do that, I needed to camp a little further along the return route to allow me to reach the park exit by mid-morning the following day. This plan suggested that I camp near the Pool of Bethesda (an old favourite of mine) or a little further along the track, where there are pencil pines at the foot of the Wall adjacent to Lake Salome.

I laboured once again with the heavy pack and climbed gradually through the pencil pines, reaching the wonderful open meadows of Damascus Vale about 2.30. I paused to photograph Hall's Buttress[147], picture perfect across the Vale, with a small clump of pines in the middle ground. Took a 'selfie'

---

146 Keen 'canyon walkers' come highly recommended for general camp use or rocky river crossings.

147 Now called King Solomon's Throne.

too, having worked out how to operate the self-timer on the Nikon. Passing over Damascus Gate, I descended the 'boards' on the other side and was soon at the side path to the pool by about 3.00.

I left my pack at the junction and circled the Pool of Bethesda to reach a good picture vantage point on the far side. The sky was still blue, with wispy, wind driven clouds; the water on the pool surface was peaceful. The Buttress cast a reflection on the water, not perfect, but nice, never the less. I took a few shots, hoping some might turn out well[148,] though wary of the mid-afternoon light and high degree of contrast.

Back on the main track, I veered off at the pines and made camp close to the foot of the Wall about 4.00. It was a pleasant spot...a little windy, but sheltered, with water and heaps of pine firewood. I had a log to sit on while enjoying a hot meal and some coffee. While there, I bandaged some sore spots on my heels[149] and arranged all my kit for the evening. The tent was up and the weather was changing slowly. By 6.15 it began to spit as I turned in to read and listen to music. By 8.30 it had turned to persistent, heavy rain. I emerged, shivering a bit and threw the fly over the tent frame and secured it with stones. After a little adjustment[150], it was fine and I enjoyed a dry, comfy night.

DAY 4: TUESDAY 12 JANUARY 2016, OUT WITH A BROKEN FISHING ROD

The walk out from Lake Salome has been described in my earlier accounts so will not be repeated here. I took the broken 'two piecer' in to Compleat Angler in Melbourne, only to be told it was not repairable. So I guess this was fishing tip that never got started. You have to laugh. Next time, I will carry the rod in a PVC tube!

---

148 They were not too bad, though not among the best I have taken from this spot.
149 Elastoplast fabric patches are ideal for mild blisters.
150 It is vital to keep the fly off the tent fabric, hence the requirement to anchor the fly securely.

Recent Tasmanian Trips, 10a, Three Capes by Kayak, 2018

Kayaking trip to the Three Capes, Tasman Peninsula, 2018

Introduction

This was a commercially organised four-day sea kayaking trip to explore the rugged capes of the Tasman Peninsula. There were about ten in the group, two guides (one on shore and one paddling) and from memory we had three double kayaks and two singles. We all met in Hobart at the Old Woolstore Apartments at the start of day 1.

It was very special for me as I knew the capes were best viewed from the sea and as a bonus, my son John got time away from his Border Force customs work and was able to join the team. We paddled by day and came ashore each evening, staying at a well-appointed holiday rental called The Bolthole. The guides did the cooking there while we, mostly wrecked from the day's exertion, had hot showers and enjoyed pre dinner drinks (and after).

It was an arduous experience overall, made more awkward by some gastric problems I arrived with which troubled me a fair bit but not to the extent that it spoiled the trip. As a result, I did not keep a day to day diary of the trip, as it was quite short anyway.

The trip included some short shore based walks with visits to historic convict operated coal mines as well as land based views of some of the coastline we had previously traversed at sea.

The Tasman Peninsula is almost an island, being surrounded by the Tasman Sea to the south and east, Storm Bay to the west and to the north by Norfolk Bay but connected to the mainland by a narrow isthmus, the Eaglehawk Neck. The coastline, largely covered by national park, is made up of spectacular dolerite cliffs, beautiful sandy beaches and sheltered bays, making it an ideal paddling destination. We encountered an abundance of flora and fauna, both on the water and on short but spectacular hikes.

The kayaks were single and double sit-in expedition sea kayaks with rudder. These are stable, easy to paddle and control. They are very forgiving and are suited for everyone from beginners to experts. On day one we had a thorough briefing on all aspects of sea kayaking techniques with ample time to practice and familiarise ourselves with the kayaks. We used 220 cm Werner Skagits. All were split paddles for easy adjustment to suit one's style.

Other equipment supplied include a pfd (life jacket), one 20-litre dry bag, a set of pogies (paddling mittens), a splash skirt[151] and for those who needed it, a cagoule (an over-the-head style jacket that has seals on the waist, wrist and neck offering protection from wind and rain).

DAY 1: 14 JANUARY 2018

We start with a morning pick up (around 8am) from the Hobart hotel for the two-hour drive to Fortescue Bay, in the heart of the Tasman National Park. This morning's paddle was towards Cape Huoy, one of the highlights of the Three Capes Track.

The weather was calm and allowed us to make our way to the base of the Candle Stick, a mecca for rock climbers from around the world and conveniently located beside a seal haul-out. We paused here while Australian fur seals played in the water around us. We then paddled underneath the candlestick to the open sea beyond.

Returning to the shelter of the bay we explored hidden coves and enjoyed a picnic lunch before heading back to our accommodation, not pausing for a quick swim on the way. Paddling distance approximately about fifteen kilometres.

---

[151] This attaches to the kayak, effectively being a barrier to water entering the boat.

DAY 2: 15 JANUARY 2018

we launched the kayaks from the shelter of Pirates Bay and experienced true ocean paddling as we paddled south past the Tasman Arch (pausing directly underneath the arch itself) and passed the Blowhole. Towering sea cliffs, deep sea caves and abundant marine life were highlights of the day's paddle.

Lunch was enjoyed at Bivouac Bay where we stretched our legs on a hike with great views over the sea cliffs. We then transferred back to the Bolthole.

Paddling distance was again around fifteen kilometres.

DAY 3: 16 JANUARY 2018

A more gentle day after a rather torrid second day. We drove across to the Lime Bay area, for a short paddle to the infamous convict coal mines historic site. After a picnic lunch, we again stretched our legs and explored the area, seeing the remains of the convict cells that made up the coal mining penal settlement.

We continued our paddle north, past delicate sandstone cliffs and sandy beaches to finish at Lime Bay. On the back to the Bolthole, we did a cliff walk along the coast so as to see the Tasman Arch and the Blowhole from above. At the Blowhole, there was an ice cream van! Paddling distance twelve kilometres.

DAY 4: 17 JANUARY 2018

In the morning, we visited the Remarkable Cave and followed that with a 2.5 km hike to the summit of Mount Brown, descending to the surf beach looking out to Cape Pillar in the east.

Then we returned to the water near Crescent Bay and paddled north to the Port Arthur convict settlement, then on further north past Garden Point, finishing up at the nearby boat ramp and celebrating with fresh oysters on the beach.

Verdict: somewhat strenuous paddling into the spray in bad weather and rough sea, but on the whole the weather was kind to us. Well worth the effort.

The journey begins at Fortescue Bay and leads to Cape Huoy

Cape Huoy featuring the Candlestick and the legendary Totem Pole

Paddled through the arch, then on to lunch amid the rounded stones, Cape Huoy behind

Setting off for Tasman Arch and Waterloo Bay

The Tasman Arch, seen from the cliff edge

Paddling Lime Bay, near the convict settlement

The penal coal mining settlement *Convict cells*

Calmer water once in the harbour

Journey's end with beer and fresh oysters

John and I in a tandem kayak

Later Tasmanian Trips, 11

Rafting down the Franklin River in southwest Tasmania in December 2022

Day 1: 2 December 2022

Left the surf cottage on the Great Ocean Road at Anglesea in Victoria after my last online meeting for 2022. Free at last! I passed through Torquay en route to the Geelong ferry terminal and arrived in good time for the evening sailing to Devonport. Got the car[152] loaded eventually on to deck 6 and found my recliner chair B17 on deck 8. The ferry was very well set up, though I did very little ship exploration. There was an excellent bar and hot food buffet, so I enjoyed a hot roast beef and vegetables with a sweet pavlova to finish. And, of course, I took the opportunity to reopen my account with Boag's true Tasmanian beer in the form of a cold pint.

We set sail just before 9.00 pm. The shore lights grew dimmer and more distant and the light faded as we left the blinking channel lights and headed into open sea. Cabin lights were dimmed and most of the 'recliners' were soon rugged up and dozing. The car decks were locked so there was no going below to get any extra clothes.

I plugged in the iPad and phone charger and soon dozed off. It was a bit uncomfortable — a bit like trying to sleep when flying economy class. We were awakened at 6.15 am and ordered to get ready to disembark at 7.00. It

---

152   An ageing Peugeot 206 with 150,000 km on the clock and the back seats removed to make way for all the camping gear.

was a relatively gentle crossing though I definitely felt the ship's movement when making my way to the toilet during the night.

DAY 2: 3 DECEMBER 2022

The Peugeot was released soon after docking and I made my way immediately out of Devonport, heading for Deloraine on the M1. The quiet, rural setting early that morning was reminiscent of my earlier time near[153] here and the many return visits since. It was a fine, sunny morning. I stopped for breakfast at a café in the main street of Deloraine and fuelled up the car for the longer run down to Derwent Bridge. After picking up supplies for the later Pine Valley[154] walk, I was off again by about 9.00 am.

From Deloraine, the sealed road leads south to a pass over Quamby Peak before dropping down to the Great Lake. After about an hour's driving along the shore and passing numerous fishing shacks, the tar seal ended at Miena. After that, it was rough gravel all the way to Bronte Park[155], where the road was again sealed for the short run on to Derwent Bridge. The gravel section across the Central Highlands was about sixty kilometres. Back on the sealed section I passed Little Pine Lagoon, where I fly fished in the 1970s with a diamond driller from the Rosebery lead and zinc mine[156] on the West Coast. I must have arrived at Derwent Bridge about midday and checked in to my accommodation to sort gear for the following day's link up with the rafting bus. After a light lunch, I drove the six kilometres to Cynthia Bay on Lake St Clair – National Park headquarters for the southern end of the ark.

I checked at the ranger desk on hut and track conditions for the later Pine Valley walk. Also confirmed my booking for the water taxi on 12 December for transfer up to the northern end of the lake. All good.

Despite the rather hot day of thirty-one degrees, there were still patches of snow on the higher slopes of Mount Olympus. Everyone was in shorts

---

153 My parents sent me here in school holidays to do farm work at nearby Hagley, from the age of about ten.
154 See the notes on the Pine Valley walk in the Cradle Mountain . Lake St Clair National Park, following the rafting trip
155 An old Hydro Electric Commission construction camp.
156 My first full time job as a graduate mining engineer.

and singlets, many tourists and a huge number of motor cycle groups. On returning to the hotel, I washed all the road dust off the car and was myself washed up in time for a drink at the bar at 5.30 pm. Mercury draft cider with ice went down well. It was an old style country pub with timber beams and a huge open fireplace for the winter cold. The typical pub menu's offerings included 'parmi', pie 'n peas with a gravy 'floater' or, for something different, a Sri Lankan curry complete with roti bread, courtesy of the all Sri Lankan staff. Piano music tinkled away in the background and I even recognised the *Ashokan Farewell*, which my daughter Isabelle played on her violin at her mother Heather's funeral.

DAY 3: SUNDAY 4 DECEMBER 2022, RAFTING DAY 1

I awoke to a more cloudy morning and was collected by the rafter's bus about 10.15 am. Kit-wise, I was handed a large dry bag, a lilo and a wetsuit and climbed abord the full coaster sized mini bus. It took about forty-five minutes to reach the Collingwood River bridge from the hotel. This was the start of the rafting trip proper[157]. I donned my wetsuit and reef walking shoes and we were soon under way – three rubber zodiacs and two inflatable singles[158].

The water was quite docile and led to the Junction[159], where the Collingwood flows into the Franklin. We pulled in there on the stony bank for a doughnut and dried fruit. I noted a sheltered campsite above the stony beach. Now on the Franklin proper, the next section led us through the Angel Rain ravine and beyond there to the Log Jam where the boats had to be manhandled over a huge log. The next stretch was gentle and quiet with towering banks on either side of us. Dark swirls and eddies occasionally gave a glimpse of smooth dolerite rocks below the surface. We made a fly camp about an hour's paddle further down river at what is called Wizard's Rest. Brett cooked prawns and beef on the gas stove while we paddlers feasted on

---

[157] The trip begins on the Collingwood river, which joins the Franklin a short distance downstream.

[158] The larger zodiacs took four paddlers and a sweep, with waterproofed gear lashed to a carrying frame

[159] Junction Camp -I sampled a smooth river stone or two and later brought them all the way home.

savouries and a can of beer. Light rain started to fall just as our flys were up. Then we settled down for a few more Boags.

I slept fitfully that night, no doubt due in part to the sloping ground and a dry thirst[160], but eventually all was well but a little cold in the early morning.

DAY 4: MONDAY 5 DECEMBER, RAFTING DAY 2

We were woken at 6.30 am with hot coffee and warm bread topped with egg and bacon. It was a nice way to start the day, even though the river clothing was still wet from the day before[161]. More breakfast followed after we were all up and gathered around the kitchen fly.

Camp was then struck and we helped to load the rafts, lashing down the dry bags and food barrels. Off down river again at 8.30 am. Toilet protocols all adhered to[162]. The path down river was placid and benign, until we reached the Nasty Notch and had to unload the rafts and haul them past the danger. The rocks were slippery and approach shoes would have been a better choice. Onward until we arrived at the famous Irenabyss at 10.30 for a rest. Brett got out cake, fruit and chocolate, overlooking the great, brooding ravine. The Frenchman's Cap track started from a little tributary creek and rose steeply through a break in the ravine. No limb of The Cap was scheduled for this trip, which may have been just as well as rain was imminent and visibility up higher would have been poor.

Continuing down the river, most of the rapids were okay. We only lost a paddler overboard once! We stopped for a break at 1.15 and enjoyed a lunch of bread rolls with salad. As we pressed on south, the wind and rain blew right into our faces and I started to shiver with the cold. The wetsuit was not enough and my feet were cold.

A halt was called at Rafter's Rest about 4.00 pm. This was a better camp and beach, with room to erect the kitchen fly, two tents and three sleeping

---

160 I had not thought I needed a water bottle on a river trip! So I filled up two empty beer cans with water each night after that.

161 Dripping wet shorts under a wet sandy wetsuit.

162 Human waste was collected and bagged. The shit bag followed with us all the way, getting heavier each day.

flys. With the camp now set up, dry clothes were a luxury. By 5.30, Brett was serving chicken pieces on wooden skewers, with crackers, cheese and dips[163]. Another can of Boag's was followed by crumbed calamari, hot off the gas stove. The enigmatic cook reached for another 4X as he hunched over the stove, seated on a blue esky. By 6.00pm the sky had cleared, at least partially. It suggested a fine day tomorrow, reckoned to be long and hard.

DAY 5: TUESDAY 6 DECEMBER 2022 RAFTING DAY 3

Everyone woke early. It had cleared in the evening, allowing us to sleep without rain blowing in under the fly. A long day was ahead of us as we set off at 8.30. The main highlights of the day were:
- The Great Ravine;
- The Side Slip Rapid;
- The Churn – a major portage;
- Corkscrew Rapid; Corruscade rapids – another portage; and
- Thunderush – a major obstacle.

What a day! We arrived at Rafter's Basin about 4.30. The quiet reaches displayed some memorable waterfalls, some great cascades (like the Pink Blush) with others mere elfin rivulets spilling over the mossy dolerite and lower down into the mighty Franklin. I jotted down my thoughts as light fades:
- The major portages were very awkward, challenging and quite dangerous;
- Some of the rapids were grade 4;
- Solid footwear needed for any activity out of the rafts;
- A smaller, portable dry bag would have been useful just for the camera and sun glasses.

The Rafter's Basin campsite was very spacious, which was just as well as there were three other rafting parties in residence. I found a nice spot to sleep under the stars, further back from the river and up a scraggy tea tree slope. We were all pretty tired on arrival and after unloading the three rafts.

Once stripped of wet gear it was relaxing to sit in the warm late afternoon

---

163 With cauliflower, corn on the cob, fruit salad and ice cream.

sun. Brett laid out bread rolls, salad and other snacks. I found a nice spot by the river – two large flat stones – and wrote these notes while enjoying a cold Boag's draught. You could literally feel the tranquility. A marvellously tranquil setting.

Shortly before sunset, Brett produced a delightful vegan stew, followed by apple pie. After that it got noticeably cold and we all were soon clad in duvet jackets before slinking off to bed down. I laid back and looked up at the clear, night sky with stars twinkling...and drifted off to sleep.

DAY 6: WEDNESDAY 7 DECEMBER, RAFTING DAY 4

There was no rain overnight. I slept well and only had to get up once. One of the young river guides woke us up at 6.00 am with warm brioche. I stowed my gear and headed down to the river where breakfast was on: cereal, egg and bacon muffins and coffee. To save time, the toilet queue was doubled and a chain was formed to transfer all the gear down to the rafts. After a short portal in the shallows, we were off at 7.45 am

The first half hour or so was tranquil, with quiet waterfalls tumbling down from both sides of Propsting Gorge. After portage around Three Tiers rapid, we ran the Thundering Trojan without mishap. But at the next obstacle, a nasty protruding log, we ran sideways along it and stopped. Without warning, the power of the current lifted the two-tonne loaded raft and flipped it upside down over the log and tossed five of us down the river. We were thrown about in the fast current – all the time hanging on to the upturned raft for dear life.

Memories of a similar capsize in Thailand on the Me Tang River in Chiang Mai came flooding back as I was thrown about in the bubbly maelstrom and thrust against submerged rocks before finally reaching some flat water where I was able to tread water, still gripping my paddle. Clarissa and Dom righted the raft after a few tries and pulled me abord. Next, I pulled in Mat who looked for all the world like a beached whale. Somewhat recovered, but with a very sore lower left side back, we pressed on to the notorious Pig Trough, which had to be 'lined' by the guides while the rest of us took another slippery and precarious by-pass track, eventually meeting up with the rafts as the track led us back down to the water. Just below the Pig Trough, we arrived as the famous Rock Island Bend which, to my great pride and relief, I was able to photograph[164] and capture on video.

Just down from Rock Island Bend were the rocky overhangs called Newland's Cave, which offered shelter from the rain. An early stop was called for lunch and the afternoon off river. Everyone chose a nook to sleep in among the many rocky shelves. I was grateful for an electric (USB charged) lilo pump after the laborious agony of having to use the hand version. Lunch was served about 1 pm – bread rolls and salad and a strange mix of fried peas with some chilli. By about 1.30 several other groups had arrived, turning the camp into a mini village. Rocks were festooned with wetsuits and assorted wet clothing. Still no rain. My back was still sore[165]. Clarissa gave me some of her Deep Heat and I started taking the Ibuprofen with codeine, feeling grateful I had brought some with me. I was so sore I was forced to move about like a geriatric. After an hour's rest I felt a slightly better.

The afternoon was very lazy, setting up camp among the ledges of Newland's Cave. Light, intermittent rain gave way to sunny periods. Down clothing was needed. I found a cozy spot under an overhanging rock ledge and set up a sleeping area after clearing away quite a few stones and laying out my lilo, and down bag inside my Gore-Tex bivvy bag.

In the evening, Brett cooked a chicken laksa followed by a cheese and tomato pizza – this guy is a master bush chef, without question. No wonder they call him the wizard – but not to his face. He looks just like the wizard in the Harry Potter movies, but is much more grumpy and very economical with words. We turned in when darkness fell about 9 pm. I went to sleep, cozy and warm – but very sore. Dozed off listening to the river running and gazing up at the cloudy sky. I pulled the hood over my head and slept until 8.30 the following morning.

---

164 I had a small dry bag clipped to my life jacket with a small carabiner.
165 It was early in the New Year before it settled down, but the after effects plagued me for all of the following year.

DAY 7: THURSDAY 8 DECEMBER, RAFTING DAY FIVE

Today dawned mild and overcast with patches of blue sky. It was a planned rest day as yesterday's challenges were known to arouse a demand for rest. It was always tough and we had been warned it would be. A lazy breakfast followed as we crawled out of our bags one by one and stretched. The Wizard was making a special effort and produced cereals, freshly cut oranges, pancakes (served endlessly until refused) with maple syrup, jam and cream, toasted muffins fried eggs, coffee and tea.

During the morning, some of the group lay about reading 'talking books' on their tablets, while the guides (who all knew each other well) lolled about in the rafts[166], no doubt swapping versions of the previous day's calamities. They looked perfectly contented, packed in like sardines and rugged up in down and fibre pile. I sat on a flat rock and studied the river route maps, making the notes you are reading here. Feeling exceedingly stiff, sore and immobile. Another reason they always plan a rest day here – but there is another reason.

After another fine lunch or 'wraps' with the lot, it was suggested that those so inclined take the half hour rock hop up the right bank of the river (above the cave) to the base of the climb on Rock Island Bend. After a false start through thick forest, the track stopped so I turned back. That's when the riverside rock route was pointed out so, after a short rest, I set off once again. Glad I did. This time I made it, climbed to the top overlooking the dark, swirling eddies. I marvelled at being alone in this vast, remote and yet historic place – Rock Island Bend, the image[167] that saved the Franklin.

You had to admire the raging river below this lofty perch ringed with the crimson of flowering Christmas Bells[168]. It was still in my mind when I got back to camp at 5.00 pm and put on some dry, warm clothing.

For dinner the Wizard prepared a huge pot of curry and rice with music ringing out from a speaker blue toothed to his mobile phone. I played along

---

166 Hauled up and dry they made excellent padded arm chairs. I was still very sore.
167 Originally captured by Peter Dombrovskis whose Tassie wilderness calendars were very popular. He died on High Moor at the foot of Federation Peak. I knew his wife briefly.
168 One can be seen in the relevant image.

here and there on harmonica if the melody was in the key of C major[169]. Into bed at 9.30 – still sore and finding it difficult to turn over. More codeine pills to ease the pain and allow sleep.

DAY 8: FRIDAY 9 DECEMBER, RAFTING DAY SIX

The morning broke quite mild, with overcast sky despite clear breaks during the night, usually when I reached for a drink. I was very stiff getting up at 7.30 am but once upright, movement was a little less painful. Breakfast[170] was enjoyed by all, though I was happy with Nutri Grain and a little toast, with coffee from the percolating, bubbling pot. I thought it wise to get packed while most of the group was sitting around the kitchen rockery.

Today we were to shoot the Newlands rapids, the last of the serious rapids before the more docile and forgiving lower reaches of the Franklin, as it nears the confluence with the Gordon River. My phone was now recharged to 100 per cent courtesy my charging 'brick'. The phone had got down to fifty per cent and I needed it as a back-up camera. The plan was to be on the water at 11 am.

The points of interest included:
- Newland's Cascades (run to the right, 11.30);
- Eleanor's Ferry (John Franklin's wife);
- The Royal Box (a lookout perched up on the wall);
- Little Fall;
- Diana's Basin;
- The Jane River (confluence);
- Flat Island (cableway across the river, 1.30);
- Blackman's Bend;
- Limestone caves (Penghana, 4.00)
- Double Fall;
- Big Fall (portage);
- The Waves (camp).

---

169 I only had one harmonica – a large Hohner chromatic; the rest, in other keys, were back at home.

170 Cereal, toasted brioche, sausages and eggs.

I took over a single 'duck' at 12.30 and paddled solo for the rest of the day. I had one capsize (possibly at Little Fall) so arrived at the end of the day pretty sore, tired, cold and wet at the beautiful Wave camp. I set up a two-person tent, just for luxury, by the sandy beach and had all my dry clothes on and bedding laid out by dusk. There were no mosquitoes. Imagine the scene: still, placid dark water, brown as tea, flowing silently by. Overcast with intermittent drizzle but not too cold. Dinner was by headtorch and candlelight.

DAY 9: SATURDAY 10 DECEMBER, RAFTING DAY SEVEN

The day dawned clear, with mirrored reflections on a now tamed Franklin River. All were still asleep after a long Friday to reach the Veranda Cliffs where we stopped at the Wave Camp. Overnight, I was sore and took another codeine washed down with a little Cointreau I had in a metal hip flask. So, stiff as a board, I wriggled out of the tent and was immediately (after a pee) struck by the stunning silence and serenity all around me. Wave Camp takes its name no doubt from the prominent limestone[171] 'wave' across the river from the camp.

It was a late start for the group; still cooking sausages, bacon and eggs at 10 am. This was perfectly planned as the day's paddle down to the Gordon River and Sir John Falls was a shorter one. This final stage of the descent ran as follows:

- Veranda Cliffs; (by 12.30);
- Clinelarra and Pengana caves;
- Shingle Island;
- Omega Camp (confluence with the Gordon, 1.30);
- Franklin Rock;
- The Big Eddy;
- Butler Island;
- Sir John Falls (wharf and hut, 3 pm, 6 km down the Gordon).

For this last stage, wetsuits were not required as there was no more wild water. I donned wet shorts and a woollen singlet under my life jacket.

---

[171] From about Propsting Gorge, the dolerite cliffs give way to limestone, and hence caves.

The plan was to set off about midday and to stop at the junction (Omega Camp) for a rest or, if we felt okay, press on a further six kilometres to the jetty at Sir John Falls. In the end, we went all the way non-stop. At the Gordon River junction, two of the crew jumped overboard – an often repeated celebratory release! It was a way of marking the success of the harrowing descent. From there, though, it was a stiff paddle into the wind (and a possibly incoming tide as we approached Macquarie Harbour) where journey's end (at least for paddling) eventually appeared round the bend.

There was a recently restored hut not far from the falls, which were both historic and majestic. This was the place where the Franklin blockade took place. I strolled about taking it all in. Meanwhile, all the gear was stored on the jetty and the rafts deflated and rolled up into large bundles. This was in readiness for the fishing boat, arranged to pick us up at 5.30. While we waited, Brett made a late lunch, though two of the group slept, exhausted, in the two still inflated single 'duckies'.

The fishing boat *Good Intent* arrived at 5.40 pm and we were all loaded and away by 6.50. An hour after getting under way, we rendezvoused with an impressive two masted schooner called *Stormbreaker*[172] to collect wine and beer. By 8.30 pm we left the mouth of the Gordon, with Sarah Island in view. It was a long trip out to the mouth and then across Macquarie Harbour, past the historic convict settlement of Sarah Island and on to Strahan.

We arrived at 11.30 pm in darkness and tied up at the fishermen's wharf. Dog tired, we slept on the deck (cold), on the wharf itself (no better), or in the wheel house (more sensible). Still stiff, I slept on a bench seat in the galley and saw a full moon rise outside the starboard hatch.

DAY 10: SUNDAY 11 DECEMBER, RAFTING DAY EIGHT

I stirred at 7 am and walked down to Strahan for a cappuccino and toasted raisin bread. It seemed like the first decent coffee in ages. The mini bus was expected at nine o'clock. River bags were emptied and the bus left more or less on time. We made a short stop at Queenstown, where I picked up

---

[172] A tourist yacht skippered by our skipper's brother!

fresh supplies for the immediate trip following, and then at the historic Linda hamlet.

We even stopped at the Collingwood bridge where we had started our journey down river and watched another team about to set off. The water was higher for them. Their descent was going to be harder. The bus dropped me back at Derwent Bridge Hotel and I bid the crew adieu.

Stiff though I still was, back at Derwent Bridge, my walking gear was stashed in the Peugeot in readiness for the second stage of this Tassie odyssey: a walk back to Pine Valley...

Derwent Bridge hotel

Wizard's Rest camp, first night

Brett cooked and only drank Four X cans

Paddling the Irenabyss

Rafter's rest camp, second night

Rafter's Basin (third night)

Rafter's Basin camp

Heading for the Pig Trough

Rock Island Bend

Look up river from Rock Island Bend

All packed in like sardines

Wave camp

Big Fall portage

Sir John Falls

Two great rivers meet...

Liberation at the Sir John Falls landing

Mosses at Sir John Falls

Safe in the harbour....

Early breakfast in Strahan

Later Tasmanian Walks, 12

Back To Pine Valley, 2022

Notes on a short trip back to the southern end of the Cradle Mountain Lake St Clair National Park, immediately following the Franklin River descent. It was written en route and digitised in 2024. This trip was part of a trilogy, part one being the Franklin river descent, part two being Pine Valley revisited, and part three being the Three Cape walks. My partner, Susan Stevenson, joined me for the final stage, meeting me in Hobart following the Pine Valley return. I had gone ahead, taking my little Peugeot 206 on the ferry from the mainland. Susie and I returned on it together and the last few days of the account refer to the road journey back to Melbourne, seeing the Twelve Apostles, driving the popular Great Ocean Road as well as reliving my earlier, boyhood connection with Apollo Bay.

DAY 1: MONDAY 12 DECEMBER 2022

I was up early and down to the Lake St Clair jetty on the lake by 8.45 am. Boots on, pack loaded up and ready[173]. The boatman was there checking in fellow tourists no doubt interested to see the far end of Lake St Clair. We were soon off in the well fitted out Surf Cat[174], which was immeasurably quicker than any of the boats I used in earlier visits.

We arrived at the northern end, at the now renovated Narcissus Hut about 9.40. It had a generous sleeping area, toilets, water and a radio connected to the park HQ. I sat outside on the veranda and taped up my

---

173 I managed to get some cooking oil from the tourist café and kitchen at the National Park headquarters.

174 With twin outboard engines, each of 225 horsepower, I think.

blistered hands (from the earlier river trip). I filled the CamelBak with water and made a few notes in this diary before heading off for Pine Valley, about three hours walk to the north. The weather was overcast but not raining. It was 10.30 when swags were up and I set off following the Narcissus River. At this point, the track was part of the well-known and travelled Overland Track, my route leaving this main trail to the left after about an hour and a half. I stopped at the junction to don some lighter clothing but about an hour later the rain became more persistent, so much so, that when I arrived at the hut about 2pm I was fairly wet.

Along the way, there were swing bridges over the difficult river crossings of the past. I also passed a park ranger (who asked me for my park pass) on his way back from an inspection of the hut. There were two parties in residence when I arrived: one of two and the other, four. There were plenty of double sleeping bunks, a pot belly heater, good water and a clean toilet out the back.

The rain eased off a bit later in the afternoon. The temperature inside the hut was about 12 degrees[175] so we lit up the coal fired pot belly. Pretty soon it was warm and cozy as I cooked my evening meal. I had brought chicken pieces which I fried with onions with green peppers and asparagus sticks. I also had a fruit salad, complete with coffee bags and a dram.

By 7 pm we had all cooked and cleaned up as light was starting to fade. I was looking forward to a comfy sleep as I had managed to dry my Thermorest by the coal heater. I lay there listening to Harry Chapin on my little digital player before falling asleep till about 6.00 am.

DAY 2: TUESDAY 13 DECEMBER 2022

Awoke to continuing bad weather. It was overcast, rainy and very cold. I made porridge for breakfast and followed that with fried bacon and greens. In this weather, a climb back up to the Acropolis was out of the question so I decided to climb up to the Labyrinth Plateau instead, but not expecting to see very much as all the tops were whited out. The climb was arduous and

---

175 There was sign on the wall asking not to light up unless 12 degrees or less. The bunker, however, was empty of coal. And the remaining coal dust was hard to keep burning.

wet all the way and took an hour and a half. Much of the track was overhung with wet prickly heath and heavily washed out under foot. Cresting the rim of the plateau, the wind was immediately biting and I needed gloves right away.

Windswept and misty, there was little point carrying on. I headed back down, reaching the hut about midday, minus the sole of one boot. Fixed a good lunch with pumpkin soup, salami and cheese, fruit and coffee. There followed lots of wet gear to hang up. The weather remained bad into the afternoon so I took a short stroll along the Acropolis track to Cephissus Falls. To my great disappointment, nothing else was possible.

In the evening, the kerosene stove got itself blocked and would not prick to clear. As a result, dinner took ages to cook on the sputtering, useless flame. So annoying. To make matters worse, we struggled with the pot belly due to the lack of lump coal. I blew and blew, then returned to the faulty stove with cold, wet feet.

It looked as if there was no chance of an Acropolis climb the following day. The brief showing of patches of blue sky were obviously an aberration. I decided to take another look at the situation tomorrow, but most probably I would have no option but to walk out back to the lake head. The goddess mother of Pine Valley, the Acropolis, was to remain unsullied, at least for this trip.

Day 3: Wednesday 14 December

Slept well and woke at 6 am. All the others were up and moving. Everyone had agreed to walk out back to Narcissus as the weather was still quite foul with continuous rain showers and permanently wet feet. We had all departed by 8.30.

The walk down to the lake took two and three-quarter hours, with the clouds clearing only now and again then giving way to more rainfall. As I joined the Overland Track again, there were numerous 'finishing parties' streaming into the hut[176] thankful to have completed their walk and keen

---

176 Some were commercially guided parties – one of the guides was a young woman in a short leather mini!

to catch the boat back to civilisation. They crowded out the hut, spilled out on to the veranda and hung wet gear everywhere.

My plan was to stay here overnight and catch the morning boat at 9.30. I laid out my sleeping mat after drying it off[177] and fluffed up my Everest sleeping bag. Most of my kit was dry except for my socks as I was only carrying two pairs – so one pair was dried out each afternoon, only to join the other pair even if still damp. Bare feet in the hut! It was much warmer in this hut at 16 degrees. After most of the overlanders had departed, a level of peace and quiet returned to this normally tranquil place. Precocious youngsters, excited at having completed their overland journey, tended to be noisy and oblivious to those around them. I hung about, looking at all the expensive, barely used equipment, which kind of prompted me to replace some of my well used and overworked older stuff. Narcissus is the bustling terminal for this park and only thins out at the end of the day. Strange to think back to when I was last here (with my now departed brother), it was deserted. We certainly had better weather on that trip.

I made a great dinner of fried chicken and veg, as I still had onions, green pepper and asparagus. Enjoyed hot tea and chocolate[178]. Outside, from about 6 to 7 pm, the light was great for views of the surrounding peaks – Olympus and Acropolis. I saw a pair of green and yellow parrots, but failed to spot the little platypus which apparently swims around the jetty at dusk every evening. That night, the hut had about ten in residence, plus at least three tents pitched on tent platforms out the back. One pair was planning to do the lakeside walk to Cynthia Bay, which is only worth doing once in my opinion. They had gone when I woke up.

DAY 4: THURSDAY 15 DECEMBER 2022

Packed up and left the hut, catching the ferry at 9.30 to Cynthia Bay. The Shark Cat took only thirty minutes! After collecting the Peugeot, I returned to the Derwent Bridge Hotel for a re-pack of gear and lunch.

---

177   These are usually carried rolled up and strapped to the outside of the rucksack – so they get wet when it rains.

178   I had to borrow a gas stove from one of the other walking parties.

Refreshed, I drove back to Hobart and met Susie at the Astor Hotel in Macquarie Street[179]. A positively 'queer' and old worldy joint with talkative hosts. We had a nice room with an en suite bathroom – which I needed by that stage. Dinner was at Little India, corner Liverpool and Collins.

DAY 5: FRIDAY 16 DECEMBER 2022

The idea was to adjust all the kit for 'car camping' as opposed to bushwalking. There was also some gear to mend or replace. In addition, Susie had not seen Hobart before. The day went as follows:

- Replace the kero stove with a gas version at the Macpac store in the city;
- Select some decent sunglasses for Susie;
- Purchase all the groceries needed for the camp at Fortescue Bay;
- Lunch[180] at the Whaler pub in Salamanca Place ;
- Evening walk through the Liverpool Mall and Wellington Arcade.

By evening, the Peugeot was packed and we were ready to head off the next day.

---

179 Susie Stevenson, who .had flown in from Melbourne that morning. She and I got together sometime after Diane and I separated in 2016. This was the hotel all the rafter used.

180 The seafood chowder and the mussels were both to die for!

Cynthia Bay jetty Lake St Clair

Jetty, north end of the lake, Mt Olympus at rear

We used to cross on the logs...

Narcissus Hut

Pine Valley hut, 2022

Entering Pine Valley forest

Cephissus Falls

Cephissus creek below the hut

Waiting for the ferry...

Happy young arrivals – the journey ahead of them

Leaving Nacissus again...

Lunch back at the DB pub

The Whaler pub

Hobart port area

Later Tasmania Walks, 13

Three Capes Walk, 2022-23

A walking camping trip to the Tasman Peninsula, written en route.

Day 1: Saturday 17 December 2022 (3 Capes Day 1))

We left the hotel after breakfast and drove directly down Macquarie Street and on to the Tasman Bridge. Thirty minutes later we arrived at Sorell where we stocked up on supplies and refuelled. Motoring on, we stopped at Dunally for coffee and bought a dozen fresh, jumbo shucked oysters in a foil tray from an oyster farm just off the main road. Then, it was on across Eaglehawk Neck and fairly soon afterwards on to the turn-off to Fortescue Bay on an unsealed road for about twelve kilometres We had booked a spot at the camp and were checked in to site #15. After setting up the tent and fly, there was intermittent rain and it was distinctly cool.

We cooked chicken and veg for dinner, with brewed coffee and chocolate (after devouring the oysters). Crawled into the tent about 9.30 pm but were kept awake by a noisy group of Asian tourists.

Day 2: Sunday 18 December

Arose at 6.15 am to see the sky had cleared overnight to greet us with a fine, clear morning. After porridge, pikelets and coffee we set of on the Three Capes Track to Cape Hauy. It was a long walk for old legs, taking four and a half hours (a half hour more than signposted). The view from the lookout was a little disappointing as you could see neither the Candlestick nor the Totem Pole[181]. I trotted back and rejoined Susie at the Cape Pillar turnoff,

---

181 I viewed these on a previous sea kayaking trip.

about two kilometres back from the lookout. We trudged back to camp and had a siesta after lunch. It was quite a warm day with a fair bit of step climbing. We showered and felt much better. Susie helped cook an evening meal of chicken, asparagus, onion, tomato, chilli and red pepper, with an egg chucked in. There was also a little leftover cous cous as well, plus beer, wine and chocolate. Were-charged the phones and turned in with the weather still clear.

Day 3: Monday 19 December

The sky clouded over during the night presenting us with a rather subdued morning, accompanied by the sound of the waves on the nearby beach. After a rather tough previous day for anyone over seventy we had slept well. We were soon up and enjoyed a breakfast of porridge, brewed coffee and toast, with Tasmanian leatherwood honey and marmalade.

The plan was to do a short walk to Canoe Bay, hoping to get a view of Cape Hauy from across the bay, and still be back at camp for lunch. Canoe Bay was a pleasant, coastal stroll of about one hour but alas there was little view of the Lanterns on the tip of the cape. Eager to see them I left Susie at Canoe Bay and charged on over the next point and descended to Bivouac Bay. Still no view! I raced back to find Susie had been waiting for an hour and twenty minutes.

We meandered back to camp, walking barefoot across the sandy beach for the final stage of the walk. It was pleasant to remove wet walk shoes, and not only when crossing the shallow stream trickling into the emerald blue sea. Hungry, we prepared hot soup and crackers with cheese and salami, washed down with Mercury cider. After lunch it was off in the car to see the Tasman Arch, the Blowhole and Devil's Kitchen, where we enjoyed a cappuccino and an ice cream as a treat. We were back at camp by 5.30.

Day 4: Tuesday 20 December

As Port Arthur is only a short drive from Fortescue Bay we packed up our camp and left after the usual breakfast to drive to the NRMA holiday camp near the Port Arthur tourist centre. After setting up camp we stocked up on supplies at the rather limited general store and returned to camp, re-stocked with wine and beer.

In the afternoon, we strolled down to Stewart's Beach where Susie was interested in picking up some rounded stones by the shore. Back at camp we showered (using the five-minute hot water timers) and enjoyed Tasmanian grown pinot noir and pizza in the well-appointed communal kitchen. Susie was very impressed. On the other hand, I was subdued – still with a congested chest and sore after the ordeal on the river. I also had a nasty infected finger. I hoped I'd feel better for the walk to Cape Raoul.

DAY 5: WEDNESDAY 21 DECEMBER

A rest day. The plan was to follow the coastal track all the way to the old penal settlement, referred to locally as the 'Historic Site'. We set off after breakfast, losing the track at one point and ending up in the Stewart Bay resort. Further on, it was interesting to view some of the convict officers' quarters, gently restored, as well as the penal colony close-up rather than from a rocking kayak while cold and wet as was the case last time.

We backtracked to camp and arrived for lunch about two and a half hours later. The camp guest lounge was empty so we enjoyed lunch around a large coffee table: soup, cheese and SAOs, fruit and a bottle of Spreyton cider. Then it was off to the lavender farm only to find it overrun with foreign tourists, all gathered around the high-end food service like bees around the hive.

I still felt tired and stiff. For one thing, my back remained very sore from the river trip and the longest finger on my left hand was still infected[182], very tender and stubbornly refusing to settle down.

The lavender seemed to be just starting and late blooming. The beds of English roses were lovely and there was also a distillery on site. Tassie is well known for its artisanal gins and whiskeys. We had an enjoyable dinner at a café on the main road – shared to seafood chowder and the locally popular scallop curry pie floater. Both very good, the latter with chips and a dressed salad.

Later, after turning in, I lay on my back listening to kids yelling with

---

182 Finger damage from paddling and spores in the water?

glee in the dark and chasing the local wildlife. Then there were late arrivals, speaking loudly as they set up their vans or tents and flashed their torches about. Car doors slamming; car alarms winking; passers-by with headlights up; I donned ear buds and listened to music till 12.15 by which time the noisy chaos had subsided. We slept until 5.45 am when someone's alarm went off.

DAY 6: THURSDAY 22 DECEMBER

Left the camp at about eight and after a short drive towards Nubeena turned off to the left to view the Remarkable Cave. There was an easy set of steel stairs down to a good viewing spot. Further along the Nubeena Road and before Nubeena itself, we turned left on Stormlea Road and drove on until it ended in a car park which marked the start of the Cape Raoul walking track.

We did the shorter version, taking in Shipstern Bluff, as well as the Cape Raoul lookout and returned to the car about midday. We met a few others along the track, heading all the way to the cape itself some four or five kilometres from the lookout where we stopped at the junction with the Shipstern Bluff track. The views were vast and dramatic, the track well graded and gentle.

Just past Stormlea Road turn-off, the main road led straight into Nubeena where we soon found our homestay, Murray, one of two units in a complex called Chill at the far end of White Beach Road. and settled in[183]. It was a fully appointed two-bedroom home. With looming Christmas holiday closures, we replenished our food and grog at the local IGA and returned to our home via the local beach, where Susie collected abalone shells for her collection back home.

Back at the home stay complex, in a unit called Murray I lanced my infected finger and downloaded all the phone and camera images. Susie cooked beef sausages and cous cous and we enjoyed that with cheap red wine and Boag's beer. We managed to arrange a doctor appointment for the following day as my injured ribs and chest were still very bad and I had an endless need to cough.

---

183 The door lock combination was emailed to us the day before.

Day 7: Friday 23 December

It rained overnight but Susie got all the washing dried. This was good as I could not find any spare underclothes. It dawned fine, with a nice peaceful outlook over the bay, just across White Beach Road. We planned this as a rest day so I could be 'seen' medically, which nearly didn't happen as I had to fake a Covid vaccination in order to see Dr Saul who checked my chest (not too bad he said) and gave me some doxycycline. He was a former rugby player and knew of my father.

We moved on to the local café and IGA, where we bought a whole chicken to roast for Christmas and returned to the bolthole via Parsons Bay (within the larger Wedge Bay) where I learned that Pacific oysters have been largely eradicated. We waded in the calm clear waters lapping at our feet. Back at Murray, we had a sandwich lunch and spent the afternoon relaxing in our most comfortable seaside retreat. Susie put the chicken in the oven. I played some music through the iPad and Bluetooth speaker and planned tomorrow's route to our planned camp at Lime Bay.

Day 4: Saturday 23 December (3 Capes walk, day 4)
Christmas Eve at Lime Bay

We left White Beach at 8.30 am and set off for Saltwater River after collecting a bag of ice at the Nubeena IGA. By about ten o'clock we had reached the campsite at Lime Bay and paid our $13 camp fee (an envelope in the honesty box at the entrance).

First, we went back down the road a short distance to visit some old convict ruins and the site of Australia's first coal mine. The austerity of the solitary confinement cells (well restored and preserved) has a profound effect.

Back at camp, the usual lunch was enjoyed with Spreyton cider. We set up a camp among soft grasses and shady trees. Nearby, there was a toilet block with water, but no showers or electric power. Then it was off on foot on a track to Lagoon Bay, supposedly only 1.5 km away. Well, about five kilometres later we turned back as we were obviously on a newer fire trail. Rather cross, we returned to camp, all the while cursing the park staff until we were back, settled into wine and bourbon.

Mozzies were a bit of an issue, biting me right through my long johns. The doxy was making me a bit listless as well. We needed to zip up the mozzie net on the tent door as soon as we were inside for the night. Before that, though, Susie set to and cooked up meatballs and coleslaw (which she had prepared the previous night back at Murray.

DAY 5: SUNDAY 25 DECEMBER CHRISTMAS DAY AT FREYCINET

We had a restful sleep under a clear, starry sky, safe from the mozzies thanks to the Fairydown Sting mountain tent. Up early and away by 8.15, we went non-stop back through the 'neck' and stopped at Dunally again, this time for fuel and ice. After that it was goodbye to the Tasman Peninsula and quickly back to Sorell, where we turned northeast to Swansea via Triabunna, where we stopped at a French patisserie for an almond croissant and cappuccino. It was strange to see so many shops open – the local IGA, servos and cafes.

From there it was non-stop to Coles Bay and the Freycinet National Park where we had won a camp spot in the pre-Christmas ballot for site 36 in Honeymoon Bay. The sun beat down on us as we ate lunch and took a dip in the sparkling sea. Susie gathered more purple scallop shells. I found some shade and mixed a bourbon with coke and ice and marvelled at the scene before us.

We had planned for a Christmas dinner – not lunch, due to our likely late arrival at the camp. As the heat of the day subsided, we sat down to roast chicken and coleslaw, followed by Christmas pudding, with a topping of bourbon, mixed with butter and sugar. It was a most pleasant evening, sipping fine local wine and cold beer. We played some tunes on the harmonica (which the nearby neighbours said they liked) and chatted until the mozzies became a nuisance and we beat a safe retreat.

DAY 6: MONDAY 26 DECEMBER – BOXING DAY AT THE BEACH

The day broke overcast, with mist on Mount Amos But the weather cleared as the day progressed, ending up quite hot in the sun. The plan for the day was:

    Visit Sleepy Bay;

Wineglass Bay lookout;

Coles Bay (for ice and oysters);

A beach stroll and swim.

The climb up to the Wineglass Bay lookout was steep in places but only took about thirty minutes to the high saddle, with lots of tourists. Very congested but a great view.

Ice cream and lunch by the jetty and boat ramp at Coles Bay as the oyster farm was closed. Back at the camp for a snooze and afternoon swim. Nice hot showers, too, at the end of the day.

DAY 7: TUESDAY 26 DECEMBER

Fine weather continued to greet us in the morning, with the sun beating down on the tent fly as I woke. I was even in a bit of a sweat. Susie was already up and laying breakfast out on the collapsible camp table. We had coffee and toasted fruit buns while learning of a heatwave in the mainland cities. We had a glassy, smooth sea with waves lapping gently on the shore.

We drove out to Cape Tourville and were surprised by the gentleness of the walk and the superb views of Wineglass Bay and the bird colony at the Nuggets, just offshore. Then it was back to Coles Bay for an ice cream and another bag of ice for the esky. Susie wanted oysters for lunch so we drove a little way back north to Freycinet Marine Farm where we bought a dozen for $28 which we were washed down with beer and cider. Back at camp, it was time for a swim – a lovely refreshing dip – looking up at Mount Amos and the Hazards. Flat water, a gentle breeze, boats on the water. Cold showers followed to wash off the beach sand.

DAY 8: WEDNESDAY 28 DECEMBER, LAST DAY IN TASSIE

Strong, gusty winds overnight heralded an unpleasant dawn. We decided to break camp and get away early – we were booked on the ferry due to sail that evening from Devonport so we set off at 7.30 am.

The route was Coles Bay to Bicheno; on north to St Mary's then west to Deloraine, where the Raspberry Farm served fine meals. We made the ferry and boarded about 5.00 pm for the 6.45 pm sailing.

Day 9: Thursday 29 December, back in Victoria.

We docked in Geelong at 5.30 am after a rather fitful night in the recliner lounge as a result of two very noisy sleepers (endless, loud snoring). Deck 1 unloaded last but we drove off down the ramp after a relatively short wait and headed off straight through Geelong central, then Torquay (still early morning) and arrived at the Anglesea surf cottage for breakfast.

All good – the place all in order, but I was tired after the crossing and drive. I slept all afternoon, still suffering from the sore back, heavy chest and a mysteriously sore arm. It was good to have a kitchen to cook in for a change, comfortable chairs to sit in and most of all – a hot shower.

Day 10: Friday 30 December, at Anglesea

I awoke still feeling rather unwell, though my chest seemed to be clearing slowly. Did nothing all day – just rested. Susie did loads of laundry and we cleaned and dried all the camping gear. We did a brief trip to the local IGA for fresh supplies and the luxury of an ice cream. We enjoyed smoked mussels before dinner and fed the resident parrots[184]. Made a pizza for a main meal sitting at a proper table sipping wine and guzzling the Boag's beer we were still carrying.

Day 11: Saturday 31 December, New Year's Eve at Anglesea

A fine sunny day greeted us with an expected top temperature of 27 degrees. Short pants and tee shirt weather. I was feeling a little better though had a mild headache[185]. Being a pleasant morning, we had coffee at Poppies on Inverlochy Crescent and stopped on the way home to get some soluble aspirin for the fever. It was a relief to return to the bolthole free from the overcrowded madness of the village area in peak holiday season. Susie was very pleased with her trendy new purple/pink overalls which looked very attractive with a white singlet underneath.

---

184 We don't feed the white cockatoos as they become destructive and damage wooden trims.

185 Recurring Ross River virus – has been coming and going for years.

Day 12: Sunday 1 January 2024, New Year's Day at Anglesea

After thirty-one days on the road, our New Year's Eve was subdued. And, of course, day one of the new year was accompanied by traffic chaos in Anglesea. The Point Addis road was banked up for miles. We gave up stopping there and drove back to Torquay and had a quiet lunch at the Sou'West Brewery – crumbed broccoli and spicy Korean chicken. Thankfully, the traffic eased for the drive back home.

That evening, I watched the Big Bash cricket[186] and had a Herbert Adams pie for dinner. The chest was still clearing. I had two doxycycline tablets left.

Day 13: Monday 2 January 2024, at Anglesea

We went to Donohue's Beach so Susie could search for flat sandstone specimens. Then it was on to Airey's Inlet so see the lighthouse. Service at the café there was rather slow due to the holiday season, so we cancelled our order and went to the nearby Salt Brewery where we had a cheeseboard and two Salt lagers.

On the way home we picked up more fuel for the Peugeot and another ice cream. The red headed king parrot was waiting for us on return...

Day 14: Tuesday 3 January 2024

This was the last day on the 'doxy'. I was feeling better, but still coughing up a lot of phlegm. Went back to Torquay to have a drink at the Sou'West Brewery with Dave and Fiona Clark. Meatballs, fresh crisp bread with a tasty sauce for dinner.

Day 15, : Wednesday 4 January

Got up, had a cough followed by a hot shower. Feeling better. Spent the morning cleaning up the house for son John junior's arrival on Friday with his young son Mac, Susan (his girlfriend) and her daughter Maya. We put all the tools and hardware under the house and cleaned up the outside deck area. Then watched a bit of the cricket Test Australia v South Africa in Sydney at the SCG. It got washed out later in the day.

---

186   Brisbane Heat v Sydney Sixers.

I tried to take Susie to the Pirate's Cave by rounding a few bluffs (at low tide and receding) at Urquhart's Bluff, but the wind was very strong and it was rather cold. We turned back after the first rock pool.

DAY 16: THURSDAY 5 JANUARY

We packed up and cleaned the house in preparation for a quick start tomorrow. We went down the Coal Mine Road[187] and more or less got lost and returned home. Test cricket on the TV followed by BBL in the evening.

DAY 17: FRIDAY 6 JANUARY, OFF TO WARRNAMBOOL

The route followed was Airey's Inlet, Lorne (via the Great Ocean Road), Birregurra, Colac, Terang, Warrnambool.

We arrived at Jim Askew's palatial home sometime after lunch, after a long drive from Anglesea. Jim took me to the local Men's Shed where we all said hello and drank beer. Jim was a regular with the group. He and wife Jo had several grandchildren staying, which was a bit awkward as Jo was a bit unwell. Jim cooked lamb chops on the BBQ in the very large lounge area.

DAY 18: SATURDAY 7 JANUARY

Lazy day at Jim's home in Warrnambool.

    Had a swim in his indoor pool.

    Dinner at a restaurant overlooking the port precinct.

DAY 19: SUNDAY 8 JANUARY, SLOW RETURN TO ANGLESEA

In the morning, we went to a historic car show near last night's restaurant. Jim showed the way on his large BMW motorcycle and we followed and parked when we could find a spot.

Later, back at home, we said goodbye after I played some tunes for the grandchildren (which Jo seemed to like – she had been unwell and was lying down).

We eventually found our way out of the city limits and on to the B100 towards Peterborough and then Port Campbell, where we enjoyed some

---

187 The site of the now closed Anglesea coal mine, associated with the aluminium smelter.

toasted sandwiches. From there, it was on to the Twelve Apostles with great views of the Bay of Islands and the Grotto (before Peterborough). There were tourist buses everywhere and scarcely an Aussie to be seen.

We drove on and did not stop at Laver's Hill, not long later descending the Otway Ranges to Maringo and Apollo Bay, where I felt many childhood memories returning. This was where my family holidayed in the 1960s. Margaret Barrow's house, where we stayed, was still there, though the Greenacre Motel next door had gone. Opposite, the Apollo Bay Golf Club was mostly unchanged.

The beach, the breakwater and the shops were all changed. The old Bluebird Café, however, still retained its original name. The foreshore now had a rather grotesque amusement park replacing what I remembered was a mini golf and picnic area. Meals were had at the Great Ocean Road brewery and pub at the top end of town.

DAY 20: MONDAY 9 JANUARY

We camped at Skene's Creek, at a crowded caravan park just outside Apollo Bay. The neighbours were noisy (as all these places are) so we set off early and had breakfast back at Apollo Bay.

Then we set off for Lorne, stopping at Wye River to see my work friend Dave Clark, who rents a cabin there every year for the family summer holiday. Leaving Dave, it was on to Cumberland River where the attractions were koalas and Jebb's Pool. From there it was a short drive along the Ocean Road to Lorne and on home to Anglesea.

DAY 21: TUESDAY 10 JANUARY

We arrived last night rather tired after the two days of driving. We didn't unload much – just relaxed and unwound.

I still felt a bit sore and bronchial. John junior and his son Mack arrived back from the beach and we all enjoyed a dinner of meat balls with sauce . We called Scripts on Line so I could get more antibiotics and the dial-a-doctor obliged, sending an authorisation to the local pharmacy.

The evenings were cool but it was good to be back in a soft bed after forty days on the road.

DAYS 22 TO 24 WEDNESDAY TO FRIDAY, 11 TO 13 JANUARY

Beach days at the surf cottage.

DAY 25: SATURDAY 14 JANUARY

Packed up and returned to Melbourne; checked in for the following day's flight back to Cairns. Dropped the Peugeot back at John's apartment and stayed in the CBD.

Fortescue Bay camp

Fortescue Bay

On the way to Cape Hauy

Susie had a visitor...

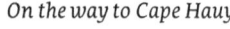

Canoe Bay

Shipstern Bluff

The Blowhole

Remarkable Cave

Port Arthur Warden's residence

Lime Bay penal colony

Looking south to cape Raoule

Lime Bay camping area

Lime Bay

Coles Bay camp site

Coles Bay

Wineglass Bay lookout

The Nuggets

Wineglass Bay from Cape Tourville

The Anglesea surf cottage

The local parrots soon greeted us

The Great Ocean Road VIC

Airey's Inlet lighthouse

The Grotto

The Bay of Islands

The Twelve Apostles

The Twelve Apostles

Epilogue

When deciding how to wrap up these nostalgic narratives, thoughts came flooding back , causing me to remember the boyhood school song, which many schools have adopted from Harrow School in the UK, where it originated.

Forty years on[188,] when afar and asunder
Parted are those who are singing today,
When you look back and forgetfully wonder
What you were like in your work and your play.
Then it may be there will often come o'er you
Glimpses of notes, like the catch of a song;
Visions of boyhood shall float them before you,
Echoes of dreamland shall bear them along.

Some of those who travelled with me are no longer with us; others I have been unable to contact and others still share the memories when we meet – the good times, the hard times and the elation upon completing each and every challenge. The changes in park management, subtle changes in parts of the routes[189] or hut upgrades[190]; the constant emergence of better equipment and finally commercial guiding – these are all parts of the reminiscences.

The task of assembling each of these trip diaries has been immensely rewarding. As I relived each often gruelling trip, the memories were refreshed and the highlights somehow enlivened again over and above the

---

188 song written by Edward Ernest Bowen and John Farmer in 1872. It was originally written for Harrow School in England.

189 Duckboards across fragile or boggy ground.

190 For example, Dixon's Kingdom and Pine Valley.

trials. Once again, I was transported there by the ageing pencil pines by the edge of the tarn, dolerite peaks reflected in the shimmering pool before me, myself tired of body but contented, and marvelling at the profoundness of the moment.

> Forty years on, growing older and older,
> Shorter in wind, as in memory long,
> Feeble of foot, and rheumatic of shoulder,
> What will it help you that once you were strong?
> God gives us bases to guard or beleaguer,
> Games to play out, whether earnest or fun,
> Fights for the fearless, and goals for the eager,
> Twenty, and thirty, and forty years on!

Now I am directed to the rainforest canopy surrounding my bush camp here in far north Queensland.

Rain has the cane drooping down the road, with the annual harvest or 'crush' not far off. The wet season rainfall drips from the bamboo and in the half-light shed by the solar powered outside lighting, the wallabies are grazing close by as I write. Frogs are glistening in the soft light, each contributing noisily to what I call 'the frog senate'[191] and the bright crimson lipstick palms are rustling gently.

As the years close in, it seems appropriate to finish with the words of John Bunyan[192], though I have taken the licence to replace the last word, 'rewarder'.

> As I walked through the wilderness of this world,
> I lighted on a certain place where was a den,
> and laid me down in that place to sleep;
> and as I slept, I dreamed a dream.

---

191 Yes, senate not sonata — I have an artwork with the same title in my bathroom, with the real thing!

192 An English writer and Puritan preacher. He is best remembered as the author of the Christian allegory The Pilgrim's Progress, 1609, which became an influential literary model.

My sword, I give to him that shall succeed me in my pilgrimage,
and my courage and skill to him that can get it.
My marks and scars I carry with me,
to be a witness for me, that I have fought his battles,
who will now be my redeemer.

www.ingramcontent.com/pod-product-compliance
Lightning Source LLC
Chambersburg PA
CBHW060351080526
44583CB00012B/259